G000123096

2002 GUIDE

THE COMPLETE GUIDE
TO THE LONGEST NATIONAL TRAIL
BY THE
SOUTH WEST COAST PATH
ASSOCIATION

(FORMERLY THE SOUTH WEST WAY ASSOCIATION)

THE SOUTH WEST COAST PATH ASSOCIATION

Registered as a charity (No. 266754)

The Association formed to promote the interest of users of the South West Coast Path

Visit our Website at www.swcp.org.uk

CHAIRMAN

Brian Panton, 5 Nicholas Gardens, Ensbury Park,
Bournemouth BH10 4BA
Tel/Fax: (01202) 526954

TREASURER

David Richardson, J.P.
44 Whitchurch Avenue
Exeter EX2 5NT
Tel/Fax: (01392) 430985

SECRETARY

Eric Wallis
'Windlestraw', Penquit, Ermington,
Devon PL21 0LU
Tel/Fax: (01752) 896237
e-mail: wallispenquit@beeb.net

ADMINISTRATOR

Sarah Vincent
25 Clobells, South Brent,
Devon TQ10 9JW
Tel/Fax: (01364) 73859
e-mail: coastpath.swcpa@virgin.net

Published by:
The South West Coast Path Association

Trade Sales and Distribution:
Halsgrove Publishing, Halsgrove House, Lower Moor Way,
Tiverton Business Park, Tiverton, Devon. EX16 6SS
Contact: Marie Lewis 01884 243242

Printed in England by Swift Print, Dawlish

ISBN 0 907055 05 2

Jacket photograph: On Carnewas Point, North Cornwall by Ronald Turner

South West
Coast Path

CONTENTS

INTRODUCTION

The South West Coast Path is a 'National Trail' funded by the Countryside Agency (formerly the Countryside Commission) and maintained on its behalf by County Councils and National Park authorities. The route is waymarked by the distinctive acorn symbol. It is by far the longest of all the Long Distance trails; it runs from Minehead in Somerset right round the South West Peninsula to South Haven Point on the south side of Poole Harbour in Dorset. As a result of the 1999/2000 survey of the Coast Path end to end using a Global Positioning System, we now have access to very precise distances - the Coast Path is 630 miles (1014 km) long. The survey, carried out by the South West Coast Path Team, included the Isle of Portland. It is interesting to note that in a contour count undertaken by this Association, it was calculated that the walker will climb over 91,000 feet (27,737 m), which is three times Mount Everest.

This Guide attempts to provide in one single unit all the basic information you need to walk the path. The information is updated annually and members are advised by newsletters of important changes during the year. We try to provide the basic information in just one small book.

A survey established that one of the chief joys of those accomplishing the Pennine Way was the sense of achievement; of a challenge met. What of our path which is twice as long and requiring far more total effort? Because of its length, few will be able to undertake to walk it as a whole. That is why as much as possible of this guide is written to be just as useful to those who only wish to walk parts of the path.

The splendid idea of making this old path around the South West Peninsula one of the first of a series of Long Distance Paths came from a war-time committee of the Ramblers' Association. The idea was put into effect by being included in the National Park and Access to the Countryside Act of 1949. Some long distance paths have now been designated as National Trails, and now have an equal basis in law with the much better known National Parks. Unfortunately, however, being authorised by Act of Parliament so long ago and despite several Opening Ceremonies, the South West Coast Path is still UNFINISHED.

The South West Coast Path Association was formed after some months' preliminary work in May 1973. It is an independent body but works in co-operation with the Ramblers' Association. The South West Coast Path Association's first aim is to secure completion of the path, and we do believe we have been responsible for many path alignment improvements, better maintenance and waymarking during our 28 year existence.

Furthermore, the South West Coast Path Association believes the Countryside Agency has been in error in two respects. Firstly it has not made it a continuous path despite its own words: 'There should be a continuous right of way along the entire length of the path.' (Countryside Agency's National Long Distance Path - Some Questions Answered.)

Secondly, in several places, the Path has been diverted from the coast for no apparent good reason, even on occasions onto main roads with no pavement. Our Association believes it would be scenically more beautiful, less hindrance to agriculture and physically safer if kept on the coast. Experience has shown that diversions away from it are unsatisfactory.

It seems that no local walking organisations were ever consulted about the path until our Association came into being. Being reasonable people we cannot expect to have everything our own way - in fact there are many legitimate interests to consider. However, to establish a path without discussing it with the people who know it best, which is exactly what the Countryside Agency was apparently trying to do, seems altogether wrong.

Our Association believes that, in a tourist-orientated area such as the South West, a continuous coastal path will be a major asset. It hopes the Path will bring more business to less frequented places and relieve some of the pressure on the South West National Parks. There is a great number of bodies interested in various parts of the Path. Our Association believes it is important that it should represent all sections, and view the Path as a whole.

The path passes along some of the finest coastal scenery in Europe, and with its enormous variety and contrast between bustling resort and quiet cove is a never-ceasing source of delight.

This path is the longest National Trail in the country. We think it is the finest, and hope you will too. We certainly know of no other that has as much contrast and variety as ours; try it!

Members receive a free Annual Guide and two Newsletters a year with up-to-date information on the state of the path.

Enquiries to: The Administrator, (see page 2)

Payment may be made using a cheque or postal order made payable to the South West Coast Path Association. We can accept the credit/debit cards shown below, providing we have the following information:

We welcome...

Card Number   Expiry Date
Full name as it appears on the card
Issue Number (Switch Cards Only)

Subscriptions: Single: £11.00; Joint: £12.50; Associations & Local Authorities: £18.50; Life Membership: £160.00; Joint Life Membership: £185.00; Non-UK Membership: £16.00.

Both the Bournemouth Coast Path and the Solent Way link in with the end of the South West Coast Path at Sandbanks, thus providing a continuous path from Minehead to Emsworth. Guide books for those trails are out of print.

THE REVERSE GUIDE

The Association has written a description of the Trail for those walking in the Poole to Minehead direction. It deals only with the path so this annual guide will be necessary for all the other information. The 'Reverse Guide' supplement is available from the Administrator at £3.50 including postage.

WEATHER

The South West Coast Path is more exposed to wind than any other long distance trail, so please pay attention to gale forecasts as well as rain. Along some sections, strong winds can be dangerous, especially when rounding exposed headlands and crossing bridges; a high backpack can act like a sail. Detailed forecasts are available on 09068 400105 for Somerset, 09068 400104 for Devon and Cornwall, and on 09068 400103 for Dorset.

A WORD TO BEGINNERS

Long Distance Path Walking

These words are not for those hardy veterans who have all the gear, have done several paths already, and know all about it. We will only say to them at least read the second paragraph of `Grading' near the beginning of the 'Trail Description' section. However, we do get a number of letters each year from those who have not ventured before on long distance paths and need some advice. This we are pleased to try and provide and we do hope those who read this will find it helpful. However, it is easy to miss out things that folk wish to know, so if you who are new read this, and are still baffled, please write to us and we will try to provide the answers. As well as perhaps helping you, it will enable us to improve this section for another year and so be of help to more people.

For Those Who Have Never Been Walking

Have you been walking at all before? If the answer is no, do not for heaven's sake try and plan several days' continuous walking. You need to do some day walks - there are some very good ones on the coast. Better still, look for the sections marked 'Easy' - start at one end and stop and turn back before you have half had enough. We say before half because it is always better to do a bit less and really enjoy it.

You can soon progress to setting out to walk a whole section either by using two cars or using public transport. One point here - if possible use the public transport to go out and walk back to your car or base. This means that you do not get yourself in a position of having to race the clock if you should take a bit more time than you thought.

If you are walking on your own, do please take additional care for, as you will appreciate, if you fall or twist an ankle there can be problems. If you are on your own therefore, you should leave a note with someone to make sure that you arrive at your destination. Not everyone is happy walking on their own and can feel lonely. There is also an added problem that you may try to do too much, so please bear this in mind.

There is no need to buy expensive equipment for the easy sections at the start; a pair of stout shoes and a rainproof is all you need. As you progress, a small rucksack or haversack for 'eats' will be needed next.

Obviously if you can join a walking club and go out with them you will collect lots of friendly advice on all sorts of gear you may care to purchase as you become more serious about walking. Maps, guides, etc., are all listed in their appropriate sections.

For Those Who Have Walked, But Not On Long Distance Trails

Day walking on long distance trails is really no different from any other kind of day walking. It is only when you contemplate several days' continuous walking that other considerations arise and there are some pitfalls which even quite experienced day walkers often overlook.

Do not be too ambitious in the mileage you plan. Do not carry too much weight of gear.

Having stated the two big points, we will elaborate. You will not be able to accomplish in daily mileage the same amount you normally cover in a day walk; you will have to settle for less. The first reason is that you will be carrying more equipment; you must for instance, have a complete change of clothing and footwear, possibly nightwear and toilet kit. For this you need a bigger rucksack so you will be carrying quite a bit more weight than you normally do. Secondly, there is what we call the 'wear' factor. For the first few days until you are really fit, it is just simply more tiring having to walk each day. The last point could be called the 'interest' factor. Usually, if you are walking a long distance path, you are further from your home base, in fresh fields and pastures new; there is more to see so you will need more time to look around.

If you usually accomplish 15 miles (24 km) a day, aim, say, for 12 (19 km). This is particularly important if you are booking ahead. You can find yourself tied to a treadmill which you cannot get off. Booking ahead has the advantage that you know there is a bed ahead. On the other hand, it does mean even if you are tired, have developed blisters, and the weather is diabolical, you have to go on. Be guided too by our `Trail Description' section and the terrain you are tackling. 6 miles (10 km), say, of a `Severe' section can equal in effort 10-12 miles (16-19 km) of an 'Easy' one.

We have stated you must carry more gear and this is true. Having said that, think long and hard about every item you imagine you may need. You will be surprised - you may find you will not want it at all. Watch particularly those extras such as cameras and binoculars - they are often a source of considerable weight. One little additional point, many rucksacks, even modern ones, are not as waterproof as you think. A plastic liner, which can be obtained quite cheaply from rambling shops, etc., as an additional inner layer, may save you that most unpleasant discovery after a long day spent in the rain that your only change of clothing is no longer dry. We would also recommend that in addition to this liner, your dry clothing should then be enclosed in further plastic bags to ensure dryness. Trainer shoes are useful for wearing at the end of the day and can be worn on some parts of the path.

A sensible idea before undertaking a long walking holiday is to take, say, a weekend of two or three days first, walking continuously as a practice.

Another point to watch especially on our Coast Path is the availability of refreshment. At main holiday times, you will get it nearly everywhere, except for the few places we especially mention in our 'Trail Description' section. Out of season, you will find it in surprisingly few places on long stretches of coast. The usual remarks about carrying stand-by supplies, therefore, certainly apply; better to carry an extra couple of bars of chocolate than to go hungry.

Walking Alone

The Association has a scheme that enables single female members who are a little nervous about walking alone to team up with other single female members. Contact the Administrator for information.

Easing The Load

On long trips it is a good idea to:

a)   Send guides, maps etc. ahead to larger post offices Poste Restante. The only snag is if you arrive on a Saturday evening.

b)   Start out with a few map-sized envelopes and the smallest available roll of sellotape

6

so that you can despatch finished guides, maps, books etc. home.

c)   many of our B & B proprietors will transfer your kit to your next destination (see p 92).

SOUTH WEST COAST PATH ASSOCIATION PUBLICATIONS

Path Descriptions by our Association are detailed accounts on all aspects of short sections of the coast path and include maps and illustrations. They cover in great detail what cannot be included in the guide book.

These Path Descriptions are all priced at £1.00 including postage. All are available from the Administrator (see page 2).

PATH DESCRIPTIONS

(Please note that as each Path Description is revised, we shall be using the new accurate distances accordingly)

Minehead to Lynmouth (22 miles / 35 km)
Lynmouth to Ilfracombe (18 miles / 30 km)
Ilfracombe to Croyde Bay (13.6 miles / 21.9 km)
Croyde Bay to Barnstaple (16 miles / 25 km)
Barnstaple to Westward Ho! (17 miles / 28 km)
Westward Ho! To Clovelly (11 miles / 18 km)
Clovelly to Hartland Quay (10 miles / 16 km)
Hartland Quay to Bude (14 miles / 22 km)
Bude to Crackington Haven (9 miles / 15 km)
Crackington Haven to Tintagel (12 miles / 20 km)
Tintagel to Port Isaac (8 miles / 13 km)
Port Isaac to Padstow (12 miles / 19 km)
Padstow to Porthcothan (12 miles / 20 km)
Porthcothan to Newquay (11.1 miles / 17.9 km)
Newquay to Perranporth (11 miles / 18 km)
Perranporth to Portreath (13 miles / 20 km)
Portreath to Hayle (12 miles / 19 km)
Hayle to Pendeen Watch (19 miles / 32 km)
Pendeen Watch to Porthcurno (15 miles / 24 km)
Porthcurno to Penzance (11 miles / 18 km)
Penzance to Porthleven (14 miles / 22.5 km)
Porthleven to The Lizard (13.9 miles / 22.3 km)
The Lizard to Helford (24 miles / 38 km)

Helford to Falmouth (10 miles / 15 km)
Falmouth to Portloe (13 miles / 22 km)
Portloe to Mevagissey (12 miles / 19 km)
Mevagissey to Fowey (17 miles / 27 km)
Fowey to Looe (12 miles / 19 km)
Looe to Portwrinkle (7.6 miles / 12.2 km)
Portwrinkle to Plymouth (13.3 miles / 21.4 km)
Plymouth (River Tamar) to Wembury (River Yealm) (14 miles / 22 km)
Warren Point (Wembury) to Bigbury-on-Sea (14 miles / 22 km)
Bigbury-on-Sea to Salcombe (13 miles / 21 km)
Salcombe to Torcross (12.9 miles / 20.8 km)
Torcross to Dartmouth (10 miles / 16 km)
Dartmouth to Brixham (11 miles / 18 km)
Brixham to Shaldon (19 miles / 30 km)
Shaldon to Sidmouth (21 miles / 32 km)
Sidmouth to Lyme Regis (17 miles / 27 km)
Lyme Regis to Abbotsbury (18 miles / 30 km)
Abbotsbury to Weymouth (14 miles / 23 km)
Isle of Portland Circuit (14 miles / 22 km)
Weymouth to Lulworth Cove (11 miles / 18 km)
Lulworth to Kimmeridge, Lulworth Range (7 miles / 11 km)
Kimmeridge to South Haven Point, Poole Harbour (20 miles / 31 km)
Alternative Inland Route, West Bexington to Osmington Mills (18 miles / 28 km)

A History of the South West Coast Path

The Association has written a history of the origins of the Coast Path. This book also includes an account of walking the Coast Path in 1854, and an account of a protracted legal case involving access to the Coast Path on the Devon / Dorset border in the mid 19th century.

Price £2.50 including postage.

The Reverse Guide

The Association has written a description of the Trail in the Poole - Land's End - Minehead direction. It deals only with the path, so this Annual Guide will be necessary for all the other information.

Price £3.50 including postage.

THE ASSOCIATION'S SHOP

Log Book

Why not keep a day by day record of your walk in an easy to carry, pocket size booklet, with a page per section in which to record your daily journey round the coast path (all 613 miles / 982 km!). Whether you do it all in one go or over a period of time, you will have a permanent record of your walks round some of the most beautiful country in the British Isles.

Price £2.75 including postage

Polo Shirt

In an attractive jade green, with the Association logo embroidered on the shirt, with 'SOUTH WEST COAST PATH' embroidered around the logo.

A good quality garment, easy to wash (65% polyester / 35% cotton), in Small, Medium, Large, Extra Large and Extra Extra Large.

Price £18.25 including postage

Sweat Shirt

In bottle green embroidered with the Association logo on the left side, and 'SOUTH WEST COAST PATH' around the logo (70% polyester / 30% cotton). It comes in five sizes, Small, Medium, Large, Extra Large and Extra Extra Large.

Price £25.00 including postage

Sleeveless Artic Fleece

In bottle green with the Association logo on the left side and two zip pockets. 100% pill resistant polyester and unlined. Sizes small, medium, large, extra large, and extra extra large.

Price £23.00 including postage

Polar Fleece Jacket

In bottle green with the Association logo on the left side and two zip pockets. 100% pill resistant, unlined, elasticated hem and cuffs. Sizes small, medium, large, extra large, and extra extra large.

Price £25.00 including postage

Cloth Badge

Good quality cloth badge, showing the Association logo, with 'SOUTH WEST COAST PATH' embroidered below, approximate size 4" x 3" (10 x 8 cm). Suitable for sewing onto shirt or rucksack, coloured logo in green and yellow on a blue background.

Price £2.70 including postage

Coast Path Embroidery

We have designed this unique counted cross stitch embroidery to celebrate the South West Coast Path. The embroidery kit contains everything you need to complete the project, and a leaflet containing full details can be obtained from the Administrator. Guidance is also given on how to personalise your embroidery to include your own completion date of the coast path.

Price £25.00 including postage

Notelets

The Coast Path Embroidery has been used as the cover design for notelets, which come in packs of 10.

Price £7.50 including postage

Whisky Tumblers

Cut glass whisky tumblers with the Association logo sand-blasted on the glass. In a presentation box.

Price £16.00, £28.00 for a pair, prices including postage. PLEASE ALLOW 28 DAYS FOR DELIVERY

Glass Beer Tankards

Glass beer tankards, plain glass with the Association logo sand-blasted onto the glass. Suitably packaged.

Price £11.50 including postage. PLEASE ALLOW 28 DAYS FOR DELIVERY

CD-ROM

Our CD-Rom is cut straight from the master files used on our web site. It contains over 350 pictures from along the Path in our acclaimed Photo Tour. It also has 33 stunning pictures especially prepared for use as computer wallpaper. It will work with Linux, Apple MACs and all versions of Microsoft Windows. If you require more technical details, check our web site.

Price £6.50 including postage

TO ORDER:- Please send details of the sizes of garments and / or quantity required, together with a cheque made payable to: **The South West Coast Path Association** to:- Sarah Vincent, The Administrator, 25 Clobells, South Brent, Devon TQ10 9JW. Tel/Fax: 01364 73859 or Eric Wallis, The Secretary, Windlestraw, Penquit, Ermington, Devon. PL21 0LU. Tel/Fax: 01752 896237.

We can also accept the credit/debit cards shown below, providing we have the following information:

Card Number   Expiry Date
Full name as it appears on the card   We welcome...
Issue Number (Switch Cards Only)

Non UK Orders: Please add £1.00 to cover extra postage.

Certificates

These are now available to persons who have walked the whole path. To members - £1.50 and to non-members - £2.50 including postage. Contact the Administrator.

BOOKS

These publications are available from bookshops. This list is not exhaustive; there are a number of other books available but we have tried hard to list all those which are really useful and even those not really useful that you might think would be.

South West Way - Minehead to Penzance

South West Way - Penzance to Poole.

Both these excellent pocket sized books are by Martin Collins. We can recommend them as most useful. Available from Cicerone Press, 2 Police Square, Milnthorpe, Cumbria, LA7 7PY at £8.99 each.

National Trail Guides - published by Aurum Press in association with the Countryside Agency. They are available from bookshops, or in case of difficulty, from Aurum Press, 25 Bedford Avenue, London WC1B 3AT. These are good guide books with good maps. An excellent venture by those involved.

Minehead to Padstow by Roland Tarr (5th Edition 2001)

Padstow to Falmouth by John Macadam (2nd Edition 1996)

Falmouth to Exmouth by Brian Le Messurier (4th Edition 2001)

Exmouth to Poole by Roland Tarr (2nd Edition 1996)

LANDFALL WALKS BOOKS - Bob Acton of Devoran has written twelve splendid books that contain well over 100 circular walks in Cornwall. These feature sections of the coast path throughout the county. They will enable walkers to progress along the coast path by basing themselves at one location. Write to Landfall Publications, Landfall, Penpol, Devoran, Truro, TR3 6NW for full list, or (Tel: 01872 862581).

Footpath Touring with Ken Ward. Land's End and The Lizard. Price £3.75 including postage. Available direct from 'Sea Chimney', South Down, Beer, EX12 3AE. An excellent guide to this section of the path by one of the co-authors of the well-known Letts Guides.

Two Moors Way (now illustrated) - by Devon Area Ramblers' Association - Price £3.00. This is not our path: one is enough! This describes the path from Lynmouth in North Devon to Ivybridge near Plymouth - and very well done it is too.

Two Moors Way by John Macadam. This is a new recreational guide published by Aurum Press and Ordnance Survey. £12.99.

Classic Walks Cornwall - 56 half day circular walks involving the coast path. From Cornish Publications Ltd, PO Box 12, Perranporth. £4.99 plus 75p P&P.

Classic Walks Devon - 60 Half-day Circular Walks - Many involving the coast path (as for Classic Walks Cornwall).

Most Tourist Information Centres (see our Accommodation section) have good supplies of leaflets and books relating to their local areas. We suggest you telephone or write to them and ask what is available.

THE NATIONAL TRUST 'COAST OF DEVON' LEAFLETS

A series of detailed leaflets with maps is available covering much of the coastline owned by the National Trust in Devon. Each leaflet contains good maps and information on the history, flora and fauna and general information of the areas.

They are available from National Trust shops in Devon or from the Devon Regional Office, Killerton House, Broadclyst, Exeter, EX5 3LE, Tel: 01392 881691; Fax: 01392 881954 at 75p each plus post and packing: (see guidelines overleaf).

The West Exmoor Coast	Wembury and Aymer Cove
Watersmeet and Countisbury	Salcombe Estuary
Bideford Bay to Welcombe Mouth	Dartmouth and South Devon
	Ilfracombe to Croyde

THE NATIONAL TRUST 'COAST OF CORNWALL' LEAFLETS

A series of detailed leaflets with maps, covering the coastline owned by the National Trust in Cornwall. Each leaflet contains information of the history, flora and fauna of the area as well as general information on points of interest. Available from National Trust shops in Cornwall or from the Cornwall Regional Office, Lanhydrock, Bodmin, Cornwall PL30 4DE. Tel: 01208 74281 Fax: 01208 77887.

Please make cheques payable to The National Trust and include postage & packing (see guidelines below).

No 1	Bude to Morwenstow	80p
No 2	Crackington Haven	70p
No 3	Boscastle	80p
No 4	Tintagel	80p
No 5	Polzeath to Port Quin	70p
No 6	Trevose to Watergate Bay, including Bedruthan Steps (not NT)	70p
No 7	Crantock to Holywell Bay	70p
No 8	St. Agnes and Chapel Porth	70p
No 9	Godrevy to Portreath	70p
No 10	West Penwith: St. Ives to Pendeen	90p
No 11	West Penwith: Levant to Penberth	90p
No 12	Loe Pool and Mount's Bay	80p
No 13	Lizard, West Coast	80p
No 14	Lizard, Kynance, Lizard Point & Bass Point	80p
No 15	Lizard, East Coast, Landewednack to St. Keverne	80p
No 16	Helford River	80p
No 17	Trelissick	80p
No 18/19	The Roseland and St Anthony Head	80p
No 19	St Anthony Battery	70p

No 20	Nare Head and the Dodman	80p
No 21	Fowey	90p
No 22	East Cornwall	80p

Country Walks Leaflet : Cotehele Estate	90p
Country Walks Leaflet : Lanhydrock	£1.00

Focus on Wildlife   £1.99

When ordering, please add the following rates for postage and packaging:

Quantity	1st Class	2nd	Quantity	1st Class	2nd	Quantity	1st Class	2nd
1	27p	19p	7	70p	55p	13-14	£1.17	93p
2	39p	31p	8-9	80p	64p	15-16	£1.30	£1.05
3-4	49p	38p	10-11	92p	73p	17-19	£1.60	£1.25
5-6	60p	45p	12	£1.04	83p	20-22	£2.00	£1.45

THE NATIONAL TRUST WESSEX REGION

The following illustrated guided walks leaflets are available from the Wessex Regional Office. To order copies, please write to: The Box Office, The National Trust, Wessex Regional Office, Eastleigh Court, Bishopstrow, Warminster, Wiltshire, BA12 9HW enclosing a cheque or postal order to include 50p towards postage and packing. Cheques should be made payable to 'the National Trust (Enterprises) Ltd.' Alternatively, you may call 01985 843601 and pay by credit card.

Isle of Purbeck (5 walks)	£2.75	
Holnicote (Horner Wood)		
- Valley Walk		£0.60
- Hill Walk	£0.60	
Golden Cap - Walks from Stonebarrow	£0.50	
Golden Cap - Walks from Langdon Hill Wood	£0.50	
Explore Holnicote	£1.00	
Holnicote - Bossington and Coastline Walk	£0.60	
Holnicote - Allerford and Selworthy woods walk	£0.60	
Cerne Abbas Giant and Dorset Hill Forts	£1.50	
Exploring Corfe Common	£0.50	
Holnicote - Dunkery and Horner Wood	£0.60	
Holnicote - Luccombe and Woodland	£0.60	
Holnicote - Selworthy and Bury Castle	£0.60	
Holnicote - Upland Archaeology	£0.60	

NATIONAL TRUST REGIONAL MARKETING AND COMMUNICATIONS MANAGERS

Devon Regional Office, Killerton House, Broadclyst, Exeter, Devon EX5 3LE (Tel: 01392 881691).

Wessex Regional Office, (for Dorset and Somerset) Eastleigh Court, Bishopstrow, Warminster, Wilts. BA12 9HW (Tel: 01985 843600).

Cornwall Regional Office, Lanhydrock, Bodmin, Cornwall PL30 4DE (Tel: 01208 74281)

All Long Distance Paths

We recommend the Long Distance Walker's Handbook: 6th Edition: Completely revised and updated. Contact - Brian Smith, 10 Temple Park Close, Leeds, West Yorkshire LS15 0JJ (Tel: 0113 264 2205). (£11.99 inc postage)

Information on Long Distance Routes can also be obtained from the Ramblers' Association, 1/5 Wandsworth Road, London SW8 2XX. (Tel: 020 7339 8500)

The South West Coast Path

Rail Links

South West Coast Path
National Park
Area of Outstanding Natural Beauty
Heritage Coast
County Boundary

0   50km

RAILWAYS

Throughout the year there is a regular service of direct First Great Western Trains linking London Paddington with Taunton, Exeter St. David's, Newton Abbot, Plymouth and Cornwall. There are also regular Virgin Cross Country Trains' services linking Birmingham, the North West, North East and Scotland with Taunton, Exeter St. David's, Plymouth, Cornwall, Bournemouth and Poole. All these services offer a range of on-train facilities including catering and on most First Great Western services during the school holidays, coach E is dedicated for the use of families. During the high season (May to September), demand for seats is high so it is recommended that seats are reserved in advance to ensure a comfortable journey. On Saturdays, additional services run to and from the West Country to the Midlands, North of England and London with a direct service operated between London and Newquay during the summer only.

There is a regular South West Trains' service linking London Waterloo with Bournemouth, Poole, Wareham (for Swanage), and Weymouth for those who intend to walk the Dorset end of The South West Coast Path. East Devon is served by an approximate two hourly service from London Waterloo to Axminster (for Lyme Regis and Seaton) and Honiton (for Sidmouth). In addition to these services South West Trains also offer a service of trains linking London Waterloo, Basingstoke, Salisbury, Exeter Central and Paignton.

Wales & Borders Trains offers long distance trains in the South West. They link Cardiff, Manchester, and Bristol with Penzance, Plymouth, Paignton and Exeter. A wide variety of attractive reduced-rate fares is often available, details of which can be obtained at Stations and Travel Centres. To obtain train information, call the National Rail Enquiries Service on 08457 484950 (24 hours a day), and to book tickets and reserve seats call 0870 9000 773 (0800-2000 Mon-Sat, 0900-1700 Sun). The web address is www.walesandborderstrains.co.uk

Wessex Trains offers long distance and most local trains in the South West. The long distance trains link Cardiff and Bristol with Exeter, Penzance, Plymouth, Portsmouth, Salisbury, Southampton and Weymouth. The local services on the branch lines of Devon and Cornwall offer connections into and out of First Great Western, Wales and Borders, South West Trains and Virgin Train services. Most Wessex Trains local routes also operate on Sundays during the summer months with the first five asterisked * below operating a Sunday service during the winter months too.

* Westbury - Yeovil - Weymouth	Liskeard - Looe
* Exeter - Barnstaple	Par - Newquay
* Exeter - Exmouth	Truro - Falmouth
* Newton Abbot -Torquay - Paignton	St Erth - St Ives
* Plymouth - Gunnislake	

To obtain train information, call the National Rail Enquiries Service on 08457 484950 (24 hours a day), and to book tickets and reserve seats call 0870 9000 773 (0800-2000 Mon-Sat, 0900-1700 Sun). The web address is www.wessextrains.co.uk

Private Branch Line Railways

Bishops Lydeard to Minehead - The West Somerset Railway PLC runs steam trains through 20 scenic miles (32 km) to Minehead. Bishops Lydeard is 4 miles (6 km) outside Taunton and easily accessible by bus. The service operates between March and October. For details contact the company at 'The Station', Minehead TA24 5BG (Tel: 01643 704996).

Paignton to Kingswear (Dartmouth) - For the rambler who is also a railway enthusiast, the Paignton and Dartmouth Railway is a `must'. This most attractive line runs from Paignton to Goodrington, Churston and Kingswear and operates preserved Great Western steam locomotives and rolling-stock. The line passes through some delightful coastal and river scenery, and a trip on the railway could easily be combined with a walk to make a very pleasant day out. It operates from March to December. For details contact - Queens Park Station, Torbay Road, Paignton TQ4 6AF (Tel: 01803 555872).

Bodmin Parkway to Bodmin Town is a service that could prove useful for those requiring bus transport to the coast. (Tel: 01208 73666).

BUS SERVICES

A new National Transport Enquiry Service has been established. For all timetable enquiries in South West England, call Traveline on 0870 6082608

Tourist Information Centres can help with bus enquiries. For details of all coastal TICs see our Accommodation section of the back of this book.

ACCESS TO THE START OF THE PATH:
Access to the start of the path can be made locally and from outside the region, with Southern National's bus service 28 linking Minehead to the Great Western Rail Line at Taunton.

Service 28 Taunton-Minehead currently operates on an hourly frequency up to the early evenings from Monday to Saturdays. On Sundays service 28 operates less frequently. For service 28 timetable enquiries telephone Southern National - Taunton. (Tel: 01823 272033).

National Express operates direct services to Minehead. For more information about national coach services to the South West, telephone National Express (Tel: 0990 808080) (this is charged at local call rates).

BUS INFORMATION:
Listed below, in path order, are details of services and information available from County Councils and local bus operators; it is intended for guidance use only. All information provided is correct at the time of going to print; responsibility for any inaccuracies or changes cannot be accepted by County Councils or bus operators. For up to date bus service information, telephone the relevant numbers given in the following paragraphs.

SOMERSET:
For service 28 from Taunton to Minehead and services 31, X31, and 31C from Taunton to Lyme Regis and Weymouth contact Southern National Ltd, The Bus Station, Tower Street, Taunton, TA1 4AF (Tel: 01823 272033).

ATMOS Ltd Transport Services (part of the W S Atkins Group) on behalf of Somerset County Council produces timetable booklets twice a year in Spring and Autumn. The 5 booklets are based on the District Council areas and are available from Libraries and TIC offices. A countywide bus map is also produced annually listing all the services in the county. In addition a leaflet showing the network of Sunday services is now also available. All literature can be obtained from ATMOS Ltd Transport Services, Atmos House, Crown Industrial Estate, Priorswood, Taunton, TA2 8QY (01823-251151).

NORTH DEVON:
The North Devon coast has a range of bus services which may be of use to coastal walkers. The greatest choice of coastal destinations is provided from Barnstaple. The principal services are: 309/310 Barnstaple to Lynton; Services 1, 2 & 30 Barnstaple to Ilfracombe; 308 Barnstaple to Georgeham (and Woolacombe in the summer); 1, Barnstaple to Bideford and Westward Ho!; 2 Barnstaple to Appledore and 319 Barnstaple to Bideford, Clovelly, Hartland to Bude 119 - two trips on Tuesdays and Fridays. Note that the number prefix refers to the bus route number. During the summer, service 300 operates daily from Barnstaple to Ilfracombe, Lynton and Minehead, with glorious coastal views along much of the route.

From Bideford there are frequent services to the coast. The principal services are 2, Bideford to Appledore; 1 Bideford to Westward Ho! and 319 Bideford to Clovelly, Hartland to Bude 119 - two trips on Tuesdays and Fridays.

Those who are not walking the entire path in one go may find the Western National X9 service from Exeter to Bude a useful link to or from the coast.

The above services are operated by First Red Bus North Devon Ltd., First Western National for timetable enquiries telephone Devon County Council's DEVONBUS ENQUIRY LINE - Barnstaple (Tel: 01271 382800) or Exeter (Tel: 01392 382800), Monday to Friday 0830 - 1700hrs.

Devon County Council produces timetable guides summer and winter entitled 'North Devon Public Transport Guide'. They are available from Tourist Information Centres, Libraries, bus operators or by telephoning the DevonBus enquiry line (number given above). Email: devonbus@devon.gov.uk Website: www.devon.gov.uk/devonbus

CORNWALL:
Cornwall County Council, in conjunction with First Western National, produces a series of 5 area public transport timetables. The booklets, published twice yearly in May and September, cover: 1 Penzance, St Ives, Camborne and Redruth; 2 Truro, Falmouth and Helston; 3 Newquay and St Austell; 4 North Cornwall; 5 South East Cornwall. Complete sets are available from the Passenger Transport Unit, Cornwall County Council, County Hall, Truro, TR1 3AY (Tel: 01872 322142) price £1.50, with cheques made payable to Cornwall County Council. The timetables can also be obtained free locally from bus stations, Tourist Information Centres and libraries, as can a county public transport map showing all bus and rail routes, with a summary of frequencies.

There is no comprehensive county bus enquiry number in Cornwall. First Western National bus information is available from Western House, Tabernacle Street, Truro, TR1 2EJ. Their enquiry lines are West Cornwall (Tel: 01209 719988), East Cornwall (Tel: 01208 79898). Details on Truronian Services can be obtained from 24 Lemon Street, Truro, TR1 2LS (Tel: 01872 273453) for services between Perranporth, Truro, Helston, Falmouth and The Lizard. Information on other operators can be obtained from Cornwall County Council's Passenger Transport Unit.

The principal routes serving coastal areas are:

First Western National Services: 1 Penzance to Land's End, 2 Penzance to Helston to Falmouth, 15 (summer only) St Ives to Land's End, 16/17 Penzance to St Ives, 86/87 Truro to Perranporth to Newquay, 88/89 Truro to Falmouth, 24 St Austell to Fowey, 26 St Austell to Mevagissey, 55 Bodmin Parkway Station to Bodmin to Wadebridge to Padstow, 124 Wadebridge to Port Isaac, 122 Wadebridge to Tintagel to Bude, X9 Exeter to Bude, X10 Exeter to Boscastle and Tintagel, 57 (summer only) Newquay to Padstow to St Ives.

Truronian Service T1 Perranporth to St Agnes to Truro to Helston to The Lizard, T34 Redruth to Helston. Liskeard and District Omnibus Co Liskeard to Looe and Polperro, Hambleys Coaches Polperro to Looe to Plymouth, Polruan Bus (summer only) Polruan to Polperro to Looe. Western Greyhound Service 592 Truro to Newquay, 594 Truro to Wadebridge, and 556 (summer only) Newquay to Padstow.

SOUTH DEVON:
The coastline between Plymouth and Exeter is accessible by bus from many inland towns. The principal services are:

80 Plymouth to Torpoint; 33/B and 34/B Plymouth City Centre and Admirals Hard for Cremyll Ferry (buses meet ferry and through ticket available); 7A Union Street (short walk from Cremyll Ferry) to Mountbatten (and Bovisand in the summer); 49 Plymouth to Heybrook Bay; 48 Plymouth to Wembury; 94 Plymouth to Noss Mayo; 92 Plymouth to Salcombe; 93 Plymouth to Kingsbridge & Dartmouth; X80 Plymouth to Paignton & Torquay; X38 Plymouth to Exeter; 87 Ivybridge to Bigbury-on-Sea; 164 Totnes to Kingsbridge; 111 Totnes to Dartmouth; 162 Kingsbridge to Hope Cove; 606 Kingsbridge to Salcombe; 120 Kingswear to Torquay; 22, 23, 24 Kingswear to Brixham; 12 Brixham & Paignton to Torquay and Newton Abbot; 85 Torquay to Teignmouth, Dawlish and Exeter; 85A Newton Abbot to Teignmouth, Dawlish and Exeter.

The above services are operated by First Western National, Tallo Ho!, Plymouth Citybus and Stagecoach. For timetable enquiries telephone Devon County Council's Devon Bus enquiry line: 01392 382800, Monday to Friday 0830 - 1700.

Western National produces timetable guides summer and winter for the South Devon area. They are available from the Travel Office at Plymouth Bus Station or by telephoning the Devon bus enquiry line, or Western National enquiries 01752 402060.

Plymouth Citybus map and services are available from the Public Transport Department, Plymouth City Council, Civic Centre, Plymouth, PL1 2EW.

EAST DEVON:
The East Devon coastline is accessible by bus from Exeter, Ottery St. Mary, Honiton and Axminster. The principal services are:

X53 Exeter to Beer, Seaton, Lyme Regis, Bridport, Weymouth; 20 Taunton to Seaton; 57 Exeter to Exmouth, Budleigh Salterton and Sidmouth; 52 Exeter to Sidmouth; 382 Ottery St. Mary to Sidmouth; 340 Honiton to Sidmouth; 885 Axminster to Seaton; 31 Taunton to Axminster & Lyme Regis (and continues to Bridport, Dorchester and Weymouth); 899 Sidmouth to Lyme Regis. On

Summer Sundays service 378 operates along the East Devon coast from Exeter to Sidmouth, Seaton, Axmouth and Lyme Regis.

The above services are operated by Stagecoach, First Red Bus Services, Axe Valley Mini-Travel and First Southern National. For timetable enquiries telephone Devon County Council's **DevonBus enquiry line** - Exeter (Tel: 01392 382800) or Barnstaple (Tel: 01271 382800), Monday to Friday 0830-1700.

Devon County Council produces timetable guides summer and winter, entitled 'East Devon Public Transport Guide'- they are available from Tourist Information Centres, libraries, bus operators or by telephoning the DevonBus enquiry line.

Bus Map - Other useful information provided by Devon County Council includes the public transport map. This depicts all bus routes and railway lines throughout the county and gives a summary of service frequency. It is available from Tourist Information Centres, libraries and bus stations or by telephoning the DevonBus enquiry line.

DORSET:
The Dorset Coast is accessible by bus from various inland points with train connections for the distant traveller. The principal routes are listed below.

Service 31 provides hourly journeys on Mondays to Saturdays between Weymouth - Dorchester - Bridport - Lyme Regis - Axminster. This service also operates until late evening with a two hourly Sunday service. Most buses will connect with trains at Axminster and Dorchester South. Passengers will also benefit from low floor buses that provide easy access and greater comfort. Please contact First Southern National, 80 The Esplanade, Weymouth DT4 7AA Tel: 01305 783645.

Service 103 operates a Monday to Saturday service between Dorchester and Lulworth/Durdle Door. It also calls at Wool railway station. For details contact First Southern National, see above. Services to Lulworth from Swanage and Wareham are operated by Swanage Taxis, tel: 01305 783645 and to Lulworth from Weymouth by Weaverbus, tel: 01305 834730. Both these services call at Wool railway station.

Service X53 operates between Weymouth - Lyme Regis - Exeter travelling along the coast between Weymouth and Bridport. Operates Monday to Saturday and provides four return journeys. This service is operated by First Southern National, see above.

Service 150 operates from Bournemouth - Swanage via Sandbanks Ferry with Service 142/3/4 operating from Poole - Swanage via Wareham and Corfe Castle. Both services run Monday - Saturday and Sundays. Please contact Wilts & Dorset Ltd, Travel Office, Bus Station, Poole BH15 1SN. Tel: 01202 673555.

Service 152 operates from Sandbanks Ferry to Poole Bus Station 5 minutes walk to railway station. No Sunday service from October to April. Please contact Wilts & Dorset Ltd, as above.

Dorset County Council annually produces a series of local public transport timetables listing bus and rail services and companies by area. A county-wide Bus and Rail Map listing all services in rural Dorset with frequency guide is also produced together with two Heritage Coast maps providing enhanced map details and timetables. These are available from Tourist Information Centres or The Passenger Transport Section, Dorset County Council, County Hall, Dorchester DT1 1XJ. Tel: 01305 225165, d.fiddik@dorset-cc.gov.uk

SEA TRANSPORT AND COASTAL CRUISES

The famous pleasure steamers Waverley and Balmoral provide both cruises and transport, to and from the Exmoor Coast.

From May until late September these big and fast sea-going ships provide transport between South Wales, Bristol, North Somerset, and the Exmoor Coast.

Sailings are to and from Ilfracombe, Lynmouth & Minehead. The timetable is subject to the Bristol Channel tides which have the second highest rise and fall in the world. Free copies of the full programme are available from Waverley Excursions Ltd., Gwalia Buildings, Barry Docks, CF62 5QR - telephone 01412 432224 or from Tourist Information Centres in West Somerset and North Devon.

USEFUL ADDRESSES

Countryside Agency, South West Region, Bridge House, Sion Place, Bristol, BS8 4AS.
(Tel: 0117 973 9966).
Countrywide Holidays Association, Miry Lane, Wigan, Lancs. WN3 4AG.
Exmoor National Park Authority, Exmoor House, Dulverton, Somerset TA22 9HI
(Tel: 01398 323665).
HF Holidays Ltd, Imperial House, Edgware Road, Colindale, London NW9 5AL
(Tel: 020 8905 9558).
Ramblers' Association, Second Floor, Camelford House, 87-90 Albert Embankment, London, SE1
7TW

COUNTY COUNCILS

Somerset County Council, County Hall, Taunton, TA1 4DY (Tel: 01823 355455).
Devon County Council, County Hall, Exeter, EX2 4QW (Tel: 01392 382000).
Cornwall County Council, County Hall, Truro, TR1 3BE (Tel: 01872 322000).
Dorset County Council, County Hall, Dorchester, DT1 1XJ (Tel: 01305 251000).

Addresses of Ramblers' Association contacts in the West Country

Devon - Mrs E. M. Linfoot, 14 Bladen Cottages, Blackborough, Cullompton, EX15 2HJ.
Cornwall - Mrs C. James, Chy-vean, Tresillian, Truro, TR2 4BN.
Dorset - Mr D. Riches, 43 Wyke Road, Weymouth, DT4 9QQ.
Somerset - Mr A. Harding, 21 Hollam Drive, Dulverton, TA22 9EL.

MAPS

1:50,000 Map. Ordnance Survey

The Metric 1:50,000 Landranger Series needed to cover the coast from Minehead in Somerset
to Studland in Dorset are as follows, working round the coast from Minehead.

181	Minehead & Brendon Hills	200	Newquay & Bodmin
180	Barnstaple & Ilfracombe	201	Plymouth & Launceston
190	Bude & Clovelly	202	Torbay & South Dartmoor
200	Newquay & Bodmin	192	Exeter & Sidmouth
204	Truro & Falmouth	193	Taunton & Lyme Regis
203	Land's End & The Lizard	194	Dorchester & Weymouth
204	Truro & Falmouth	195	Bournemouth & Purbeck

The two tourist 1" maps of Dartmoor and Exmoor available are of no advantage except that
Exmoor could be used instead of Map 181 and nearly all 180.

1:25,000 Maps. Ordnance Survey

In path order, from Minehead the coast path on $2\frac{1}{2}$" maps.

Outdoor Leisure 9	- Exmoor
Explorer 139	- Bideford, Ilfracombe and Barnstaple
Explorer 126	- Clovelly, Hartland and Bideford
Explorer 111	- Bude, Boscastle and Tintagel
Explorer 109	- Bodmin Moor (depicts coast path from Boscastle to Portgaverne)
Explorer 106	- Newquay, Padstow, Wadebridge and Port Isaac
Explorer 104	- Redruth, St Agnes, Camborne and Perranporth
Explorer 102	- Land's End, Penzance, St Ives
Explorer 103	- The Lizard
Explorer 105	- Falmouth and Mevagissey
Explorer 107	- St Austell, Fowey and Looe

Explorer 108	- Looe, Rame Head
Outdoor Leisure 20	- Plymouth and South Devon
Explorer 110	- Torquay and Dawlish
Explorer 115	- Exmouth and Sidmouth
Explorer 116	- Lyme Regis and Bridport
Outdoor Leisure 15	- Purbeck and South Dorset

All these maps may be obtained from bookshops. They may also be obtained from KenRoy Thompson Limited, 25 Cobourg Street, Plymouth, PL1 1SR (Tel: 01752 227693) POST FREE TO UK MEMBERS OF THE SOUTH WEST COAST PATH ASSOCIATION (Credit cards accepted).

TAXIS

Coast Path walking can be arduous in places but some of the hard work can be eliminated. We have been informed that the use of local taxis can ease the muscles. Transport is not for the walker, naturally, but for rucksack transfer from B&B to B&B. Local taxi firms will be pleased to give a price for the service. Consult yellow pages or ask the locals for details of taxi operators.

NATIONAL TAXI HOTLINE
Many taxi operators subscribe to the 'National Taxi Hotline' which works on a Freephone number - 0800 654321. When you dial that number your call will be automatically routed through to the subscribing taxi operator nearest to your location and you have your taxi.

We think it a grand scheme. It is free so no worries about having the appropriate coins when you are tired, wet through and fed up.

BANKS

We suggest you contact your own bank for a list of where their branches along the trail are located. Probably a Girobank account or Post Office National Savings account would prove to be the most convenient as there are small Post Offices in most villages. Overseas visitors should be wary of the above. It did not run smoothly for an Australian walker in 2001. For those, we suggest bringing your cashpoint card.

TELEPHONES

We urge you to consider buying BT Phonecards or BT Chargecards. Life is easier when you do not have to seek change for a call box.

MOBILE PHONES

These are always useful to have whilst on the Coast Path. However, do not rely on them as coverage is not always good in the South West. You may also have difficulty in obtaining top-up cards in some areas.

ORGANISED WALKING HOLIDAYS

We have compiled a list of organisations that run either self-guided or guided coast path holidays. Some also provide baggage transfer services. For a copy of this list please write to the Administrator and enclose £1.50 to cover printing, postage and administration time.

MARCH 2002
LOW WATER
From 31st, add 1 hour for BST

Days	Morning Time	Afternoon Time
1 Fr	0109	1335
2 Sa	0151	1416
3 Su	0230	1454
4 Mo	0308	1531
5 Tu	0346	1609
6 We	0428	1654
7 Th	0522	1754
8 Fr	0640	1929
9 Sa	0838	2115
10 Su	0948	2211
11 Mo	1037	2256
12 Tu	1119	2335
13 We	1157	-
14 Th	0011	1232
15 Fr	0044	1302
16 Sa	0111	1327
17 Su	0135	1350
18 Mo	0157	1412
19 Tu	0219	1436
20 We	0246	1504
21 Th	0320	1543
22 Fr	0410	1643
23 Sa	0538	1832
24 Su	0728	2006
25 Mo	0851	2122
26 Tu	0958	2224
27 We	1054	2316
28 Th	1143	-
29 Fr	0003	1230
30 Sa	0048	1312
31 Su	0129	1352

APRIL 2002
LOW WATER
add 1 hour for BST

Days	Morning Time	Afternoon Time
1 Mo	0208	1429
2 Tu	0244	1505
3 We	0321	1541
4 Th	0402	1624
5 Fr	0454	1722
6 Sa	0608	1848
7 Su	0810	2044
8 Mo	0921	2142
9 Tu	1008	2226
10 We	1049	2305
11 Th	1126	2341
12 Fr	1159	-
13 Sa	0012	1229
14 Su	0041	1256
15 Mo	0107	1322
16 Tu	0132	1347
17 We	0158	1414
18 Th	0228	1445
19 Fr	0305	1527
20 Sa	0358	1630
21 Su	0527	1812
22 Mo	0707	1944
23 Tu	0829	2059
24 We	0935	2200
25 Th	1030	2253
26 Fr	1119	2340
27 Sa	-	1205
28 Su	0024	1248
29 Mo	0106	1328
30 Tu	0145	1405

MAY 2002
LOW WATER
add 1 hour for BST

Days	Morning Time	Afternoon Time
1 We	0223	1442
2 Th	0301	1519
3 Fr	0342	1602
4 Sa	0433	1657
5 Su	0539	1809
6 Mo	0706	1939
7 Tu	0830	2052
8 We	0923	2142
9 Th	1006	2224
10 Fr	1045	2302
11 Sa	1120	2336
12 Su	1153	-
13 Mo	0009	1226
14 Tu	0041	1258
15 We	0113	1329
16 Th	0146	1403
17 Fr	0223	1440
18 Sa	0306	1528
19 Su	0403	1633
20 Mo	0520	1755
21 Tu	0644	1917
22 We	0800	2030
23 Th	0906	2132
24 Fr	1003	2226
25 Sa	1054	2316
26 Su	1141	-
27 Mo	0001	1225
28 Tu	0045	1306
29 We	0126	1345
30 Th	0206	1423
31 Fr	0245	1501

JUNE 2002
LOW WATER
add 1 hour for BST

Days	Morning Time	Afternoon Time	Days	Morning Time	Afternoon Time
1 Sa	0325	1542	16 Su	0312	1532
2 Su	0411	1630	17 Mo	0405	1627
3 Mo	0505	1728	18 Tu	0505	1732
4 Tu	0608	1834	19 We	0614	1843
5 We	0713	1940	20 Th	0725	1955
6 Th	0815	2040	21 Fr	0834	2102
7 Fr	0908	2132	22 Sa	0936	2202
8 Sa	0955	2218	23 Su	1031	2255
9 Su	1038	2300	24 Mo	1120	2343
10 Mo	1119	2340	25 Tu	-	1206
11 Tu	1159	-	26 We	0029	1250
12 We	0020	1239	27 Th	0112	1330
13 Th	0101	1319	28 Fr	0152	1408
14 Fr	0142	1400	29 Sa	0230	1444
15 Sa	0225	1444	30 Su	0307	1520

JULY 2002
LOW WATER
add 1 hour for BST

Days	Morning Time	Afternoon Time	Days	Morning Time	Afternoon Time
1 Mo	0343	1557	16 Tu	0353	1611
2 Tu	0424	1640	17 We	0442	1703
3 We	0512	1734	18 Th	0539	1805
4 Th	0609	1837	19 Fr	0646	1918
5 Fr	0710	1940	20 Sa	0801	2035
6 Sa	0811	2040	21 Su	0913	2144
7 Su	0908	2137	22 Mo	1015	2242
8 Mo	1001	2229	23 Tu	1107	2332
9 Tu	1051	2318	24 We	1154	-
10 We	1139	-	25 Th	0017	1237
11 Th	0005	1227	26 Fr	0100	1316
12 Fr	0052	1313	27 Sa	0138	1351
13 Sa	0138	1357	28 Su	0211	1423
14 Su	0223	1441	29 Mo	0242	1451
15 Mo	0308	1525	30 Tu	0309	1518
			31 We	0337	1546

AUGUST 2002
LOW WATER
add 1 hour for BST

Days	Morning Time	Afternoon Time
1 Th	0410	1623
2 Fr	0457	1723
3 Sa	0607	1845
4 Su	0722	1959
5 Mo	0831	2105
6 Tu	0933	2205
7 We	1031	2301
8 Th	1124	2352
9 Fr	-	1214
10 Sa	0041	1302
11 Su	0127	1346
12 Mo	0211	1428
13 Tu	0252	1508
14 We	0332	1548
15 Th	0414	1633
16 Fr	0502	1729
17 Sa	0605	1844
18 Su	0732	2019
19 Mo	0902	2136
20 Tu	1006	2233
21 We	1056	2321
22 Th	1140	-
23 Fr	0003	1221
24 Sa	0042	1257
25 Su	0116	1328
26 Mo	0145	1355
27 Tu	0210	1418
28 We	0231	1437
29 Th	0252	1459
30 Fr	0317	1529
31 Sa	0352	1614

SEPTEMBER 2002
LOW WATER
add 1 hour for BST

Days	Morning Time	Afternoon Time
1 Su	0449	1742
2 Mo	0638	1926
3 Tu	0803	2042
4 We	0913	2148
5 Th	1014	2245
6 Fr	1108	2336
7 Sa	1157	-
8 Su	0023	1244
9 Mo	0108	1327
10 Tu	0150	1407
11 We	0229	1445
12 Th	0307	1523
13 Fr	0345	1605
14 Sa	0429	1658
15 Su	0529	1816
16 Mo	0710	2014
17 Tu	0854	2128
18 We	0952	2218
19 Th	1038	2301
20 Fr	1119	2340
21 Sa	1156	-
22 Su	0015	1230
23 Mo	0047	1259
24 Tu	0113	1323
25 We	0135	1344
26 Th	0155	1403
27 Fr	0216	1426
28 Sa	0240	1456
29 Su	0314	1539
30 Mo	0405	1654

OCTOBER 2002
LOW WATER
until 27th, add 1 hour for BST

Days	Morning Time	Afternoon Time
1 Tu	0557	1900
2 We	0739	2022
3 Th	0854	2129
4 Fr	0955	2224
5 Sa	1048	2314
6 Su	1136	-
7 Mo	0000	1221
8 Tu	0044	1303
9 We	0125	1343
10 Th	0204	1422
11 Fr	0241	1500
12 Sa	0318	1542
13 Su	0402	1635
14 Mo	0502	1752
15 Tu	0641	1955
16 We	0829	2103
17 Th	0925	2151
18 Fr	1009	2231
19 Sa	1048	2308
20 Su	1124	2342
21 Mo	1157	-
22 Tu	0012	1226
23 We	0038	1252
24 Th	0103	1315
25 Fr	0126	1339
26 Sa	0150	1406
27 Su	0218	1439
28 Mo	0255	1524
29 Tu	0348	1641
30 We	0529	1833
31 Th	0712	1956

NOVEMBER 2002
LOW WATER

Days	Morning Time	Afternoon Time	Days	Morning Time	Afternoon Time
1 Fr	0828	2103	16 Sa	0928	2151
2 Sa	0930	2159	17 Su	1009	2229
3 Su	1023	2249	18 Mo	1047	2304
4 Mo	1111	2336	19 Tu	1122	2336
5 Tu	1157	-	20 We	1154	-
6 We	0019	1241	21 Th	0006	1225
7 Th	0101	1322	22 Fr	0037	1255
8 Fr	0141	1402	23 Sa	0107	1326
9 Sa	0219	1442	24 Su	0138	1400
10 Su	0258	1525	25 Mo	0212	1439
11 Mo	0342	1616	26 Tu	0254	1528
12 Tu	0437	1723	27 We	0349	1636
13 We	0553	1856	28 Th	0507	1801
14 Th	0732	2016	29 Fr	0635	1921
15 Fr	0839	2108	30 Sa	0753	2031

DECEMBER 2002
LOW WATER

Days	Morning Time	Afternoon Time	Days	Morning Time	Afternoon Time
1 Su	0859	2131	16 Mo	0919	2141
2 Mo	0956	2224	17 Tu	1005	2223
3 Tu	1048	2313	18 We	1046	2302
4 We	1136	2359	19 Th	1125	2341
5 Th	-	1221	20 Fr	-	1204
6 Fr	0042	1306	21 Sa	0019	1243
7 Sa	0124	1348	22 Su	0057	1322
8 Su	0204	1430	23 Mo	0135	1402
9 Mo	0244	1512	24 Tu	0215	1444
10 Tu	0325	1556	25 We	0258	1530
11 We	0411	1646	26 Th	0346	1623
12 Th	0506	1746	27 Fr	0443	1725
13 Fr	0611	1853	28 Sa	0552	1837
14 Sa	0722	1958	29 Su	0710	1952
15 Su	0826	2054	30 Mo	0825	2101
			31 Tu	0931	2202

DOGS

For many years most district councils and unitary authorities have implemented dog bans on beaches generally from 1st May to 31st October. Our Association and most of the general public regard this as a sensible measure.

There are several sections of the South West Coast Path that cross beaches and are officially marked as such. These beaches are Croyde Bay in Devon, Harlyn Bay, Constantine, Treyarnon and Perranporth in Cornwall, and Studland in Dorset.

The routing of the Coast Path (with its designation as a National Trail) across these beaches means that they are public rights of way. Our enquiries now reveal that a public right of way DOES carry precedence over seasonal regulations banning dogs, and ultimately any walker in the process of walking along, but not stopping on, these sections of the path may be accompanied by a dog under TOTAL control.

However we strongly recommend the following:-
a) If an alternative route is provided and signposted, that you use it.
b) That residents near to dog ban beaches use other walks and do not use the beach path during the ban period.
c) Total control means that the dog should be on a short (not extendable) lead.
d) That your progress should be as unobtrusive as possible to other beach users. To aid this, close attention should be paid to the actual route marked on the map.
e) Lastly, but most importantly that, should the worst happen, any dog mess MUST be removed from the beach.

RIVER CROSSINGS

The walker tends to view that feet are the only certain method of progress - and why not? Unfortunately, the absolute purist would need to be an olympic-class swimmer not to have to use ferries on the South West Coast Path. However, a certain amount of scepticism is helpful, absolute reliance on ferries is not advised.

There are other ferries available on the Path which walkers may wish to use for diversions or shortcuts. We have attempted to list those directly necessary.

Tide Tables (see pages 19 and 20)

The tide tables included in this edition refer to the times of low water at Devonport. These tables will act as a guide for those wishing to wade across the Gannel (Newquay), Gillan Creek, and the Erme and Avon (Bigbury-on-Sea). Please be sure to read the warnings given under each section. We have been criticised for being too cautious over the times we suggest for wading the rivers, and know that some walkers cross at other times. We believe our attitude is correct as there certainly are dangers, but you may wish to try at low tide on other occasions to see if conditions will permit a safe crossing. Variations in barometric pressure can affect tide levels. Remember there are different levels daily of low water; if in doubt seek local knowledge.

Newquay (The Gannel)	Deduct 30 minutes	Gillan Harbour	Deduct 15 minutes
R. Erme	As at Devonport	Bigbury/Bantham (R.Avon)	As at Devonport

*The Tide Tables on pages 19 and 20 are Crown Copyright. Produced from Admiralty Tide Tables with the permission of the Controller of Her Majesty's Stationery Office.

SUGGESTED ITINERARY

For some the fun of planning their own itinerary is a major part of the enjoyment of their holiday. If you are one of these, DO NOT READ THIS SECTION.

On the other hand there are some who have been put off tackling our path because they just could not see how to pack 630 miles' (1014 km) walking into a normal holiday. The answer is, of course, you cannot. Our Path, we reckon, needs about eight weeks to accomplish. That being so, we have tried to divide it up sensibly into eight roughly equal sections. Obviously, if we are going to suggest weekly stages, the beginning and end of each one must have reasonable accommodation and public transport. That presents a problem in itself, so after some thought we have broken it down into four 7-day and four 6-day weeks. Obviously not everybody will take a day off per week on their walk. That being the case, some will find they progress further along the Coast Path than our suggested itinerary. As usual, we would be very glad to hear from anyone who has tried one of our weeks and to hear their comments on it.

If you are a seasoned walker then there is a lot to be said for walking the whole path, albeit at different times, in our usual anticlockwise order. However, if you are not experienced, then obviously we should point out that the North Cornwall week, the third one in our schedule, is much the easiest if you want to start with something less demanding.

To keep the weeks set out below in a simple format the information is only an outline. IT IS ESSENTIAL TO CONSULT THE DETAIL IN THE REST OF THE GUIDE TO EFFECTIVELY PLAN YOUR HOLIDAY. Distances can vary depending on where you actually stay. Furthermore, our distances are only approximate because they are all 'rounded'.

After some of the place names we have added 'River Crossing'. You are advised to consult the appropriate section in this book for ferry and low tide suggestions.

Kilometres	Miles	Week 1 (Seven days)	
		MINEHEAD Rail Services to Taunton & S. National to Minehead Direct Nat. Express coach services.	
15	10	PORLOCK WEIR	
20	12	LYNMOUTH/LYNTON	
21	13	COMBE MARTIN	
20	13	WOOLACOMBE	
27	16	BRAUNTON	
20	12	INSTOW	
18	11	WESTWARD HO! (via Bideford)	Filers/Red Bus to Barnstaple & Rail services to Exeter. Direct Nat. Express coach services.
141	87		

		Week 2 (Seven days)	
		WESTWARD HO! Rail services to Barnstaple & Filers/Red Bus to Westward Ho! Direct Nat. Express coach services	
18	11	CLOVELLY	
16	10	HARTLAND QUAY	
25	15	BUDE	
16	10	CRACKINGTON HAVEN	
18	11	TINTAGEL	
15	9	PORT ISAAC	
19	12	PADSTOW (River Crossing)	First Western National bus to Bodmin Parkway Railway Station (Great Western Main Line)
127	78		

		Week 3 (Six days)	
		PADSTOW Rail services to Bodmin Parkway (Great Western Main Line). First Western National Bus to Padstow	
22	14	PORTHCOTHAN	
18	11	NEWQUAY (River Crossing)	
18	11	PERRANPORTH	
20	12	PORTREATH	
20	12	HAYLE	
9	6	ST IVES	Numerous bus services or rail service to St Erth (Great Western Main Line)
107	66		

		Week 4 (Six days)	
		ST IVES	Numerous bus services or rail service from St Erth (Great Western Main Line)
22	14	PENDEEN	
15	9	SENNEN COVE	

Kilometres	Miles		
19	12	LAMORNA	
15	9	MARAZION	
17	11	PORTHLEVEN	
22	13	LIZARD TOWN	Truronian bus service to Truro Railway Station (Great Western Main Line)
110	69		

Week 5 (Six days)

Kilometres	Miles		
		LIZARD TOWN	Rail service to Truro (Great Western Main Line) Truronian bus service.
17	11	COVERACK	
21	13	HELFORD (River Crossing)	
16	10	FALMOUTH (River Crossing)	
22	14	PORTLOE	
20	12	MEVAGISSEY	
19	12	PAR	Rail services (Great Western Main Line)
115	72		

Week 6 (Seven days)

Kilometres	Miles		
		PAR	Rail services (Great Western Main Line)
21	13	POLPERRO	
20	12	PORTWRINKLE	
21	13	PLYMOUTH (River Crossing)	
24	15	WEMBURY POINT (River Crossing)	
22	14	BIGBURY-ON-SEA (River Crossing)	
22	14	SALCOMBE	
21	13	TORCROSS	First Western National service Dartmouth - Kingsbridge - Plymouth
151	94		

Week 7 (Six days)

Kilometres	Miles		
		TORCROSS	First Western National service Plymouth - Kingsbridge - Dartmouth
16	10	DARTMOUTH (River Crossing)	
17	11	BRIXHAM	
17	11	BABBACOMBE	
27	16	EXMOUTH (via Starcross/Exmouth Ferry)	
21	13	SIDMOUTH	
17	11	SEATON	Bus services to Sidmouth, Lyme Regis, Honiton and Exeter
115	72		

Week 8 (Seven days)

Kilometres	Miles		
		SEATON	Bus services from Exeter, Honiton, Lyme Regis and Sidmouth
23	14	SEATOWN (Dorset)	
19	12	ABBOTSBURY	
17	11	FERRY BRIDGE (Wyke Regis)	
21	13	ISLE OF PORTLAND	
23	14	LULWORTH	
23	14	WORTH MATRAVERS *	
22	14	SOUTH HAVEN POINT	Ferry-Sandbanks, Wilts & Dorset to Poole or Bournemouth & Rail services Nat. Express coach services from Bournemouth to London
148	92		

* See pages 84 & 85 for opening times of Army Ranges and alternative routes.

THE SOUTH WEST COAST PATH

General

This is a series of notes on the state of the path which we hope will help you in your walking. Obviously it is very difficult to keep something as extensive as this both up-to-date and concise. Suggestions for improvement or amendments will always be welcome. We can only keep you right up-to-date with the state of the path if YOU will keep us posted about conditions as you find them on any stretch of the path. Your fellow members will be grateful, and so will we.

If you have any complaints about ordinary maintenance or signposting on the path, please write either to the Exmoor National Park Authority or the relevant County Council, Devon, Cornwall or Dorset. They should see this is done, and what is generally not realised is that any work carried out is 75% grant aided from the Countryside Agency for official National Trails such as the South West Coast Path. If you have any major problems or difficulties we would always be glad to be advised as well.

Each section has a reference to the Ordnance Survey map relevant to it - Outdoor Leisure (OS OL) and Explorer (OS E).

Towns and villages are now marked T or V respectively but the places at the end of each section appear as the first entry in the next one. We obviously stick our necks out to try and classify towns and villages. To us a town should have a reasonable range of shops, maybe even something as exotic as a laundrette. Villages should at least have a pub and a village store open all the year round, and a bus service. There are, of course, numerous other places you can get refreshment in season, but precious few out of it. Please note that all sections end at reasonable access points, usually having parking facilities.

Places which can be reached by rail are marked.

Distances

As a result of the 1999/2000 survey of the Coast Path end to end using a Global Positioning System, we now have access to very precise distances. The survey, carried out by the South West Coast Path Team, included the Isle of Portland - having done so we have become optimistic about our lobbying for the inclusion of The Isle into the official route. We have, therefore, jumped the gun and adjusted our book to include it.

We now know the Coast Path to be 630 miles (1014 km) long. This includes the Isle of Portland. When one considers we estimated the Coast Path to be 613 miles end to end, without including The Isle, we were not far out.

The section distances are shown in four columns.

The first - distance of the section in kilometres
The second - cumulative distance in kilometres
The third - distance of the section in miles
The fourth - cumulative distance in miles

The distances are measured along the officially designated route of the Coast Path, not along any diversions we suggest offering more scenic experiences than the route installed by the authorities.

Grading

Each section is graded as Easy, Moderate, Strenuous or Severe. Please note we no longer take into consideration lack of escape routes, distances from public transport, etc; it is purely a question of physical difficulty. We will try to highlight in the sections other considerations when they apply.
We would like to underline one point; the whole of our path is certainly not easy. Some parts of it are but other parts are not. We have had a number of letters from people who have walked The Pennine Way and who have been literally amazed at the severity of some of our tougher sections. Perhaps as a further comment we may add that recently we walked two 6 mile (10 km) adjacent sections. The time taken for one was 50% more than the time taken for the other. This may give additional emphasis to the importance of studying terrain if you wish to compute time.

Section Timing

We have introduced estimated timings for those wanting to know approximately how long each section may take to walk.

We consider these times to be a fair average. There are those who will complete sections quicker or slower than our estimations. We have NOT allowed for refreshment stops or for looking at views. However, it is important to remember that many factors can influence the speed at which you walk, e.g. weather, the amount of gear carried, an unexpected diversion etc., and you should always allow adequate time for your walk, especially if you are relying on public transport at the end of your walk.

These timings relate to the official route of the South West Coast Path only, and not to any of our suggested alternatives.

THE REVERSE GUIDE - POOLE TO MINEHEAD

The Association has written a description of the Trail for those walking in the Poole to Minehead direction. It deals only with the path so this annual guide will be necessary for all the other information. The Reverse Guide supplement is available from the Administrator at £3.50 including postage.

THE TRAIL DESCRIPTION - Minehead to Poole

FOLLOW THE NATIONAL TRAIL WAYMARK (THE ACORN SYMBOL)

CAUTION

This guide book describes the *official* route of the National Trail known as the South West Coast Path. Along its whole length it is maintained by the county councils of Devon, Cornwall and Dorset; the National Trust and Exmoor National Park.

Where you find we have little to say about the route we consider that it is highly unlikely that the walker will run the risk of going astray.

We are sometimes asked if you require a map as well as a guide book and our advice is certainly yes. One does not get as badly lost on the Coast Path as you can on inland paths, but a map is an asset nonetheless. Furthermore many walkers derive much interest from looking at their route in relation to the rest of the countryside on ordinary walks, and the same applies just as much, if not more so, on our Coast Path. The National Trail Guides offer a partial solution with their maps, but even these are not as useful as a map sheet.

Those who set forth upon this beautiful trail must remember it is mainly a cliff top path - in places it can be a very high cliff top. WE STRESS IT IS UNWISE TO LEAVE THE PATH ON THE SEAWARD SIDE OF ANY OF IT. THESE PATHS ARE SAFE BUT IF YOU LEAVE THEM YOU CAN PUT YOURSELF IN DANGER.

Now and again we suggest an alternative path away from the officially designated route. This will be for a more scenic and enjoyable experience. The above authorities have failed to create them as the designated route despite our representations over many years.

These alternative, recommended paths follow rights of way and in a few instances 'permissive routes' which are maintained by the landowner.

THIS ASSOCIATION STRESSES THAT WALKERS SHOULD NOT WANDER OFF THESE PATHS, ESPECIALLY SEAWARD OF THEM.

YOU CAN FALL A LONG WAY IF YOU DO. IF YOU FALL A LONG WAY - YOU CAN DIE.

LIABILITY DISCLAIMER

Information included or available through the South West Coast Path Association (SWCPA) is given in good faith and is believed to be accurate and correct at the time of going to print - however it cannot be guaranteed not to include inaccuracies or typographical errors.

Advice received via the SWCPA should not be relied upon for personal decisions and you should take into account the weather and your own capabilities before following the walks set out in this Guide. It is for the individual concerned to weigh up the risks of each of the walks described in this book.

The SWCPA makes no representations about the suitability of walks to any one person and will accept no liability for any loss or damage suffered as a result of relying on this book: it should be used for guidance only.

In no event shall the SWCPA be liable for any personal injury or any loss suffered as a result of using this publication.

FOOTNOTES

In certain sections we have added footnotes commenting on two books where you may be led astray. These are as follows:

'CP'   -   Martin Collins' two South West Way books by Cicerone Press.
'NTG' -   Four National Trail Guides - published by Aurum Press in association with the Countryside Agency.

| 1 | Minehead to Porlock Weir (Car Park) | OS OL9 (T) Minehead |

Grading: Official Route - Moderate
Alternative - Strenuous

Distance - 15.3 15.3 9.5 9.5

Timing: 4.5 hours

See also our Minehead to Lynmouth Path Description.

The South West Coast Path starts from Quay Steps, 100 yards (91 m) or so beyond the Red Lion Hotel. This is opposite the celebratory marker on the sea front of a pair of hands holding a map. This was sculpted by Owen Cunningham to the design of local art student Sarah Ward, and was opened on 14th February, 2001. The construction of this striking piece of art was managed by the South West Coast Path Team and part funded by donations from our South West Coast Path Association members.

You cross the road and walk between two cottages on the sea front.

The official route, although a good moorland walk, does not follow the traditional coastal route. Strong walkers looking for something better can start at the westerly end of the sea front road, proceed via Greenaleigh Farm to Burgundy Chapel and then make a steep ascent up North Hill. An easier alternative to this first piece is at Greenaleigh Farm, immediately before the house and the signpost 'To Burgundy Chapel and Beach' to fork left and then turn back, signposted 'North Hill'. This path zigzags back to pick up the official route, so avoiding the steep climb after Burgundy Chapel.

When taking the steep ascent from Burgundy Chapel at the T-junction go left - the path to the right goes only to a view point - and at the next junction go forward.

When you have gained the summit of North Hill, there is an acorn sign pointing to Selworthy and Bossington. Follow the line of this until you come to the next coast path sign, where there is a right fork marked 'Rugged Cliff Top Path'. Ordinary walkers should proceed forward on the official route but the more adventurous can fork right and proceed, walking seaward by what is a well-defined path.

Alternative - Rugged Coast Path

The 'Rugged Cliff Top Path' is a splendid alternative to the official path, with good views to seaward. It is well marked, but there are signs prohibiting dogs. At the stile take the left fork and soon you follow the rough track down by a boggy stream to the bottom of Grexy Combe at 937 481. From here take the well-defined diagonal path leading up the hill to the wall which is the National Trust boundary. This wall can be followed towards the sea at first and then along parallel to the sea all the way to Western Brockholes. After Western Brockholes the path bears inland, but is well signposted and rejoins the official path behind Hurlstone Point.

Coast Path continues

Those who have taken the official route, when reaching Bossington Hill should take the definitive right of way which goes down Hurlstone Combe. There is a much more spectacular route around Hurlstone Point which can be used apart from gale force conditions. If you stay on the official path, take care to descend the path to the left of Hurlstone Point and do not be tempted to take the more obvious path to the left (no signpost) contouring round Bossington Hill.

The official path goes inland from Hurlstone Point via Bossington and then out to the sea again. However, because of high storms the pebble ridge has been pushed back over the path and a deep impassable gully has been formed. You can take the path that has been signposted to Porlock from the road to Bossington Beach, missing the pebble ridge. An alternative is to walk on the first part of the Coast Path at the back of the pebble ridge past the lime kilns and then turn left at the signpost marked 'Footpath to Porlock Avoiding Flooded Marsh'. This will bring you to Sparkhayes Lane and into Porlock.

At Porlock the Visitor Centre and the Doverhay Museum are both worth a visit. The Ship Inn is an historic old pub. St Dubricius' Church is famous for its effigy monuments.

If you do not want to go to Porlock, follow the route of a new permissive path that is shortly to be opened up at the edge of the flooded lagoon to Porlock Weir, enabling you to see the wildlife around the lagoon. We hope that this will be opened by the time you read this.

To get to Porlock Weir from Porlock you take the road on the right - NOT the one that turns right past the Visitor Centre and is signposted to Porlock Weir - (unless you want to walk along the road) but the next turning on the right past the village hall and there is a footpath on the right that takes you through the woods at the back of West Porlock.

2 | Porlock Weir to Lynmouth (Visitor Centre) OS OL9

Grading: Moderate   Distance -   19.8   35.1   12.3   21.8

Timing: 4.5 hours

See also our Minehead to Lynmouth Path Description

The path leaves Porlock Weir in front of the Anchor Hotel; turn left at the sign for Culbone.

This path is well marked. At Culbone turn right if you want to visit the small church. There is also a refreshment hut where you help yourself and leave your payment. From the church, retrace your steps up the path and turn right onto the Coast Path; in about 300 yards (275 m) turn right into Culbone and Embelle Woods and on into Yenworthy Woods. This path through the woods has been reopened as the Official Coast Path.

When you get to Yenworthy Combe there is a sign to the Pinetum, where there is a pleasant diversion. There are some unusually mature examples of trees planted between 1840 and 1860 and several are over 100 feet tall. There is also a trout pond off the stream and an icehouse which was cut into the cool, shaded bank of the stream. A tunnel leads to a deep cemented pit which was sealed by two tightly fitting doors to hold ice throughout the year for use in the kitchens before electricity.

At the end of the Pinetum is a new permissive path through woods that has been opened up called 'Ben's Path' south of Home Farm that rejoins the Coast Path. Before you get on to Ben's Path you may like to go to Glenthorne Beach. You will see the remains of a jetty, which was built to land heavy building materials for the estate when overland routes were impractical. There is also the remains of a boathouse, coal store and lime kiln. The limestone and coal were brought over from South Wales.

Proceed to Sister's Fountain, where there is a legend that Jesus drank here with Joseph of Arimathea on his way to Glastonbury. Continue uphill through a pair of wild boar head gateposts, which was the entrance to the Victorian Woodland Lodge, which usually has barking Jack Russell dogs in its garden.

At Caddow Combe, the official route is again signposted inland 'Countisbury 1.5 miles'. The surefooted might prefer the right of way signposted 'Lighthouse' which proceeds out to the Foreland Point Lighthouse. Just before the entrance to the lighthouse where the wall commences on the right, the path takes off up the bank to the left. The beginning is clearly marked because the authorities tell you they no longer maintain the path. This path is more exposed than the official route and careful walking is advised. It has magnificent views if you are surefooted and the weather is calm.

The National Trust has a good path which can be taken down the seaward side of the main A39 coastal road so avoiding the upper reaches of Countisbury Hill. Lower down the hill the path joins the road but a new path on the seaward side ensures that you will not get run down.

You come out on the foreshore. Walk along into Lynmouth crossing the footbridge, and there turn right down to the sea front turning left up the steps before the cliff railway, that is assuming you are a purist and are not actually going to use the railway which you can well do if you wish! If you use the railway you do suffer slightly at the top in that you will have to walk nearly into Lynton and then out again to regain the North Walk. After all, it serves you right for not having walked the whole way!

It is interesting to know that at Lynmouth you can now walk Devon's coast to coast route by using the Two Moors Way to Ivybridge then the Erme Valley Trail which links into the Erme/Plym Trail to Plymouth. Guide books to the above are available from Lynton TIC (see page 131).

3	Lynmouth to Combe Martin (Car Park)	OS OL9 (T) Lynton/Lynmouth

Grading: Strenuous	Distance -	21.4	56.5	13.3	35.1

Timing: 7 hours

See also our Lynmouth to Ilfracombe Path Description.

Please note there is a long, lonely section onward from Heddon's Mouth to Combe Martin without any chance of refreshment.

The path itself out from Lynton is a Victorian idea for a coastal footpath called the North Walk and although to our modern ideas, tarmac might not be the ideal footpath medium, it is a very fine high level walk indeed. This takes you very happily up to Castle Rock. Unfortunately, the official route is then on the road all the way through to Woody Bay.

However, there are diversions which will save you some road walking. The first takes off to the right after the turning circle (roundabout) at the end of the Valley of Rocks and then goes in a loop back, to come out by the Lodge at the beginning of Lee Abbey. The second alternative is a left turn immediately opposite Lee Abbey which is labelled 'Woodland Walk' (each end) and rejoins the road about 0.75 mile (1200 m) further along.

If you do not follow the 'Woodland Walk' but follow the road past the toll house and refreshment stop (seasonal), you will climb up a hill and come across a new footpath on your right, that goes along the field adge to Crock Point and through the woods at Crock Pits. This is an excellent addition to the Coast Path, taking you off a busy road, with some stunning coastal walks, and we thank the Exmoor Park Authority for making this possible.

This is one of the finest pieces of Coast Path in North Devon and should not be missed by anyone who is reasonably surefooted, or unless weather conditions are very bad. The path takes off just before the Woody Bay Hotel opposite the Red House and the beginning of the path is marked by a signpost on the right which says 'Public Footpath to Woody Bay Beach 0.75 mile'. This path comes out on another road where you turn up left. There will be another sign 'Footpath Hunter's Inn 2.25 miles'. You will cross a stile with a sign 'Heddon Valley Hunter's Inn'. This is a superb path which is now the new official route. It is much nearer the coast giving splendid views. When the path reaches the Heddon Valley path, the official route is as follows. Continue ahead/left towards Hunter's Inn. On reaching the stone bridge over the Heddon River on your right, cross over it, pass through the gate and on reaching the next path across turn hard left. Continue for 100 yards (91 m) or so to the signpost on the right to Combe Martin.

Alternative Route
For a very pleasant alternative down to the beach and restored lime kiln follow these directions. Turn hard right and walk down by the river to Heddon's Mouth, crossing the bridge by the picnic area. Carry on to the beach and the lime kiln. Return to the picnic area by the bridge and continue through the picnic area, keeping the river on your left. In a while ignore the path going down on your left. Pass through the gate and continue for 100 yards (91 m) or so to the signpost on the right to Combe Martin.

Coast Path continues

Whichever route you have taken, continue as follows. Follow this path up to the right, through the gate and on up; there are seats on the way up! Continue up the path and various steps and on reaching the few steps near the top, carry on round to your right, where the path now levels off. More lovely views of the Heddon Valley open up. Carry on round the headland at Peter Rock (beware if windy) and along the Coast Path for a good 0.5 mile (800 m) until you start heading inland and reach the path going across you by the stone wall, with the Coast Path sign up to your left. Whilst in the valley of Heddon's Mouth, those requiring refreshment have easy access to the Hunter's Inn and the National Trust shop selling very good ice cream.

Just west of East Cleave you will regain the old official route passing along High Cliff and North Cleave. At map reference 628 482 take the short walk across open heathland to avoid the walk up to the old Trentishoe Down Road.

As there are many sheep tracks by Sherrycombe, we suggest you follow the grass track along the top of the combe to the inland end of it to pick up the path down.

When ascending Great Hangman from Sherrycombe you reach a seat. Keep alongside the wall on your left. There is a number of well-walked paths going out to the right but they are all wrong! From Great Hangman the path is clear to Little Hangman where more stunning views are available.

When you come to the shelter above Combe Martin, turn right on the unmarked path; this has the better views.

4	Combe Martin to Ilfracombe (Harbour)	OS OL9 (T) Combe Martin

---

Grading: Moderate, Strenuous in parts	Distance-	8.6	65.1	5.3	40.4

Timing: 2.5 hours

See also our Lynmouth to Ilfracombe Path Description.

The path leaves the lime kiln car park, passing the Exmoor National Park Visitor centre; fork right and join the A399 road. Turn right (Seaside Hill Road) above the beach. Turn right onto a narrow tarmac lane, which climbs steeply to rejoin the A399 road.

Walk on the slightly raised path along the road side through two gates. Having gone along a path beside a field to the flight of steps, you should turn left up the newish slip road back to the main road and to the brow, passing the bus shelter. You then turn right to follow the road down to the old main road with a bus shelter over to the right, which is now used as an information point for the Heritage Coast. Here you turn left beside the entrance to the Sandy Cove Hotel to follow a track towards Watermouth Cove.

Watermouth Castle, built 1825, comes into view. At Watermouth it is possible to cross the foreshore at low tide to a flight of steps; take care as the rocks can be slippery. This is not possible at high tide when one has to continue along the road with no pavement for approximately 200 yards (185 m) and there is then a stile off right into the woods. Take care whilst walking this road section.

The next section of the path is very pleasant on the western side of Watermouth and continues out and around Widmouth Head. This section provides some very spectacular walking; we particularly commend the view back from Widmouth Head over Watermouth, whatever the state of the tide or sea. This will be your last good viewpoint of the dramatic setting of the Great Hangman and the Little Hangman eastwards above Combe Martin. After Widmouth Head the path continues in front of the coastguard cottages going to Rillage Point.

This fine section ends with a road walk down into Hele. Turn right and look out for some steps on the far left of the beach. The path then zigzags passing Beacon Point with a fine view of Ilfracombe, until it reaches the top of Hillsborough. There are several paths to choose from here but they all end up in Ilfracombe. We have asked for an additional waymark to route you onto the harbour road.

5 | Ilfracombe to Lee Bay

OS E139 (T) Ilfracombe

Grading: Easy to moderate	Distance-	5.3	70.4	3.3	43.7

Timing: 1.5 hours

See also our Ilfracombe to Croyde Bay Path Description.

Walk along the edge of the harbour, bear left at the slip and then right into Broad Street. At a T-junction, turn left into Capstone Road next to the Sandpiper Inn. After about 170 yards (150 m), turn right and walk around Capstone Point. Follow the path from Capstone Point down to Wilder beach and now take the flight of steps that goes up the back of the Landmark Theatre. Follow this path up to the top of the gardens and the gate by a shelter. Pass through this gate and bear right to walk along Granville road, before bearing right onto an unmetalled road which takes you to the Torrs Walk: it is well waymarked.

At the top of the Torrs Walk bear right and follow the path down the field to the stile in the corner. Continue ahead around the hill and beware of the steep drop on your right, to the stile. Now cross the field to the old coach road ahead, bearing right onto it and follow it all the way to Flat Point. Along Flat Point the Coast Path follows the route of the old coach road. (Flat Point is National Trust land with its open access policy, and it can be roamed at your own risk and offers good sites for picnic stops.) Passing through a field gate your route is along a narrow, pleasant road down into Lee.

Refreshments are available all year round at the Grampus Inn in Lee village, which is only a minor diversion from the coast.

6 | Lee Bay to Woolacombe

OS E139 (V) Lee Bay

Grading: Strenuous, becoming easy	Distance -	6.4	76.8	4.0	47.7

Timing: 2 hours

See also our Ilfracombe to Croyde Bay Path Description.

This section will take you longer to walk than you think as it includes some up and down work but is a lovely piece of path to walk.

Proceed up the road from Lee, turn right onto a path by the National Trust sign 'Damage Cliff'. To the left of the path are the remains of a pre war golf course. Before Bull Point the path crosses two steep valleys, Hilly Mouth and Bennets Water. The lighthouse is one of the few manned stations left in the country. Rockham has a fine stretch of sand that is very popular in the summer. Morte Point is a spectacular jagged slate ridge rather like a dinosaur's back emerging from the sea. Offshore is the often submerged Morte Stone and this 'Rock of Death' was aptly named in the last century. At certain states of the tide an awesome tidal race can be seen; many ships have been wrecked off here.

7 | Woolacombe to Croyde Bay (Beach)

OS E139 (T) Woolacombe

Grading: Moderate	Distance -	10.2	87.0	6.3	54.0

Timing: 3 hours

See also our Ilfracombe to Croyde Bay Path Description.

This section starts at the Waterfall Hotel and runs parallel to the Esplanade road, then turns up Chalacombe road. This is now waymarked but a vital waymark has been removed to indicate where the route turns off the road into the warren. This path is about where the National Trust sign has been placed. The official route stays in the Warren; the alignment shown on 139 OS Explorer map is incorrect.

This section starts rather poorly along the road south from Woolacombe and tries hard to lose itself in the enormous dunes. Waymarking, however, has been improved and you should not go astray. A possible alternative is to walk the Marine Drive which gives fine views. If the tide is out it is easier to walk Woolacombe Beach but it should not be attempted on a flood tide as you may not be able to get off the beach at Vention.

If you have used the official path, it leaves the Warren by a set of steep steps. At the top turn right and after 500 yards (460 m) a path leaves the official route; this takes you down to a car park (refreshments and toilets). Pass to the left of the caravan site, over a stile and up the cliff slope to rejoin the official route to Baggy Point.

The high level path out to Baggy Point is pleasant. If the visibility is good you will get a good chance as you turn the corner to look at the path for a number of miles ahead across Bideford Bay. At Baggy Point itself, when you have turned the corner, do bear right on to the lower path; it is no further and provides much better sea views.

Passing the National Trust car park, there is a road walk of about 545 yards (500 m) before the turn off to the beach. Do not be tempted to use the first slipway as it would be very difficult walking over the rocks.

8 | Croyde Bay to Barnstaple (Long Bridge)   OS E139 (V) Croyde

| Grading: Easy | Distance - | 23.1 | 110.1 | 14.4 | 68.4 |

Timing: 5.25 hours

See also our Croyde Bay to Barnstaple Path Description.

Distances are measured walking via Crow Point, and around Horsey Island, through Velator to join the disused railway track all the way to Barnstaple.

The path crosses the top of Croyde beach, and on to the low cliffs at Down End, turns left and after reaching the old coastguard lookout, one has to cross the main B3231 road. This is a very busy road so take great care as you cross over the road which has to be done at this point. Walkers are advised NOT to take dogs onto this beach between May and September.

Turn left and walk downhill a short way to reach some stone steps. After a short climb, the path contours round Saunton Down, parallel to and above the road.

From this path there are some spectacular views down the length of Saunton Sands, and if clear, across the estuary to Appledore. On the hillside to the left some ancient cultivation terraces can be seen.

The large flat-roofed building is the five-star Saunton Sands Hotel owned by the Brend family. Wonderful food; they welcome all, including walkers.

At this point you are confronted with three routes from which to choose:-

1. *The official route* crosses the B3231 road and passes around the hotel and descends to the large Saunton Sands car park. (The refreshment hut is open from Easter to the end of September.)

   Continue in an easterly direction across the car park and pick up a sandy lane near some holiday chalets. At the end of this lane you return to the B3231 road.

   Take care now as there is 400 yards (365 m) of that road to walk along until just past the Saunton Golf Club driveway. Turn right here. The path then wanders around the landward side of the golf course. It is well marked.

2. This route does not involve crossing the B3231. At the bottom of the slope before the road, turn left onto a public footpath. You climb steeply with the path bearing right. It passes near to Saunton Court and continues on to the B3231 road opposite the red brick house. You then follow the official route as described in Option 1 above.

   This diversion eliminates 400 yards (365 m) of very dangerous road walking. The Heritage Coast Service suggests this route and we have asked for signs to be installed.

3. This third choice is probably the one preferred by most walkers. Cross over the B3231. Pass around the Saunton Sands Hotel and descend to the large car park. Walk south along the beach via Airy Point to Crow Point. After 3.5 miles (5.5 km) along the beach, just after the

groyne watch out for a slatted wooden catwalk on your left. This is your beach exit so walk along this to Broad Sands. As you do so you will have regained the official route.

The official route after options 1 and 2 now enters the Braunton Burrows nature reserve.

These burrows are renowned for their great wealth and diversity of their plant life, and over 400 species of flowering plants have been recorded here.

When the Burrows car park is reached the path uses the so-called American road to Broad Sands. It should be noted that the American road is often flooded across making this section of the walk sometimes difficult.

Arriving at Broad Sands, either by the Burrows walk or the beach walk (Option 3), the path becomes a little vague, but keep the estuary on your right hand side and you cannot go wrong. Head for the white cottage on the estuary side.

The route now follows the estuary side on top of the Great Sea Bank. The path keeps to the top of this sea wall all the way to Velator. If you wish to visit Braunton turn left at Velator and walk along the old railway track into the village.

From Velator the route now follows the old Barnstaple to Ilfracombe railway track into Barnstaple: the railway was closed in 1970.

In the summer months, the walker will have a problem on this section of the path, as not only is it the South West Coast Path, but it is also a cycle track used by many hundreds of cyclists. Few bikes seem to have any audible means of warning you of their approach, so walking can become very hazardous. After leaving Velator you will pass the old railway station at Wrafton and after about 1 mile (1500 m) the path suddenly emerges onto the estuary side. When the tide is high it presents a very fine picture and in the winter months there are many ducks and waders to observe.

After Heanton Court, a possible stop for refreshments, continue following the old railway track which follows the banks of the estuary to Barnstaple. By the time this Guide is published the new bridge over the River Yeo should be in place. Cross the new bridge and continue along beside the wharf towards the old Long Bridge over the river in Barnstaple.

9 | Barnstaple to Westward Ho! (Amusement Arcade)
OS E139 & OS E126 (T) Barnstaple (Trains); (T) Bideford

| Grading: Easy | Distance - | 30.7 | 140.8 | 19.1 | 87.5 |

Timing: 7 hours

See also our Barnstaple to Westward Ho! Path Description.

Distances are measured walking through to Bideford: approximately 6 miles (10 km) can be avoided by using the Instow to Appledore Ferry, but this is seasonal and subject to the tide.

Having passed the old Barnstaple railway station, you soon pass a new recreation area with seating, a good spot for a break. Continue along beside the river to the Long Bridge and take the steps up to the left which bring you onto the bridge. Cross the bridge - there is no need to cross the road. On the other side of the bridge pass the Leaderflush/Shapland works on your right and then turn right by the roundabout. Follow this road and when it bears right, cross over to pick up the path ahead behind the houses. Follow this to where it joins the Tarka Trail by the old railway bridge, bearing right along the old railway track. Again be aware of cyclists as you follow this all the way to Instow where there is the option of using the ferry, tides and weather conditions permitting. However, remember the official route of the South West Coast Path is in to Bideford.

Contact Mr Ommanney   Easter to October 7 days per week - every 15 mins
The Sea Chest   Tidal - Approximately two hours each side of high water
Market Street
Appledore EX39 1PW
Tel: 01237 476191

It may also be possible for pre-organised parties to use the ferry out of season - please telephone for further details.

Please note, however, that absolute reliance on ferries is not advised, so if the ferry is not running, rejoin the old railway track by the old level crossing and signal box.

Continue on to Bideford under the new Bideford bridge. The old Bideford railway station is the base of the Hartland Coast Heritage Service. Refreshments are available in season in the reconditioned railway carriage.

Cross the Bideford Long Bridge, turn right and walk along the quay. Continue walking by the riverside path now named Landivisau Walk (Bideford's twin town in France) keeping the car park on your left. At the end of the car park there is a waymarked lane passing the Bideford RFC stadium. Continue walking on a road to pass under the new high level road bridge, then up a rough track, turn right by the waymark, and walk down a narrow track. This rejoins the riverside by a small beach at Lower Cleave. There is some more road walking passing the Yeoldon House Hotel. Be sure to keep to the waymarked lane; do not stray up any of the many private drives. After the second war tank traps, fork right and the route enters the National Trust property of Borrough Farm. This is a very pleasant section through some riverside woods with fine views back up the river to Bideford.

There is now a steep descent to another small beach with stepping stones over a marshy area. After the second National Trust sign turn right. There are now two options here. Use the low tide route except at high tide as it is the more attractive route and can be taken in all cases but high tide. These routes are both well waymarked. With the steps now provided it is not difficult to negotiate the breach in the sea wall. Having done that the path turns inland to meet up with the high tide route. Follow the waymarked route around the Appledore shipyard to reach the road, turn right and into Appledore via Myrtle Street.

At Appledore plenty of accommodation and refreshment places are available. Along the Quay you meet the ferry slipway from Instow. The route now continues into old Appledore, passing the homes of the old sailing captains to near the lifeboat house. Walk along the side of the road past the DCC recycling centre and out towards the mouth of the Taw/Torridge estuary.

Here for some distance you are walking on the seaward side of the dunes turning to the golf links side to pass Sandy Mere, then it is a straight walk into Westward Ho!. At most states of the tide it is possible to walk the beach, but be warned, the sand can be rather soft in places. Westward Ho! has plenty of accommodation but refreshment places are limited out of season.

10   Westward Ho! to Clovelly (Mount Pleasant)   OS E126 (T) Westward Ho!

Grading: Strenuous	Distance -	18	158.8	11.2	98.7

Timing: 6 hours

See also our Westward Ho! to Clovelly Path Description.

After passing the last of the holiday chalets, the path follows the track of the old Bideford to Westward Ho! railway. This is a fine stretch of the Coast Path over Cornborough and Abbotsham cliffs. At Greencliff a very poor coal was once mined. The path now climbs steeply over Cockington cliffs only to drop again to sea level to cross a pebble beach before climbing again via a wooden staircase, to cross Babbacombe cliffs. At Peppercombe turn inland to cross the stream and then the path meanders through Sloo Woods to join the new section through Worthygate Wood.

NOTE: The route shown on OS Explorer map 126 at Gauter Pool is wrong. The path does not turn to the south but goes on through the woods dropping to Buck's Mills.

At Buck's Mills refreshments are available and a walk down to the old Quay is worthwhile. On leaving Barton Wood, keep to the bottom edge of the field until you cross a bridge into Hobby Drive. The walk along the Hobby Drive is nearly 3 miles (5 km) long, and takes longer than you think. There is a path which takes you off the Hobby Drive down to the harbour; by walking down it and then up to the village street again, you can rejoin the Coast Path.

Grading: Moderate to strenuous   Distance -   16.6   175.4   10.3   109.0

Timing: 5 hours

See also our Clovelly to Hartland Quay Path Description.

This is a very fine section indeed, what coastal walking is all about! Allow yourself plenty of time to really enjoy it. You leave Clovelly by following the coast path sign through the large gate in the wall/fence on the left of the road going down the hill - do not go down the hill. Follow the track round to the right, to the coast path signpost, where you follow the path down to the right (yellow waymark). After a while you pass through the kissing-gate and follow the fence on your right until reaching the small kissing-gate in the shrubbery. Follow this path and soon a covered seat appears on the right. Carry on through the shrubbery and through the next two kissing-gates. After a while turn right at the T-junction, following the coast path sign, and right again at the next fork. Soon you come to an original seat called the 'Angels Wings', with nice woodcarvings. On reaching the track, take the coast path hard to the right - do not go along the track. Follow this path to a wonderful viewpoint before it descends steeply into a valley to a track. Go right and before going immediately left and immediately right again there is an easy detour that is very worthwhile. Having turned right off the steep descent, go ahead instead of sharp left up the track beside the cliff edge. When this track levels out, look out for some indistinct steps up to the right and follow these to a cutting in the rock which take you through to a marvellous lookout platform with lovely views.

Returning back through the rock cutting, turn right and go down to the old shelter, passing through the pointed-arch doorway. Further excellent views along the coast to the waterfall open up before you. There is a further viewpoint past the shelter but the views are quite restricted. We now recommend that you return back to the coast path sign bearing right down to the main track where you turn hard right to follow this track down the valley to the shore. Go down the narrow path, crossing the stream by the stepping stones. Pause at the shore and notice the rock formations and the waterfall along the coast to your left (at low tide). Also note the old lime kiln. Now follow the grass track inland past the lime kiln and old building. Shortly take the Coast Path up to your right. Half way up follow the steps to the right ignoring the path going on ahead. On reaching the top, cross the stile by the NT sign for Brownsham.

The path proceeds through one field and over another stile which is multistepped on the eastern side, then across another field to the stile in the right hand fence, and then proceed down the steps, across the bridge at the bottom, turning left, and then take the first turning on the right. This is the more seaward route and is now the official path. We asked for this path and are grateful to the National Trust for having provided it. At Becklands there is a small memorial plaque in memory of the crew of a Wellington bomber that crashed into these cliffs in April 1942.

The route now continues practically on the coast all the way to Eldern Point and then on to Shipload Bay. The true coastal path from Shipload Bay to Barley Bay seaward of the radar station is now open and freely available. (Seasonal refreshment hut - Hartland Point car park.)

The path down into the Smoothlands Valley and out to Damehole Point is a wonderful part of the coast path. Those requiring further exercise may like to walk over the cliff top on the north of the Smoothlands Valley and it does give wonderful views, but it is not the official path. We confidently recommend Damehole Point itself to the sure-footed as not only being one of the most dramatic pieces of definitive Right of Way in the whole country but also as an ideal picnic spot.

To cross Abbey River the path goes inland behind the cottage to a stone bridge.

After crossing Abbey River, those who want the most scenic route should not turn left as directed at the next coastal path sign. Continue right out to the coast at Dyer's Lookout and then turn left up the cliff edge. It is a little further but scenically much better. On reaching the old Rocket House by the road inland to Stoke, bear right to follow the path downhill to Hartland Quay, soon picking up the small road down to the seasonal refreshments, museum, toilets and hotel.

12   Hartland Quay to Bude (Canal Bridge)   OS E126 & E111

Grading: Severe	Distance -	24.8	200.2	15.4	124.4

Timing: 8.5 hours

See also our Hartland Quay to Bude Path Description.

This is a most rewarding but very tough section. It will almost surely take you longer than you think although the beginning is comparatively mild. Before reaching Bude you will have crossed ten river valleys. A word of caution - there are no refreshment facilities other than the seasonal opportunities at Morwenstow and Sandy Mouth, so you should consider adding to your load at Hartland Quay.

The path from Hartland Quay is largely track and becomes a grassy footpath behind St Catherine's Tor. There is then a climb up and down to the waterfall at Speke Mill's Mouth. In our opinion this is the most dramatic waterfall on the whole of the path and we do not forget Pentargon ahead.

The path keeps to the eastern side of the stream for about 150 yards (135 m) then crosses it by a new wooden footbridge. Follow the signs up the valley to the east of Swansford Hill. The path over Swansford Hill is still walkable but should not be attempted in strong wind conditions.

Take care at Sandhole Cliff after joining the metalled road to watch for the signpost after about a 0.33 mile (500 m) directing you to turn right to rejoin the Coast Path. If you miss this you may find yourself doing about a 2 mile (3 km) walk down the road to Welcombe Mouth. Our Association has been urging the North Devon Coast and Countryside Service to install a true coast path along Sandhole Cliff; those who have been this way before will notice that they have installed half of what we requested.

On the descent into Marsland Mouth, look out for a little stone building, once the seaside lookout of the author, Ronald Duncan. It will provide a shelter from the elements.

As you come across the Cornish Border you will start to find a series of extremely helpful and well-thought-out posts. You might smile at the first which says 'Cornwall' but thereafter not only do they point the way in each direction, but they also tell you where you are down the shank of the post. Our thanks and appreciation to whoever had this idea - surely the best yet!

The diversion to visit Morwenstow Church is worth consideration. In season refreshments are available at the old rectory. The eccentric Parson Hawker was vicar here in 1830; look out for his hut which he constructed out of driftwood on Vicarage Cliff, when you regain the Coast Path.

At Steeple Point there is a tendency to keep too far inland. The official path keeps well to seaward. To cross the stream in Coombe Valley (where there are refreshments and toilets), there is a footbridge.

At Duckpool a new path has been created which takes you slightly inland away from the original path. This is marked with a white arrow where you will soon cross a new footbridge and rejoin the original path.

At Sandy Mouth there is a National Trust cafe. In season it is a welcome refreshment point, but watch the daylight as there is no electricity and the cafe surely closes at darkness at the latest.

The walking now becomes easier. Soon after Northcott Mouth, Crooklets Beach is reached. Keep to the cliffs passing the cricket pitch. This is the official route and the best way into Bude.

13   Bude to Crackington Haven (Beach)   OS E111 (T) Bude

Grading: Strenuous	Distance -	16.4	216.6	10.2	134.6

Timing: 4.75 hours

See also our Bude to Crackington Haven Path Description.

A colourful free guide to the coast is available at the Bude Tourist Information Centre.

Bude has good shops and accommodation, being a fair-sized town. Before you leave do try a short beach walk to the north on the falling tide and look at those cliffs - alternating bands of sandstone and shale in beautiful curving waves and with eroding continuations of the strata extending out across the beach. This pattern has been with you since Hartland, but as you go south there will soon be a series of changes - from tightly compressed folds to violent crumplings and igneous intrusions of a much more complex nature.

The southbound path starts from the sea lock on the historic Bude Canal, climbs to the cliff top at Compass Point and on to Efford Beacon. Looking back if the tide is out, the magnificent beach stretches before you for several miles going absolutely due north, with the dish aerials of the satellite tracking station visible beyond. To the south east if the weather is clear the high tors of Dartmoor can be seen, and to the south. west the prominent outline of Cambeak on the south side of the Crackington Haven inlet.

The path over Efford Down and on to Upton is easy enough to follow, and then it is sandwiched between the cliff edge and the road to Widemouth. The beach at Widemouth is popular for swimming and surfing. Toilets, cafes and accommodation are available, but apart from the fine beach with its prominent Black Rock, an unusual stack of slump breccia, Widemouth is not attractive; but be prepared, there will be no more facilities until you reach Crackington Haven.

South of Widemouth the path follows the low cliff for a short distance and then diverts inland slightly at Wanson Mouth to join the coast road by the stream valley. Turn west and climb up to Penhalt Cliff. Major subsidence is occurring and the coast path has long gone, but don't blame the County Council, you will see that the road is going as well! At the southern end of the cliff top car park the Coast Path proper recommences through a field and then descends steeply into Millook Haven.

Those with a geological interest should go on to the stony beach to view the remarkable chevron folded rock strata in the cliff on the north side - a classic textbook photograph and in sharp contrast to the curving folds to the north beyond Widemouth.

Follow the steep road beyond the stream crossing in Millook for a short distance, then branch right on to the cliff top path at Raven's Beak. From here the path climbs steadily but is fairly easy going all the way to Chipman Point. Note the ancient stunted oak wood in the area of Dizzard Point. The stream valley at Chipman Point is steep and deep, one of a series ahead, some with spectacular waterfalls cascading over into the rocky beach below. A tough ascent, then a further drop into the valley at Cleave Strand followed by a ridge walk at Castle Point giving tremendous views. The descent to the Coxford Water stream is severe and the climb onwards to Pencannow Point will certainly exercise the heart/lung system. Pause to recover and enjoy the views before the descent into Crackington Haven.

CP - Dizzard Point - The path is nearer the coast than the map suggests.

14 | Crackington Haven to Boscastle (Footbridge) OS E111 (V) Crackington Haven

Grading: Strenuous   Distance -   10.9   227.5   6.8   141.4

Timing: 3.75 hours

See also our Crackington Haven to Tintagel Path Description.

At Crackington Haven it is usually safe for a swim, but never go out of your depth on Cornwall's north coast. There are toilets and a seasonal shop, pub and cafe, and a long, tough, remote stretch ahead. The folds in the rock strata are remarkable, with interesting patterns down on the beach at Tremoutha Haven. Take particular care to the west of the Cambeak headland - keep away from the cliff edges and just admire the views - Hartland and Lundy Island to the north; Tintagel and Rumps Point to the south.

The path is now relatively level and generally stays above the massive landslip zone at Strangles Beach. There is a good path down through the landslip to the beach, which is interesting and pleasant at low tide, but it is an arduous climb back. At the northern end of the beach is the conspicuous Northern Door rock arch. There is access to the road and car parking at the National Trust Trevigue Farm (Coast Information Centre).

Ahead looms High Cliff, the highest point on the Coast Path in Cornwall and best avoided when a gale is blowing. Just before High Cliff the path goes round the back of a small stream valley where there is a diversity of minor paths, but then just aim for the top. The southbound descent from High Cliff is precipitously steep so take it slowly, then the path up through the massive landfall at Rusey Cliff twists and turns through the brambles and gorse. This is a major geological fault zone. The path is easier to follow than it used to be, but the ground here is soily and the vegetation grows rampantly in summer which presents a continuing problem to the County Council which has difficulty keeping it cleared back.

Once at the top of Rusey Cliff there follows an easier stretch through grassy sheep fields, with the approach to Buckator now being more coastal than shown in earlier guides.

The sheer black cliff of Buckator hangs over the sea inlet, with impressive white bands of quartz running through, quite different from the brown and grey cliffs of predominantly sandstone to the north. The path dips slightly to cross a marshy stream where stepping stones provide firm footing, then continues on at high level to Fire Beacon Point. Here the descent is steep but there are attractive slate steps on the most precipitous part. The path then keeps close to the cliff edge and into the Pentargon inlet where an impressive waterfall cascades down to the sea. The best view of this is now from the southern side, cliff falls having caused the path on the north side to be diverted and the old viewpoint has been lost. You are advised NOT to leave the official Coast Path to attempt a better view of this Waterfall. It is a long way down.

Further cliff falls seem imminent on the south side of Pentargon, but from here on it is easy going into Boscastle. Aim for the white mast atop Penally Hill, then follow the path to the beautiful harbour inlet and past the Youth Hostel into the village of Boscastle. Penally Point is well worth the detour, an exciting viewpoint, but the slate rock is dangerously slippery when wet. Note the extraordinary small scale distortions in the strata alongside the path.

15 | Boscastle to Tintagel (Haven)   OS E109 (V) Boscastle

Grading: Moderate   Distance -   7.4   234.9   4.6   146.0

Timing: 2.25 hours

See also our Crackington Haven to Tintagel Path Description.

There are shops, pubs, toilets, accommodation and an excellent Heritage Coast Centre in Boscastle, and the old village up the lane by the Wellington Hotel is well worth exploring.

The next section on to Tintagel is shorter and easier then the two previous sections. The path leaves from the south side of the harbour and climbs steeply past the gully to Eastern Blackapit to the Willapark headland with its prominent white watch tower. Go up to the watch tower, or take the short cut across the back of the headland past the ancient Forrabury strip field system now preserved by the National Trust. The path soon descends into the stream valley of Grower Gut - there are some granite stepping stones to help you if the water is in flood. Further on the path turns sharp right to keep to the seaward side of the Manor House and onto a prominent headland which overlooks Short Island. If you are a birdwatcher, here is a good place to stop, picnic and observe through binoculars. Both Short Island and its neighbour Long Island are densely populated with breeding seabirds during the early summer, including guillemots, razorbills and a few puffins. Always look down on the water; they tend to float around in groups when off duty.

As you go on past Firebeacon Hill look for the Ladies Window rock arch in the gully to the right - walking west it is easy to miss this attractive photo opportunity. From here to Rocky Valley the going is level, but do look back to the dramatic pinnacles below Trevalga Cliff. On your left you are soon confronted by a conspicuous cliff top caravan/camp site - the path runs seaward of it. Trewethet Gut is a dangerous and eroding inlet that has necessitated a slight diversion of the path, and then you descend into the exquisite Rocky Valley. Look for seals in the surging sea as you cross the footbridge, and for the dippers that feed in the water of the stream. There is a path through Rocky Valley to the coast road, where cars may be parked.

From the footbridge a steep climb to high level again, and you find yourself overlooking Bossiney Haven. There is a crossroad of paths giving access to the beach from Bossinney village, and indeed this is an excellent place for a swim just after low tide. But the Coast Path goes on straight ahead and bears right to another prominent headland called Willapark, the second in just 2 miles. Again birdwatchers should go to the end and scan The Sisters and the ocean through binoculars. There are often terns, gannets and even shearwaters further out, but beware the precipitous cliff edge as you return to the path. Then on to Barras Nose headland, dominated by that awful hotel eyesore, and down to Tintagel Haven below the Castle ruins. Here there are toilets and a cafe.

Grading: Severe   Distance -   14.7   249.6   9.1   155.1

Timing: 4.75 hours

See also our Tintagel to Port Isaac Path Description.

Tintagel has many shops, cafes and guest houses. The Old Post Office, owned and restored by the National Trust, dates back to the fourteenth century when it was no doubt a house of some importance.

Around The Island and down in Tintagel Haven there is some interesting and complex geology with older rocks (Devonian) overthrust on top of more recent rocks (carboniferous), and bands of lava and tuff. The severe erosion, which is no doubt compounded by these faults and thrusts, is making access to The Island increasingly difficult to maintain. In the shelter of Tintagel Haven sailing ships used to be loaded with the high quality slate that is still extracted from several quarries inland away from this highly disturbed coastal zone.

The path to Trebarwith Strand climbs up from Tintagel Haven below and to the left of the Castle entrance and gives an excellent view of the rocks on the south face of The Island. From here on and past St Materiana's Church it is easy going. The Youth Hostel at Dunderhole Point was once a quarry office building. The best route, for glorious views, is the National Trust path out around the headlands of Penhallic Point, rather than the boring official route across three fields. There are further old quarries ahead as you approach Hole Beach and Trebarwith Strand, and surprisingly sailing ships were loaded under the cliffs at Penhallic Point, where the remains of the wharf can still be seen. The path drops down by the toilets in Trebarwith Strand, and opposite is a welcome pub serving hot food. The beach is worth exploring at low tide, but watch that you don't get cut off, and do be warned that swimming can be dangerous here.

From here to Port Isaac the path is long and very tough in parts. The descents to the valley streams and up again on the other side are about the steepest on the whole of the Coast Path. Do not leave Trebarwith Strand unless you have food, energy and plenty of time in hand. The climb up out of Trebarwith Strand, which is stepped almost all the way, will give you a foretaste of what lies ahead. And having reached the top, you must go all the way down again into Backways Cove, then up again to a more restful level stretch for about 1 mile (1500 m) to the stream valley behind Tregardock Beach, where you are confronted by a detached and eroding piece of the cliff known as The Mountain. As you descend on the inland side of The Mountain you will meet a crossroad of paths from Tregardock village to the beach. The beach is worth a visit at low tide but your route lies straight ahead and you have quite a long way to go.

From here the stretch marked on the maps as Tregardock Cliff is easy enough, but at Jacket's Point the deepest and steepest valley of all lies before you - the commencement of The National Trust Dannonchapel property. An excellent job has been done on the path, the stream crossing and the staircase of steps on the ascent on the south side. However having reached the top, you drop down again into yet another deep valley. There are more steps up on the south side of the valley, then you go over to the Barrett's Zawn stream valley where another mineworking adit faces you. This gave donkeys burdened with slate access to Barrett's Zawn beach - don't even think about it as this tunnel is collapsing.

On the climb up round the Barrett's Zawn cliffs you will certainly see that there have been massive rock falls and that another will occur any time. You then descend very steeply on the south side into the next stream valley at Ranie Point, and as you slide down the stony slope you may well feel that the path here could be improved. Some walkers evidently complain about the staircases of steps on these valley sides, but they are so exceptionally steep we believe that steps are the best option and we have been urging the hard-pressed County Council to put some here.

Now at last the path levels out through the sheep meadows with just a small valley to cross at St Illickswell Gug where a boardwalk takes you across the marsh. When you reach the road at Cartway Cove the official path is directly opposite and drops down by the side of the hotel at Portgaverne. But, for the best views, take the path to the right and go round the headland and if the tide is out walk along the old harbour quay, where sailing ships were once loaded with slate. Either way there is then a short road walk up to the cliff car park at Port Isaac. Go through this past the public toilets and follow the well-signed path round to overlook the attractive inlet and thence the village street.

| Grading: Strenuous | Distance - | 14.2 | 263.8 | 8.8 | 163.9 |

Timing: 4.25 hours

See also our Port Isaac to Padstow Path Description.

Port Isaac is a gem, with narrow streets and tiny cottages which are no doubt easier to look at than to live in. There are two excellent pubs and one of the cafes is in an extremely old and crooked little building. Do take time to explore the back streets and the small fish market, and see if you can find Squeeze-ee-belly Alley!

Another tough walk lies ahead and there are no facilities until you reach Polzeath, but the scenery is superb. Take the road to the right behind the fish market and past more toilets. The path bears right along the cliff in front of two prominent guest houses and takes you on past Lobber Point then down into Pine Haven. From here on the path is relatively new and apart from an unpleasant fenced corridor cutting off Varley Head, it really is magnificent, and keeps close to the cliff edge all the way to Port Quin. The fence stays on your left for over a mile of steep ups and downs, but it does protect you from the enormous herd of beef cattle that generally roams the meadows during the summer. Watch out for the peregrines that hunt along this stretch, the occasional adder basking in the sun, and seals on the rocks below.

At Kellan Head The Rumps promontory faces you at the far end of Portquin Bay. Then as you turn the corner the path overlooks the beautiful Port Quin inlet and descends to the village, once a busy little pilchard port, but there are no facilities here now although there is a tap marked drinking water on the wall in front of you as you descend the steps into the harbour. Follow the road westbound until half way up the steep hill where a new slate stile gives access to the south side of the inlet. You are on National Trust land and free to explore Doyden Point, formed from rocks of greenstone. The path follows the stream valley some distance in front of the old Prison Governor's House, and soon passes two fenced mineshafts where you might still find interesting mineral samples amongst the loose spoil material nearby - but keep away from the dangerous cliff edge.

At Trevan Point there is a sharp descent to Epphaven Cove which, with its neighbour Lundy Bay, has a beautiful beach at low tide. You then enter a surprisingly wooded valley where in late spring you will hear the delightful call of the willow warbler. As you climb up out of the bay look out for the startling Lundy Hole behind a protective fence on your right. On the cliff top again as you approach The Rumps you will see the earth ramparts of an Iron Age Fort in the lower ground in front of the headland. When you get there the detour through the entrance and on round the rocks overlooking The Mouls island is well worthwhile and can give good seabird watching; puffins nest on The Mouls most years.

It is then quite easy going on to Pentire Point, another headland formed from pillow lava. A perfect cross-section can be seen in the small vertical rock face on your left as you leave The Rumps headland, the rounded hollow shapes having been formed of molten lava under the sea. The walling stone alongside the path reveals the structure of small holes in the rock caused by gases and steam, but do not remove pieces as samples; the National Trust spends much time and money maintaining these walls and they provide wind shelter for the sheep.

There are many good viewpoints on the Coast Path, but that from Pentire Point is one of the best. In clear conditions south to Trevose Head and beyond, and north to Bude, the satellite tracking station and even Hartland Quay and Lundy Island are visible, but you will need binoculars! Then follows an easy descent into Polzeath with the Camel Estuary before you and Stepper Point with its Daymark Tower on the opposite side. In contrast to the last 20 miles of perfection, the cliff top housing and car parking in New and Old Polzeath are unfortunate, but the sea, the sand and the surf are magnificent. There are toilets on the left as you reach the road beyond Pentireglaze Haven. The path continues along the cliff edge to the village centre and gives access to the beach on the way.

Grading: Easy

Distance -   4.7   268.5   2.9   166.8

Timing: 1.25 hours

See also our Port Isaac to Padstow Path Description.

Polzeath is a surfers' paradise with several shops, cafes, accommodation and campsites. On the left by the park is a small Tourist Information Centre and there are toilets opposite.

Follow the road past the beach car park and take the path right by the cottages where the road bends sharp left on the steep hill. The path follows the edge of Tristram Cliff where you can watch the expertise of the surfers. From here to Daymer Bay the path along The Greenaway is intensively walked throughout the year, and measures have had to be taken to discourage people from wandering off the route and scarring the fragile turf with alternative tracks. In fact this path is so good it is now classed as suitable for wheelchair users, which is almost unique on the Coast Path. There are houses on your left, but the coastal scene is beautiful with a rocky sea-washed platform below - the haunt of curlews, redshanks, grey plover and oystercatchers, with the headlands of Stepper Point and Pentire Point in the background. Many fishing and pleasure boats can be observed entering and leaving from Padstow, some 2 miles (3 km) up the Camel Estuary.

Just off Trebetherick Point is the Doom Bar, noticeable only at low tide when the waves are breaking over the sand; there were many wrecks here during the days of sail when ships were largely at the mercy of wind and tide. There are toilets and a cafe in Daymer Bay car park and the beach is one of the safest for a swim - but keep out of the estuary channel at low tide.

The Coast Path goes down the steps on to the beach and then through the dunes and over a footbridge just below Brea Hill. To visit little St Enodoc Church, which was once buried beneath the blown sand, turn left midway along the dunes and follow the white markers across the golf course. You must then retrace your route back to the dunes, or you can go on through the golf course to rejoin the Coast Path in the dunes on the far side of Brea Hill, but this is a busy golf course and you may wish you had a protective helmet and visor. Your route through the golf course is marked by large white painted rocks. From the footbridge you can go either way round Brea Hill, or straight over the top! Alternatively, if the tide is out you can walk along the beach to Rock and the Padstow ferry. All routes are pleasant and the sheltered estuary surroundings make quite a change from the exposed cliffs that you have been used to. The official path goes through a hollow just behind the dunes on the south side of Brea Hill, a Site of Special Scientific Interest for the rare plant life that thrives on the calcium-rich sand. At the southern end the path branches left to a higher level and on to Rock car park, but you can continue on along the beach, except at very high tide. There are toilets in the car park and the ferry landing is on the shore below. Be warned however that at exceptionally low tides the ferry may sail from quite some distance downstream in front of the dunes, so keep a lookout as you walk.

Rock/Padstow (River Camel)
Black Tor Ferry
Padstow Harbour Commissioners,
Harbour Office, West Quay,
Padstow, Cornwall PL28 8AQ.
Tel: Padstow (01841) 532239
Fax: (01841) 533346

Ferry operates all year at 20 min intervals
No Sunday service from last
Sunday in October to
1st Sunday in April
(or Easter if earlier)

We understand that this ferry company is no longer keen to issue single fares, but we have been told that they will do so for genuine walkers on request and accordingly you should ask for a single fare if that is what you require.

The Saints' Way, Cornwall's coast to coast path from Padstow to Fowey starts here. A guide book is available from Padstow TIC (see page 131).

19 | Padstow to Trevone (Car Park)

Grading: Easy   Distance -   9.1   277.6   5.7   172.5

Timing: 2.5 hours

See also our Padstow to Porthcothan Path Description.

Normally the Padstow ferry will take you into the harbour, but at low tide it will deposit you a short distance downstream at St Saviour's Point, just below the path to Stepper Point. Do not take this as an opportunity to cut out Padstow; you should go into the town and explore. The harbour area, the narrow lanes in the old town and up to St Petroc's Church are attractive and fairly traffic free. A glass of beer and a genuine Cornish steak pasty make an excellent traditional lunch. A visit to the Tourist Information Centre on the harbour is recommended, and on your way it is interesting to look at the places of origin of the many fishing boats - all ports from the Hebrides to the Channel Islands!

The Coast Path starts on your left at the north end of the harbour and is wide and well trodden. In the early summer blackcaps and warblers sing in the wooded stream valley at St George's Cove. From Gun Point you can, if the tide is out, take a short cut across the beach to Hawker's Cove by the prominent old Lifeboat House. If the tide is in you can enjoy a quiet swim; this is a very pleasant and usually wind sheltered beach. Go round the back of the old pilots' houses from Hawker's Cove and then climb up to Stepper Point, with its disused coastguard lookout and the stone-built Daymark Tower. From this high ground there is a remarkable panorama behind you and on a clear day you will see the granite tors of Bodmin Moor in the distance.

So now you are back on the exposed Atlantic Coast. Approaching the precipitous inlet of Butter Hole Cove, look out for the small Pepper Hole a few yards to the right of the path. There follows a long easy stretch to Gunver Head, followed by a steep descent to the small stream valley. The rocky pinnacles of the Merope Islands just behind you are spectacular. After a short climb up again you will see the Marble Cliff and Porthmissen Bridge ahead. The cliff comprises many bands of hard limestone and softer shale on which razorbills, guillemots and kittiwakes nest in the summer. At Roundhole Point the path skirts the impressive Round Hole collapsed cave which should be approached with caution, and then descends to the car park at Trevone.

20 | Trevone to Porthcothan (Footbridge)

Grading: Easy   Distance -   12.7   290.3   7.9   180.4

Timing: 3.5 hours

See also our Padstow to Porthcothan Path Description.

There are toilets, a cafe and a good beach in Trevone, but little else of interest to the walker, except perhaps some bed and breakfast accommodation. The path passes behind the little headland on the south side of the bay and follows the cliff edge round rocky Newtrain Bay. There are refreshments, toilets and a beautiful beach at Harlyn.

The stream generally has to be crossed via the road bridge, and then the path follows the beach for about 330 yards (300 m) before climbing slightly into the dunes and so on past the end of the bay to Cataclews Point. The hard erosion-resistant dolerite rock here was used to make the polished font in Padstow Church. In Mother Ivey's Bay there are some unpleasant man-made features which mar the coastal scene, including an often foul smelling sewage discharge which frequently contaminates the nearby beaches. There is a huge and conspicuous caravan site near Trevose Farm, and access to the headland by the new Padstow Lifeboat Station is barred by an ugly concrete and mesh fence, reminiscent of prison camps which is in sharp contrast to the old tamarisk hedges nearby. How sadly all this compares with the painstaking remedial and conservation work that has been carried out by the National Trust on long stretches of the coast to the north of the Camel Estuary.

At Trevose Head you can generally visit the immaculately kept lighthouse, but keep away when the fog horn is blowing. On a clear day you will see the granite hills of West Penwith behind St Ives to the south and the satellite tracking dish aerials beyond Bude to the north. Turning south, the path passes yet another large Round Hole as it descends to Booby's Bay. There is something of a rocky scramble to get through to Constantine Bay, but it is beautiful here with a particularly attractive beach at low tide - not really safe for swimming unfortunately. Beyond the dunes the path leaves the beach to go round Treyarnon Point, revealing another attractive beach at Treyarnon Bay. The Youth Hostel is on the left, and in the car park area there are toilets and refreshments. If you are intent on swimming, observe the safety notices which will certainly tell you not to do so at low tide.

An unusually indented coastline follows beyond Trethias Island, but the path cuts across the narrower headlands. Between Pepper Cove and Warren Cove are the ramparts of an Iron Age Fort, and in Fox Cove you may see the remains of a ship which ran aground in 1969. Minnows Islands and the cove beyond are quite spectacular. The path turns into Porthcothan Bay, descending through the protected National Trust strip which contrasts with the housing development on the opposite side. To reach Porthcothan's pub, the Tredrea Inn, take the road before the bridge and go uphill for approximately 500 yards (458 m).

21 | Porthcothan to Newquay (Harbour)   OS E106

Grading: Moderate   Distance -   17.9   308.2   11.1   191.5

Timing: 5 hours

See also our Porthcothan to Newquay Path Description.

Porthcothan has toilets, a shop, limited accommodation and a pub. The path leaves past the shop and keeps in front of the houses and on round the headland overlooking Trescore Islands. There is a short steep descent into Porth Mear valley, a popular spot for birdwatchers, and an equally short steep climb up again, then it is an easy walk to Park Head, another spectacular viewpoint. As you approach Park Head you will come across a National Trust landmark stone - keep to the path to the left of the landmark as there are numerous landslips here and signs warn to keep well inland of the white posts because of cliff falls. Ahead lies the famous Carnewas property of the National Trust, with a beautiful beach at low tide. As you leave Park Head you will see that the cliff is slowly sliding down, although it has been like this for many years. Bedruthan beach itself has a recurring accessibility problem due to the dangerous condition of the cliffs, but a great deal of money is being spent on the long flight of steps down. If the tide is on its way out, it is worth going down to explore the pools, caves and the rock stacks, Bedruthan Steps, but don't get cut off and don't even think about swimming. The National Trust cafe and Information Centre in the car park are open throughout the summer.

Bedruthan Steps can be busy, but you will soon find yourself on a quieter stretch of path to Trenance Point. A steady descent into Mawgan Porth follows where the Coast Path crosses the beach. This is one of the few beaches in North Cornwall where dogs are permitted in the summer. At Mawgan Porth there are toilets, shops, cafés, and a pub. The road must be used here for a very short distance in order to cross the stream. The southbound path leaves to the right on the sharp road bend on the hill out of Mawgan Porth. Then follows a long high level stretch to Watergate Bay, with minor descents at Beacon Cove and Stem Cove, between which across Griffin's Point headland are the ramparts of another Iron Age Fort. Just inland is the airport and RAF station at St Mawgan, and you may find yourself being targeted by high-powered military jet aircraft as they come in to land. Ahead lies the magnificent Watergate Beach, but the path remains at high level until it crosses the road behind the Watergate Bay Hotel into Watergate itself, where there are toilets, cafés and a pub.

After crossing the stream bridge by the car park, where there are toilets, the path leaves to the right from the road to Newquay and again climbs to the high cliff top where it remains all the way to Whipsiderry. Here some ugly cliff top development has been permitted, but the coastal scene is great, with Newquay and Towan Head in the background. The cliffs at Whipsiderry are high and precipitous, but there are steps down to the beach and some caves to explore. There are new Coast Path signs here which take you along the pavement down the hill to Porth Beach. However you might prefer to take the original route that starts with a narrow path between a hotel and the cliff edge, and then leads you on to Trevelgue Head. You might then choose to cross the footbridge onto the island where a rough sea can be most spectacular.

You must now return to Porth Beach where there are toilets, cafés, beach shops and pubs. You may then walk along the beach which is signposted from the Mermaid Inn, rather than taking the official route, joining the path opposite the Porth Beach Hotel at the Porth Beach car park - from here it crosses the headland between Porth and Lusty Glaze. This short cut avoids the road and takes you round the cliff edge at Lusty Glaze and into the Barrowfields Park. You are then on the road into Newquay town centre, but if the tide is out, you can walk along the magnificent beach from Lusty Glaze or from Barrowfields all the way to the harbour.

22 | Newquay to Holywell (Beach)   OS E104 (T) Newquay (Trains); (V) Crantock

Grading: Moderate   Distance -   **10.2   318.4   6.3   197.8**

Timing: 4.5 hours (Official Route)

See also our Newquay to Perranporth Path Description.

Newquay is the biggest town on the north coast and the pedestrianised shopping centre is quite attractive. There is no shortage of restaurants, pubs and accommodation here, and there is even a railway station! But do explore the beaches and the harbour before you leave, and if the tide is out you can gain access to the coast path by the steps at the back of the harbour.

The Coast Path leaves just above the harbour and climbs past the old Huer's Hut to Towan Head. In the cliffs below the Hut is a noisy kittiwake colony and this is a very good spot to observe the differences between kittiwakes, fulmars, black-headed gulls and the rest. Towan Head is particularly good for seabird watching; with binoculars you may spot gannets, petrels and shearwaters further out.

From Towan Head the path follows along the back of Fistral Beach. This is probably the most popular surfing beach in the British Isles and international competitions are held here. The path climbs to the cliffs at the southern end, passing in front of the housing development at Pentire, then across the headland at The Warren over to The Gannel river estuary.

There are four ways that you can cross the River Gannel, three of which are available, tide permitting, throughout the year. The distances via the Penpol crossing assume that you have walked via Fern Pit; the same applies to the other two crossings of Trenance Footbridge and the A3075 main road route. However, it is possible to reach the Trenance and Trevemper crossings from the town itself.

1. Newquay to Crantock via Penpol

This is now the official crossing of the River Gannel. Up river there is ferry and a tidal footbridge off Trevean Lane which crosses over to Penpol Creek. If you are at Fern Pit and need to go upstream, go east (inland) along Riverside Crescent, Riverside Avenue, Fistral Crescent, turn right into Pentire Crescent, continue along Penmere Drive and turn right into Trevean Way, then turn right at the coast path sign. Be warned; there is an earlier footpath sign to Crantock - DO NOT take it because you may find it is under water. Having crossed the Gannel, turn right to follow an estuary side path. Presently it becomes a track and you pass a house on the right, then some bungalows and can soon turn right down into the National Trust car park at Rushey Green. Take the exit practically opposite where you came in. There is a seasonal cafe close to the car park. (Note that the NTG refers to this crossing as being at the bottom of Trethellan Hill).

2. Newquay to Crantock via Fern Pit Ferry Crossing (summer only); (deduct approx. 2 miles / 3 km)

Newquay/Crantock (River Gannel)   Spring Bank Holiday
Fern Pit Cafe and Ferry   End of May to mid-September
Proprietor - G A Northey   continuous 7 days a week
Fern Pit, Riverside Crescent, Newquay. TR7 1PJ.
Tel: 01637 873181

You have to pass Fern Pit to reach the official crossing of the Gannel. If the ferry is running, it is a comfortable and scenic way to cross; there is even a cafe on the Newquay side so that you can while away your waiting time with refreshment. However, neither the ferry nor the footbridge, which is used at low tide instead of the ferry, is available when the cafe is closed.

3. Newquay to Crantock via Trenance Footbridge (add approx. 3 miles / 4.8 km)

Further up stream again, just before the estuary becomes a river, there is another footbridge which we call 'Trenance'. It is beside the new A3075 Gannel Road just before the boating lake on the left and its junction with Trevemper Road. If you are in Newquay and know the tides are against you, the quickest way to get here is to walk down the new Gannel Road (A3075). On the other side of the footbridge, walk forward for about 165 yards (150 m) keeping the hawthorn hedge on your left, until you come to a clearing on your left, offering various routes for you to choose. You can either turn right through the pedestrian gate that is a permissive path (this path is dependent on the tide, and should be navigable for two hours either side of low tide) or, if you have any doubts about the tide, you are advised to take the old bridleway through the big gate going towards Trevemper. Proceed forwards uphill and having gone over the brow, turn right before you get to the tarmac. You walk via Treringey coming to Penpol Creek and so on, to Rushey Green as described above.

4. Newquay to Crantock via the A3075 (add approx. 4.5 miles / 7.2 km)

However if all these crossings fail there is the A3075 main road itself, which is the only all-states-of- the-tide and all-seasons route. Those taking the A3075 should proceed along it until just after the roundabout where the A392 branches off. In about 100 yards (90 m) take the little unsigned lane on the right. You immediately pass a partly ruined barn on your right and soon you pass a house on the outskirts of Trevemper. Then as the road bears left, go forward and right. Pass through a gate and turn left to go via Treringey to Penpol Creek and so on to Rushey Green. Needless to say the A3075, although the one route that is always certain is quite the longest and certainly the most uninteresting.

Coast Path continues

Crantock Beach is attractive at low tide and can give good views of terns fishing in the Gannel below the cliffs of Pentire Point East. The path passes behind the dunes to the National Trust car park at Rushey Green, then westwards through the dunes to the cliffs of Pentire Point West. Alternatively you may walk along the beach to gain access to the path by scrambling up at the western end of the dunes.

Porth Joke is a sheltered sandy inlet, then follows a climb to Kelsey Head, another Iron Age site. From here in the distance can be seen St Agnes Head with Bawden Rocks offshore. Holywell Beach lies before you and the path descends to the dunes and then into Holywell. Those continuing onwards can take advantage of the splendid new National Trust footbridge across the river seaward of the village.

NTG Page 35 (Map) The official path goes out onto Towan Head and back.

23 Holywell to Perranporth (Beach car park) OS E104

Grading: Moderate. Sand dune route - Strenuous. Distances - 7.3 325.7 4.5 202.3

Timing: 2 hours

See also our Newquay to Perranporth Path Description.

The path cuts across Penhale Point headland and then skirts the seaward edge of the rather ugly Penhale Camp, where there is a short fenced section. The army presence here has however served to preserve the beautiful wild dunes area inland from being overrun by campsites and chalets, and it now deserves to be protected as a nature reserve. The path goes out to Ligger Point and you get the first good view of the long Perran Beach.

The easiest path, if the tide permits, is now along the great stretch of firm beach to Perranporth rather than over the dunes. Even if, as is sometimes the case, you can only walk part-way along the beach it is worth going down to do this, there being a number of 'escape routes' up from the beach going south. The important point to watch if you want an easy descent to the beach is to fork left along the sandy path after the old wooden stile; the right fork is quicker but much steeper. It is essential that you stay on the marked route through the dunes as there is recent news of collapsing mine shafts.

The official path takes you towards the dunes where you will see the rusty coloured Perran Iron Lode in the cliff quarry. The path descends behind this and follows the back of the beach for almost a mile then climbs up through the dunes behind the rock cliff at Cotty's Point. The incoming tide will reach the foot of the cliff here but there are escape steps to the dunes at each side, and if the tide is out you can continue on along the beach rather than going over the top. The path descends to the back of the beach just south of Cotty's Point, crosses the stream by a footbridge and so takes you into the town or the car park where there are toilets.

24 | Perranporth to St Agnes (Trevaunance Cove)   OS E104 (T) Perranporth

Grading: Moderate	Distance -	6.0	331.7	3.7	206.0

Timing: 2 hours

See also our Perranporth to Portreath Path Description.

Perranporth is a busy holiday centre during the summer and has good shops and accommodation. The eroding rock stacks at the southern end of the beach are interesting, and may be explored using the beach access at the far end of the car park in front of the hotel terrace. Round the corner you will find a staircase from the beach up to the cliff car park at Droskyn Point. The official route leaves west from the town car park and follows the hill up Cliff Road, but just to the left of the Atlantic House Hotel there are some steps up and a footpath which takes you past the Droskyn Point car park. Whichever way you have chosen, keep inland of the prominent castellated building and on along Tregundy Lane to the end of the houses. The southbound Coast Path is signposted half left at the entrance drive to the Youth Hostel and the South West Water sewage pumping station. It then descends slightly to the right before climbing to the cliffs overlooking Shag Rock.

From here on you will see increasing evidence of mining activity. The path is fairly level going, passing the small outcrop of granite at Cligga Head which has been quarried and displays conspicuous stripes of greisen (for the chemistry of which you must consult the textbooks!). The mineralisation along the coast here and to the south is attributable to the intrusion of the granite which extends over a considerable area below the surface. Walking southbound through the quarry and mineworkings, you are unlikely to lose the path. Hanover Cove is named after a shipwreck. The Hanover was lost in a storm in December 1763 on route from Lisbon to Falmouth: all hands were lost plus a cargo of gold. It is rumoured that there is £50m of gold still onboard. The rock formations around the cove are dramatic and green copper stains the cliffs. There are many mineshafts in this area capped with conical steel mesh which allows access for bats.

The long stretch to Trevellas Porth is level easy going alongside the airfield perimeter; you will progress much faster here than you did further north. There is a sharp descent into Trevellas Coombe where there are many mine workings with their decaying buildings. Go upstream to the bridge which crosses the stream in front of the Blue Hills engine house and then right over the top to Trevaunance Cove. The southern path is the recommended route here, as the current official path passes close to the cliff edge. Cross over the road and turn right behind the four storey grey rendered housing block to pick up the official path. If you go down into the cove, where there is a seasonal café and toilets, a footpath behind the Jubilee Terrace and steps take you back up to the Coast Path.

It is possible to cross the beach from Trevellas Porth to Trevaunance Cove at low tide, but be warned that the boulders are dangerously slippery. Surprisingly there was once a harbour under the cliff on the west side of Trevaunance Cove, but all you will find now is a tumbled mass of granite blocks.

25 | St Agnes to Porthtowan (Commodore Inn)   OS E104 (V) St Agnes

Grading: Moderate	Distance -	7.4	339.1	4.6	210.6

Timing: 2 hours

See also our Perranporth to Portreath Path Description.

From the top the Coast Path stays at high level out to St Agnes Head, passing many mineshafts and waste tips on the way. Here you are circumnavigating St Agnes Beacon, a small outcrop of granite 0.5 mile (800 m) back from the coast. As the path turns south, you will see Godrevy Lighthouse across the bay, with St Ives and the massive granite of Penwith beyond. The going is relatively easy and soon you will pass the much-photographed Towanroath Engine House, part of the Wheal Coates tin and copper mine and now preserved by the National Trust. The path then descends into Chapel Porth where there is a car park, toilets and a seasonal cafe. At low tide, if you walk some distance north along the beach, you will see a streak of copper ore in the cliff beneath the Towanroath shaft.

The southbound path leaves The National Trust car park, travelling inland for 200 yards (185 m) on the right of the small stream, before joining the wide rough track to Mulgram Hill, then there is a good cliff top walk to Porthtowan. The path descends to the back of the beach and on past the car park where there are toilets. The transition from mining to tourism here has produced some unattractive features, but the beach is beautiful and extensive at low tide, from Tobban Horse in the south to Chapel Porth in the north.

26 | Porthtowan to Portreath (Harbour)   OS E104 (V) Porthtowan

Grading: Strenuous   Distance -   6.3   345.4   3.9   214.5

Timing: 1.75 hours

See also our Perranporth to Portreath Path Description.

Porthtowan is popular for surfing and has accommodation, a pub, a few shops and seasonal cafes. To find the southbound path turn right along West Beach Road then left up the narrow road to the cliff top. On the headland the path turns south, passing many mineworkings, and keeps some distance back from the crumbling and dangerous cliff edge. At the steep valley drop to Sally's Bottom, where steps have been installed on either side, then on reaching high level again you find yourself walking alongside the unattractive Nancekuke fence which encloses the large military establishment just inland. It stays with us for over a mile and almost to Portreath, where the Daymark above the harbour entrance can be seen ahead. The path turns south just before you reach the Daymark, avoiding another dangerous cliff edge, and joins the road down to the harbour. The long narrow inlet is unusual, but the protective pier which extends over the rocks on the south side is now out of bounds; too many people have been swept off by waves breaking over.

27 | Portreath to Hayle (White Hart Hotel)   OS E104 & E102 (V) Portreath

Grading: Moderate   Distance -   19.9   365.3   12.4   226.9

Timing: 5.5 hours

See also our Portreath to Hayle Path Description.

There are shops, cafes and bed and breakfast accommodation in Portreath, but the beach is small in comparison with most on this coast. To gain the southbound path go round the harbour to the beach car park, then to the right up Battery Hill. Where this road drops to the beach again at the western end, the Coast Path branches left up the valley. In approximately 5 yards (5 m) there is a low National Trust sign marking Western Hill. The official Coast Path begins with well made steps and leads round Western Hill; you have views from here after your initial effort to gain the cliff top.

At Bassett's Cove you go through a big car park and start several miles of easy cliff top walking. There are practically no signs, but there are only two points at which you are likely to go astray: for 1.5 miles (2.5 km) you get closer to the road and then start to get away from it again; after a further 0.5 mile (800 m) you should observe a small field ahead and to your left; here you have to fork right and then turn right.

You pass Hell's Mouth which has a seasonal cafe just across the road, then when you are approaching another field you come out onto a track where you turn right, but this time do not take the next right as it is a beach path only.

There is then a very pleasant walk around Navax and Godrevy Points; there are good views out to sea, ahead to St Ives and what to many is a surprise southwards. You then have to negotiate a big car park but by keeping well to seaward you can miss most of it and the road that leads to it.

You will find Godrevy Cafe, which is open from 10am till sunset during November to February and from 10am till 6pm the rest of the year. It also closes every Monday, except for bank holiday Mondays, and on Christmas Day and Boxing Day. To find the Red River footbridge leave the car park's southwestern corner along a board walk. You will see the bridge to your left. After crossing it walk seaward along the bank of the river.

The walking is easy along the shingle bank which takes you towards a lifeguard hut. You then begin a stretch following way-posts which are well sited and lead you accurately, provided you follow the arrows carefully. As the waymarks sometimes become firewood for barbecues and as the path zigzags, you may find yourself heading too far inland, in which case you just head for the sea.

Once Black Cliff is behind you, avoid taking the route to the beach and walk towards a chalet called Silver Spray. Leave this house to your right and walk along a line of chalets on your left. Keep straight on. You soon go through a car park and take the track which follows the old quay. You then cross a swing bridge and turn right into Hayle and continue on to the White Hart Hotel.

28 | Hayle to St Ives (Western Pier)   OS E102 (T) Hayle (Trains); (V) Lelant (Trains)

Grading: Moderate   Distance -   9.0   374.3   5.6   232.5

Timing: 2.5 hours

See also our Hayle to Pendeen Watch Path Description.

Distance is measured from the railway viaduct / the White Hart Hotel at Hayle, around the estuary to Lelant then along the coast to St Ives.

Note that between Lelant and Marazion there is a cross peninsula path, St Michael's Way. This could be used to make a circular trip around Penwith by walking round the coast and then coming back inland from Penzance or Marazion to Carbis Bay.

From the viaduct, the quickest but dreariest route is straight along the main road, Carnsew Road. There is a longer but somewhat more attractive alternative not to be missed by bird watchers. Go along the road passing the 30 decontrol sign and at the end of the long building on the right is a footpath signposted 'The Weir half a mile'. At the end of a tall hedge bear right, then bear left by a bridge. Then as the ground widens bear left again to walk along a lagoon embankment. Presently you come out again on the main road and have to turn right. Whichever way you did that first stretch from Hayle, turn right on the A3074 signposted St Ives, passing the Old Quay House.

Here again is decision time as for some incredible reason the official path continues along the A3074 road through Lelant. At the end of the main street, where the main road bears left, you go ahead on a minor road to the church. If you wish to do this, fair enough, but we recommend a quieter alternative of the same length below.

After the Old Quay House go along the road passing under the railway bridge. Then turn right, signposted 'St Ives Park and Ride'. When you come to a toilet block cut through to the road on your left in front of the price board for the car park. Follow the road to your right which eventually comes out at Lelant Church.

At the church continue on the same line, go ahead across the golf course and under the railway again. Here turn left to proceed along the seaward side of the railway. Eventually you come onto a pedestrian level crossing and then bear right; on the descent avoid two beach paths on your right.

About 200 yards (185 m) before Carbis Bay there is an opportunity to go down to the beach and save yourself one last hill. If you stay with the path you go up to join a road and turn right down this. Circle round the inland side of the cafe complex to leave Carbis Bay on a tarmac path above the beach but to seaward of the hotel.

Ascend, crossing a railway footbridge, then keep ahead avoiding the path on the left. Continue along ignoring 'Private road pedestrians only' on the right. The path becomes a minor road where the road bears left and there is another private road on your right; go ahead. Cross the railway again on a more substantial old fashioned bridge to bear right and downhill. You come down to Porthminster Cafe and then you can walk either side of the little park, continuing along below the railway station.

For those interested there is a coast to coast walk from St Ives to Marazion. There is a guide leaflet to St Michael's Way available from the TIC (see page 131).

Grading: Severe   Distance -   **22.3   396.6   13.9   246.4**

Timing: 7 hours

See also our Hayle to Pendeen Watch Path Description.

You are now starting on the longest and most deserted stretch of coast on the whole South West Coast Path, so think about accommodation. Out of season you will have to walk three whole sections, 22 miles (35 km), even in season two sections, 17 miles (27 km), before you find refreshment on the path. You can divert as listed below inland but this will increase the distance and all suggestions are subject to some seasonal closing and opening hours. There is not even a telephone box on the path. It is magnificent walking, but do not start out unprepared.

Refreshment possibilities are Zennor, Bosigran Farm, Pendeen/Botallack and St Just. There is sometimes a mobile snack wagon in Cape Cornwall car park (on the path).

One other warning, the path is often rough and rocky, the terrain is severe and in places after rain surprisingly boggy; few will average 2 miles (3 km) an hour; in other words it will take you longer than you expect.

Many use St Ives as a staging post; if however you should just wish to walk through, continue along the path below the railway station by which you enter. This becomes a tarmac lane which proves to be called The Warren at its end. Keep as close as you can to the harbour until you reach its north west corner. Here you have a choice; the purists will stay with the harbour and walk out round what is called The Island or St Ives Head; it is a pleasant walk. The less pure or perhaps those with still a lot of miles to cover can cut the corner by following signs to the Tate Gallery - this will bring you out behind Porthmeor Beach. Those going out to The Island can walk right round the harbour to turn left signposted 'The Museum'.

You can walk round The Island but the interesting little St Nicholas Chapel is on the high point in the middle. When you have completed your circuit you turn right to pass along in front of the Tate Gallery.

Go along behind the beach passing the Tate Gallery ignoring the ramp going down to the beach. The road starts to rise; there is a car park on your right and the path you want starts to bear off right by some public conveniences. You pass a bowling green and continue along the deteriorating tarmac path out into the country.

One place where it is easy to go wrong because of inadequate signposting is shortly after Clodgy Point on Burthallan Cliff; a path goes inland here and currently it is better marked than the main Coast Path.

The Coast Path cuts behind the National Trust property of Pen Enys Point; if you should have time on your hands, it is a pleasant extension.

If the weather is clear, Carn Naun Point is the place to look back and gloat at what you have done. A little later, be careful just before the stream, where you should avoid a path down to the beach. You should also ignore a path running inland just after the stream. Look for seals out on the Carracks - they are often there.

You pass the old mine building at Treen Cove and come out behind Gurnard's Head. Here again if you have time it is a splendid diversion out to the Head but so often walkers are pressed for time and cut across the neck.

The area around Porthmeor Cove is particularly spectacular if you can take your eyes briefly off where you are putting your feet!

As you drop off Carn Veslan, look ahead to the ridge of Bosigran Cliff and aim for the high point (not the big hill inland with the tower). The path drops then starts to bear left uphill, crosses through a ruined wall then bears right. Shortly you do go left up another clear path but in only a few yards turn right up a more indistinct path heading for the high point. As you get nearer you pass round to the left of it to drop into the valley. Here you go across a main track used by climbers and on across a little stone bridge. You go straight up the other side, only bearing right again as you approach the top wall.

On Rosemergy cliff there is a currently unmarked four way junction; go straight ahead.

30 | Pendeen Watch to Cape Cornwall (Car Park)   OS E102 Inland (V) Pendeen; Inland (V) St Just

| Grading: Moderate | Distance - | 6.5 | 403.1 | 4.0 | 250.4 |

Timing: 1.75 hours

See also our Pendeen Watch to Porthcurno Path Description.

Remember what was said about refreshment in section 29.

The official path from Pendeen Watch goes along the road to the far end of the row of coastguard cottages and turns right.

There is a better unofficial coastal route from Pendeen Watch which you can find by walking along to the right of the road and going down along the cliffs as the road bears away from the coast. Naturally avoid the marked and fenced-off mine shaft. Presently you come opposite a close inshore islet, The Enys, with a broken-down cairn on the top. Follow the path over the shoulder to join the official route by turning right over the stream.

The route is well-defined and brings you to the old Levant Mine dressing floors. A minor inland diversion is recommended to Geevor Mine, where you will find a museum, refreshments and toilets.

Refreshments may also be obtained a pleasant 0.75 mile (1200 m) walk away by turning left at the Levant Beam Engine up a track that becomes Levant Road, into Trewellard where there is a pub, and, a few steps on the left, a seasonal tea room.

After the Levant Mine the path bears right along tracks which are not coastal and what few signs there are you may trip over but are unlikely to see! Watch for the turning out to Kenidjack Castle-it is now properly signed.

Out on Kenidjack Castle, the path goes down to a stile and reaches a track where you are signed left. You leave this track at a sign directing you right, into the valley. Continue into the valley to a cottage to bear right and cross a footbridge. The path then bears right to a junction by a ditch. The official path bears left, zigzagging uphill to turn right at the top. An easy alternative, although somewhat overgrown in places, continues right. If you take this, proceed along the path; just before a small piece of ruined wall on your left, scramble up a few yards to turn right on a similar path above, which leads to the road.

When you reach the road whichever way you came you must turn down it. The official path goes down towards Cape Cornwall but does not go out onto it. Therefore those in a hurry may prefer to turn left just before the car park, but be careful if you want refreshment as the snack wagon, if it is there, will be down in the car park. Alternatively if you have the time, go out on the Cape; it is a wonderful spot owned by the National Trust for 57 good reasons and open to all. It was once considered to be 'Land's End' so maybe it has had a lucky escape!

31 | Cape Cornwall to Sennen Cove (Beach Car Park)   OS E102

| Grading: Moderate | Distance - | 8.1 | 411.2 | 5.0 | 255.4 |

Timing: 2.5 hours

See also our Pendeen Watch to Porthcurno Path Description.

After Cape Cornwall you climb up the track to Ballowall Barrow; the road bears off left but the Coast Path goes ahead. This is probably one of the grandest sections of the whole coast path.

In the Cot Valley, turn right onto the road and follow it to the car park at the bottom where a National Trust granite sign points you across the stream.

At Carn Barges the path takes a little inland loop to avoid the worst of the sand dunes. If the tide is out a quicker option is to walk along the firm sand to Sennen Cove (all year round refreshments available).

Grading: Moderate   Distance -   10.6   421.8   6.6   262.0

Timing: 3.25 hours

See also our Pendeen Watch to Porthcurno Path Description.

Leaving Sennen Cove you pass the Round House; go on into the car park area and turn left at the public toilets. Proceed ahead shortly to turn right and then head for the battlemented look-out.

Paths from Sennen to Land's End and for several miles beyond are so ubiquitous that it is impossible usually to give precise directions, you just follow the coast and your fancy and are unlikely to go seriously astray. There has in time past been publicity in the national press about footpath access to Land's End. This in no way concerns the Coast Path which is as freely available as it has been for years.

Regarding the Land's End complex itself, you have two options. If you want to use the cafes or other facilities head straight for it. If you wish to pretend it is not there, though that may be difficult, keep right out on the coast and only look out to sea! For what it is worth the official route goes via Gleeb Cottage with its collection of animals rather than using the path nearer the sea.

The short length just before Nanjizal Cove is perhaps the best bit of a very fine section; if you are lucky enough to pass that way in early spring you will see that it was once a bulb growing area. After you have crossed the stream do not turn right at once but proceed ahead for 30 to 40 yards (28 - 36 m) then turn right.

After a climb you are heading out to Gwennap Head and Tol-Pedn-Penwith. Tol-Pedn means the holed headland and it is spectacular. To find the hole, proceed up to the Coastwatch hut and walk on a bearing of 140 degrees for 153 yards (140 m), then walk along a path which bears 190 degrees. UNLESS YOU INTEND TO BE VERY CAUTIOUS, DO NOT GO TO LOOK FOR THE HOLE: GREAT CARE IS REQUIRED. You drop down over a natural bridge with the hole on your left - walk round it, do not fall down it and then leave again on the obvious path which soon climbs back on the cliff top; you do not have to go back the way you came.

At Porthgwarra, if you turn down the slipway it is possible to make a short diversion by way of a tunnel through which boats were once hauled. The only snag with this innocent entertainment is that you will have bypassed the seasonal cafe above. If you use the cafe turn first right afterwards.

Although the path from Porthgwarra leaves by an inland route, you can walk out round Carn Scathe if you wish. To do this, when you have turned down from the cafe bear right just before granite gate posts between the cliff top and a garden. The first few yards are overgrown but you will soon be glad you went that way. When you get back to the main path turn right.

After climbing out of Porthgwarra the path levels off and stays with the cliff tops. As you descend towards Porth Chapel Beach take a short excursion out onto a granite point for glorious views of the beach. Returning to the path it descends to the back of the beach passing by St Levan's Holy Well. Do not continue down to the beach, unless you want a swim, but turn off left above it. Another rewarding diversion from the official path is out and around the headland of Pedn-mên-an-mere.

You come out into the car park behind the Minack Theatre through an unusual kissing gate. Go through the car park to leave at the other end on a path parallel to and behind the Theatre entrance. There are various warning notices but you would need to be very infirm or suffer from vertigo not to be able to go down the steps. At the bottom turn left and do not, unless you want a swim, go down to the beach but keep along the path contouring above the beach.

In Porthcurno there is a good cafe usually open from Easter to the end of the season, but you will have to make a short detour left up the valley to reach it. Also, further up the valley, is an excellent museum to celebrate that Porthcurno was once the world centre of communications.

33 | Porthcurno to Lamorna Cove (Harbour)　　　　　　　　OS E102

Grading: Strenuous	Distance -	8.8	430.6	5.5	267.5

Timing: 3.25 hours

See also our Porthcurno to Penzance Path Description.

There is again fine walking in this section and some of it easy going; however parts of it are not easy and it may well take longer than you expect.

If you have visited the cafe you can take the old path and miss out Percella Point but the views from it over Porthcurno are spectacular. After Percella Point the official path is way inland with fields between it and the cliff top. How it can be named 'the coast path' is anybody's guess. However, you will not be cheated out of a more seaward path because the National Trust has a splendid coastal route. So before you get to those fields, watch out for a path on your right leading seaward of the official route. That is the one this Association calls 'a coast path'. You can even divert from that to drop down to Pendvounder Beach for a swim. Further east along Treen Cliff this path rejoins the official one.

The next chance of a diversion is at Treryn Dinas, which is an extra not to be missed by anyone who likes a scramble, to go up and onto the famous Logan Rock.

Unfortunately you have to go back inland again to continue on your way to Penberth, a scenic gem. Cross the slipway, passing the old capstan and go up the other side outside the house to climb a cove-side path. You come up to a headland which is worth another ten minute stop.

Around St Loy the authorities have so far failed to make the good path they should, so you therefore get shunted inland then have to use what in wet weather can be a very mucky path to get to the beach. There is no path at all for a few yards, but in response to representations by this Association, a path of sorts has been formed by the authorities along the bouldery beach, but watch out for the turn inland again after about 55 yards (50 m); we have had reports of a walker missing this in misty weather and getting cut off by the tide.

Be careful on Carn Barges not to be diverted onto the inland path to Lamorna; the official and better route is round the coast. Look for the cross just before Lamorna unless you are in too much of a rush to get to the seasonal cafe.

34 | Lamorna Cove to Penzance (Railway Station)　　OS E102 (V) Mousehole; (V) Newlyn

Grading: Strenuous and then easy	Distance -	9.7	440.3	6.0	273.5

Timing: 2.5 hours

See also our Porthcurno to Penzance Path Description.

After the cafe you bear right behind the harbour and cross the bridge. You go up past a most complicated waymark which, unless you look at it carefully, almost sends you the wrong way. However keep right but with only one house still on your right.

Few find the right route into Mousehole because it is never signed properly. We will describe it here in case you would like to join that exclusive bunch. Descend the hill passing the Wild Bird Hospital on your left. There is a post box on your right with a coast path sign pointing the way you have come but not the way you are going! After 33 yards (30 m) turn right opposite 'Lowena', and at the sign for Merlin Place, head towards the rocks, St Clement's Isle, which you can see out to sea. Just before the foreshore bear left along a terrace and fork right into a car park. Go to the bottom right end of the car park to continue briefly along the harbour side. You then have to turn in again left and then first right. However those with an interest in history before turning right should go forward past the house with pillars to read the plaque on the other side. The turn right brings you out on to a busier street; bear right along it to come behind the harbour again.

A new cycle/walk way continues seaward of the road to Newlyn.

Go round the back of Newlyn Harbour passing the War Memorial then bear right over the little bridge, with the Seaman's Mission on the right. A diversion a few yards upstream takes you to the award winning Pilchard Works, a working museum. Over the bridge bear right to come out once again behind the beach. After you have passed the tennis courts or remains of them, the path comes back to the road; here you go across the corner of the beach to go up steps and walk along the promenade.

At the end of the promenade pass the swimming pool and continue round to pass Penzance Harbour and on to the railway station.

35 Penzance to Marazion (Market Place)   OS E102 (T) Penzance (Trains)

Grading: Easy

Timing: 1 hour

See also our Penzance to Porthleven Path Description

| Distance - | 5.4 | 445.7 | 3.4 | 276.9 |

Note that between Lelant and Marazion there is a cross-peninsula path, St Michael's Way. This could be used to make a circular trip around Penwith by walking round the coast and then coming back inland from Penzance or Marazion to Carbis Bay.

Completed in 2001, there is a much improved route which leaves the station car park and follows the top of the sea wall to join the official route near the heliport, and continues on the top of the sea wall towards Marazion.

As you pass the cafe known as 'The Station', you emerge onto the road and head for Marazion. Just before the large white Marazion sign, cut through to the right and after a few yards you will cross a pedestrian bridge just seaward of the road bridge. You now go just seaward of the fields/car parks and then up a side road to join the main road.

Located at Marazion is the southern end of St Michael's Way leading to St Ives. The guide to it is available from St Ives TIC (see page 131).

36 Marazion to Prussia Cove (Bessy's Cove)   OS E102 (V) Marazion

Grading: Moderate

Timing: 1.75 hours

See also our Penzance to Porthleven Path Description.

| Distance - | 6.8 | 452.5 | 4.2 | 281.1 |

Walkers are treated badly at the beginning of this section, as there is no path at all for a while and then the first coastal length is on a beach.

You go up the road in Marazion, zigzagging if you wish to use a pavement, and pass the 40 sign. When just ahead is the sign which thanks you for driving carefully, turn right into a driveway. As the driveway bears right into a private house, you go left down a little concrete staircase and then follow the path down to the shoreline. At the bottom you are on a beach, walk along to ascend some hideous metal steps.

There is a short temporary diversion for a cliff fall which starts at Trenow Cove. Follow the track indicated on the notice for 274 yards (250 m) and look out for a low yellow arrow pointing you back to the coast.

After that you should have no trouble getting to Perranuthnoe where there are refreshments in season. The path turns inland here behind some houses, comes out onto the road to go up the lane opposite. Go right at the fork passing Blue Burrow Cottage and bear right.

When you get back to the coast do not go down the track to the beach but turn left into the next field. At Cudden Point the path cuts slightly inland but then the true Coast Path goes seaward again before Little Cudden.

At Bessy's Cove the path goes up to join a track by a letter box. Continue ahead bearing right to turn right over a stone stile beside a massive gate. The official route is down the path but the parallel track to its left is easier.

Grading: Strenuous   Distance -   10.3   462.8   6.4   287.5

Timing: 3 hours

See also our Penzance to Porthleven Path Description.

The path at Prussia Cove is quite a surprise, a sunken lane between two large stone buildings. You continue along a lane with the old coastguard row up on your left to pass through a gate, after which the track becomes a path and you should fork right at the first junction.

The path later becomes a green track down to Praa Sands where there are plenty of opportunities for refreshment in season.

The presently poorly marked route takes you down on the beach to leave it again as soon as you have passed the beach cafes up wooden steps. At the top turn right and proceed along to turn left to the well marked path through the sand dunes, shortly to turn right along the road through the estate.

If you do not wish to go down on the beach there is nothing to stop you turning left after the first cafe you come to; go inland past the public conveniences and then turn back right through the car park to reach the coast. Then proceed as above from the top of the wooden steps. If you like beach walking and the tide is out you can walk the length of the beach.

Assuming you have gone through the estate, bear right at the other end to pick up the path just inland of the big stones in the road.

At Rinsey Head the path bears inland cutting off the point. You pass an old railway coach and at the top turn left and then immediately right, going through the National Trust car park. As you drop down you should see two paths ahead, one going uphill which you do not want, the other going down, which you do. Pass the restored engine house to pick up the path below it on the other side.

At Trewavas Head the path bears inland of the old mine ruins; this used to be difficult to follow but recently waymarking has been improved.

As you approach Porthleven the path becomes semi-tarmac. You pass a cross erected in memory of those buried on the cliffs in unconsecrated ground. You go through a gate, or round the gatepost to join a lane, and bear right as you reach the main road to go down to the harbour.

| 38 | Porthleven to Mullion Cove (Harbour) | OS E103 (V) Porthleven |

Grading: Moderate   Distance -   11.4   474.2   7.1   294.6

Timing: 3.25 hours

See also our Porthleven to The Lizard Path Description.

At Porthleven as so often you have to walk right round the back of the harbour and out the other side. You go beyond the battlemented tower-like building to keep up the coastal road, using Mounts Road although it says it is a cul-de-sac.

Shortly after the last building on the right, a hotel, turn left off the track into the National Trust property Parc-an-als Cliff to avoid a landfall. Over the top you pick up the track again to proceed on and down to the beach.

If you have plenty of time there is a walking route right around Loe Pool, the biggest natural lake in Cornwall.

As you cross Loe Bar look for the path going up just to the right of the field but divert to see the white cross on your right. You pick up the path you want on 126 degrees from the cross. After the path levels out you pass a wooden seat and about 100 yards (90 m) after this, fork right to pick up the old route.

At Gunwalloe Fishing Cove you come out onto a gravelly road; do not take the first right which goes down to the beach but bear right on the second turning to pass inland of a house. At the top of the hill there is a stile where walking gardeners should look left.

Above Halzephron Cove you bear round to join the old road. Turn right shortly before you come to a barrier. You enter National Trust Halzephron Cliff - do not turn right immediately but continue ahead to turn right just before the next field gate.

At Gunwalloe Church Cove there is an alternative. If you want to see the church, and it is interesting, when you join the road go right and after you have seen the church you can usually cross the beach and its stream.

If a church visit is not for you, the correct route bears left aiming for buildings which prove to be public conveniences and a very seasonal cafe. There is a sign where you join the road but it is badly sited so is not obvious. Proceed down the road with the National Trust Gunwalloe Towans sign on your right. Bear left off the road just before a turning space. Cross a bridge over a stream and turn right round the back of the beach. The path is narrow until you come to a track where you turn left uphill.

At the top there is a small car park; as soon as you have gone through this you can bear right to walk along the cliff tops and so miss a length of tarmac road.

There is a seasonal cafe at Poldhu Cove. You walk round the back of the beach on the road and go up the drive of the residential care home. Turn right off the driveway shortly before you get to the big house.

Skirt around the back of Polurrian Cove to go up the steps, then take a track to turn right on a road. Where the road bears left proceed ahead on a path. If you are a purist the coast path goes in front of the old coastguard lookout, but this bit of path is seldom cleared.

Just past the Mullion Cove Hotel the path veers right, through the car parking spaces opposite starting by an old cannon. At the bottom turn left.

39 | Mullion Cove to The Lizard (Lighthouse)   OS E103

Grading: Moderate   Distance -   10.9   485.1   6.8   301.4

Timing: 3.25 hours

See also our Porthleven to The Lizard Path Description.

This is a wonderful, spectacular section with lots of interest, and it can be accomplished without great effort. Unless the weather is inclement you will certainly enjoy this stretch. If you can arrange the transport it makes a spectacular long half day excursion.

You go up the road; a very little way turn right and then right again.

After Mullion Cove in several places there are alternative paths but usually it makes little difference which you take, except as mentioned below.

After Parc Bean Cove going up Lower Predannock Cliff you want the higher path not the lower and at the top bear right.

After Vellan Cliff just before Gew-Graze, the path veers slightly inland for a stile.

Taking the path down to Kynance Cove, as you go down aim for the further headland you can see which is Lizard Point. Later you will see a sign close to the sea where you have to turn left; go down further to cross a wide concrete bridge by a house.

There is a good, long season cafe at Kynance Cove. Unless the tide is right in, the quickest route is to cross the few yards at the back of the beach and go up the steps the other side. If the tide is right in you have to go up the drive before the cafe and bear right at the top.

Leave the car park just to the right of the public toilets.

Lizard Town is exceptionally well footpathed so if you are lodging there you have a great many options.

Turn left above the Most Southerly Cafe and go along in front of the lighthouse.

| Grading: Moderate but strenuous in parts | Distance - | 17.1 | 502.2 | 10.6 | 312.0 |

Timing: 5.75 hours

See also our The Lizard to Helford Path Description.

A word of warning; old stone stiles are made of the local serpentine which can prove very slippery when wet, so take care on wet polished rock.

Unless you suffer from vertigo, do not miss diverting right shortly after the lighthouse to see the spectacular Lion's Den, which although is only about 20 yards (18 m) off the path, is still missed by many.

You pass Housel Bay Hotel and later go through a kissing gate. The path is odd in that it keeps to the top edge of the field until the next gate, where it turns to the seaward edge again.

You pass the old Lloyd's Signal Station and come out on a drive by a house. You go along this only a short way and the Coast Path then takes off right.

At Kilcobben Cove you come just inland of the top building of the lifeboat station, walk round it and go down the first little flight of steps but then go forward and not down the long flight of steps to the lifeboat.

At Church Cove where refreshment is available, go across diagonally behind one building to go through beside a big gate. Avoid the next four right turns to go uphill and over a stile.

After Polgwidden watch for a sharp right turn going along in front of an isolated house; the wrong path goes forward and looks more impressive.

You pass the National Trust Devil's Frying Pan sign and the true Coast Path is diagonally ahead, down steps into the car park and out the other end to turn right. In fact it has lately been signposted avoiding the car park; the choice is yours. Whichever way you went you drop down a lovely path through a garden. Watch for the right turn just after you have gone over a stone stile next to a metal gate.

You drop into Cadgwith behind the beach where there is a chance of refreshment, and then start up the hill staying with the road to turn first right just past Veneth Cottage.

After Enys Head there is a poorly marked section: you come to a fork where you go left, soon there is another right turn which you ignore, then you come down to a gate where you turn right. Go down until you see the National Trust Poltesco sign on the left. Here turn right going down steps and over a bridge. Avoid both the next right turns unless you wish to see the old Poltesco serpentine works. At the next junction, as you go up, bear right and again at the next junction. Later you go through a golf course area at the end of which you bear right. You come out on a road where you turn right. If the road is busy you can presently go across and take a permissive path to the beach, but it is not as rewarding as you might hope.

At Kennack Sands (refreshments in season) the path is behind the beach towards the toilets and then is well behind the two beaches. If the tide is well out you can walk along both beaches to the far end but as the proper path, at the time of writing, is well maintained there is little gained. What you do need to watch for at the far end of the second beach is that you take the Coast Path which looks fairly insignificant starting up nearly on the cliff edge; there is a bigger, wide path going inland but do not take it. There is another minor junction shortly where you keep right again.

Care should be taken in front of Borgwitha and behind the cliff castle Carrick Luz, because you cut across the neck of the peninsula and do not go inland or seaward. Improved waymarking should mean that you do not now go astray.

There is a very steep if scenic drop to Downas Cove and up the other side. After Beagles Point there is another smaller drop; cross a bridge and go up what is almost a stone chute the other side. At the top turn right.

After Black Head there is a very fine viewpoint for looking ahead along the South Cornish Coast. The path has been much improved and for a long way goes along the top of the cliffs. After you pass a piggery the route gets complicated. You come to a track, bear left but after about 30 yards (28 m) go ahead on a path where the track bears left.

You cross an old stone stile, pass an old fashioned pump and come to a grassy area with caravans. Here turn sharp right and turn right again when you get to the tarmac drive. There is a shorter, alternative route here if needed: when you get to the drive, turn left along it, and very soon divert off right on a field path to Coverack. Go along the left side of this until just before a sign forbidding access. Here turn sharp left and go down steps; there is a junction here left which is a quick but incorrect route, right is correct and more scenic. Go down to the next junction where ahead is Chynall's Point, a cul-de-sac but part of the Coast Path. Left is your route towards Coverack.

As you enter Coverack you reach a tarmac path; turn right and go down to join a road. If you wish to do all the Coast Path, there is then a little loop that many miss. 20 yards (18 m) down the road the path goes away right above a children's playground. The path then looks as though it is going to end, but press on over a slight rise to go down steps and turn left in front of a house.

Keep right of the back of a pub into the car park, turn left and left again to pass the front of the same pub.

41 | Coverack to Helford (Ferry)   OS E103 (V) Coverack

| Grading: Moderate | Distance - | 21.1 | 523.3 | 13.1 | 325.1 |

Timing: 5.75 hours

See also our The Lizard to Helford Path Description.

This distance includes the walk around Gillan Creek. If you arrive there at low tide and paddle across, deduct 2 miles (3.2 km).

Note: Evening meals can present a problem in Helford. At busy periods the Shipwright's Arms (01326 231235) will only serve pre-booked meals. The Riverside Restaurant (01326 231443) is an alternative. There is also the Rose Tea Gardens which serves meals but shuts earlier. Think about this before leaving Coverack or you may go to bed hungry.

In Coverack the Coast Path continues behind the harbour and the beach and where the main road bears inland, go ahead up the small tarmac road. The tarmac ends just before a small rise; go over this and start to drop down and look for a path turning off right just before a gate across the road.

The path out to Lowland Point is improved, but the further you go the less evidence of path there is. However the basic ploy is to keep close to the shore, going east until you have to turn north at the point.

After Lowland Point the Coast Path goes through Dean Quarry. This Association fought hard to get the path on the coast here rather than a long diversion inland. Heed the notice for times of blasting; at these times the path will be closed but you can use the diversion if travelling north.

Most of the quarry area is well signposted, but it is important that when you come up level with the first building, you start down the steep ramp to the beach - the footpath goes left off this. Towards the end of the quarry area, signs are more scarce but keep with the track close above the sea to go down on to the beach at Godrevy Cove.

Walk just over half way along the beach, crossing the stream bed which sometimes has water but is often dry, then turn half left to circumvent a marshy area and pick up the path at the back of the beach. Here turn left until you can turn inland through fields. At present the correct path is a sunken, usually muddy, lane on your right, so that most stay in the fields to join the track up to Rosenithon.

At the T-junction in Rosenithon turn right and go up the hill. The road bears right and just after this the footpath takes off left into a field. Cross one field and a traditional Cornish stile, surely the forerunner of the modern cattle grid. Cross two more fields in the same direction and surprisingly, the stile is just below the gate you come to.

Turn left on the road then first right down into Porthoustock. From Porthoustock to Porthallow the official route again goes inland to avoid the now unused quarries around Pencra Head and Porthkerris Point. However, there is a coast path.

Coastal Route
In Porthoustock, keep right of the telephone box and pass the entrance to the beach, forking left up a bank passing in front of a thatched cottage. You soon come to a big metal gate; the pedestrian access is just to the right round the wall.

Continue along the track and take the left fork approximately 150 yards (137 m) beyond the northern end of a disused quarry, which leads to a steep uphill slope. 20 yards (18 m) beyond the top of the slope, fork right for the shorter route to Porthkerris beach, except around high water spring tides. The simpler route for any state of the tide is to proceed up along the track for a further 450 yards (410 m), and turn right onto another track through a field which leads down to behind Porthkerris beach. Walk straight up the hill opposite, passing the way up to a restaurant on the left. (Should this latter track not be open, continue on to the MOD building and turn right along the road.)

Where the road bears left, carry straight on through two fields parallel to the coast to a kissing gate. Proceed ahead up the path and then steeply down to the beach at Porthallow.

Official Route
You leave Porthoustock going up the hill, but soon, where the road bears right, go ahead on a track. You pass houses on your right, the track ends and you keep ahead into a field. Here turn steeply up the field 302 degrees joining the right hand field bank at the top. Keep close to the bank to a sunken stile in the corner then slightly more right 338 degrees to another sunken stile just left of the gate.

Bear left on the road which later bears left to Trenance; here turn right. At the next T junction look for the footpath ahead and a few yards to your right. Go down alongside a vineyard to join the road where you turn right down to Porthallow. There are seasonal refreshments available here.

For those interested in their progress along the South West Coast Path, you will pass the halfway point on reaching Porthallow.

You leave Porthallow by taking the second turning on to the beach and immediately turning left to go along the back of the foreshore and up steps, bearing right at the first junction.

As you approach Nare Point, ignore a metal kissing gate which you pass on the right to shortly turn left along a one-time track which served the lookout. You go through a gateway and when the track bears uphill, proceed ahead across a footbridge.

After the second National Trust property 'The Herra', you come to a small beach where you go across the back. You come to a second beach, Flushing Cove, where you turn right on a path behind the beach.

A very short distance beyond the beach, a footpath takes off left and it is decision time. If you know the tide is in and you want to walk round, turn left.

Gillan Creek - Walking Round
It is about 2.25 miles (3.5 km), say an hour, easy walking but nearly all road. This distance is extra to the mileage shown for the section. If time is of the essence, you can go via Manaccan and be in Helford in 3 miles (5 km), but that is of course not walking the Coast Path.

Go up the grass-centred concrete track to and along a made-up road. At a left bend the Coast Path is signed to the right of a pebbledashed house. Proceed along a short stretch of a narrow, possibly overgrown, path into a field. Keep to the hedge on the left to a six bar gate, then go diagonally across the next field over a stile just left of another gate. Turn sharp left and make for the gate just in front of a white bungalow. Go through to the farm road, then right up to the main road. Turn right here down to Carne and right again beyond the creek head to St Anthony.

Gillan Creek Crossing
No ferry but it can usually be forded from one hour before Low Tide to one hour after. Predicted low water is 15 minutes earlier than shown in the Tide Tables. But do proceed with care.

There are two possible crossing places. Proceed until you can go no further along the path by the river, descend steps to the beach and wade across towards two caravans on the far shore.

A little further upstream you can cross part way on stepping stones in two sections: however this is not the easy option it sounds because they are extremely slippery and do not go across the whole river. It is advisable to carry handfuls of sand to scatter onto the stepping stones and even then be careful. If you do not use the stepping stones, it is possible to paddle across.

Once across turn right to pass in front of the church. Turn left up the hill. About 10 yards (9 m) past a mounting block on the left, look for a path going off at an angle right, take this and turn first right. You may then see the sign which should be at the bottom.

Coast Path continues
For the short route you need to turn left just after the house on your right beyond the kissing gate. If you have time the circular route out around Dennis Head is rewarding. To walk this, proceed ahead into the open field along a vestigial track towards a wood, keep to the left of the wood but close to it. Pass round the back of it where you will find a stile on your left; you can complete the circuit of the head returning to the stile and then back along the right hand hedge. You pass through several fields but then watch out for the sharp and partially concealed right turn into the wood. (Dogs must be kept under strict control.)

You come out by an old railed hound enclosure to bear slightly right and then go up a tarmac drive with grass in the centre. At the top turn right down the road, turn left up steps just as you get to the drive of a house called Traeth Cottage; it is easy to miss; if you get to the shore you have missed it!

Go along the back of the car park, down the road, crossing the first bridge over the creek. Turn right and go along past The Shipwright's Arms to the ferry point.

---

42 Helford to Falmouth (Ferry Terminal)   OS E103 (V) Helford

---

Grading: Moderate   Distance -   16.1   539.4   10.0   335.1

Timing: 4.5 hours

See also our Helford to Falmouth Path Description.

Helford to Helford Passage - use ferry, see details below. If the ferry is not running your alternatives are probably a taxi or a walk of 13 miles (21 km). This is mostly road but you can incorporate Frenchman's Creek. (Local taxis service - Autocabs 01326 573773).

Helford Passage (Helford River). Seasonal. Helford River Boats, Helford Passage, Nr Falmouth Tel Mawnan Smith 01326 250770	April 1st to October 31st. Departs hourly - Helford Passage on the hour and Helford 10 mins. past the hour. 9am to 5pm daily. Summer months only (July and August) runs on demand from 9am to 9.30pm. All crossings subject to weather conditions.

Helford to Helford Passage (Walking route) approx. 13 miles (21 km).

This moderate to easy route, on footpaths and minor roads, is as close to the Helford River as possible.

Take the path up the hill in front of the Shipwright's Arms; you will pass houses on your right and come down to Penarvon Cove. Back at the west side of the cove you will need to turn inland. Follow this track up a road where you turn right then left onto a farm track. This will lead you to the permissive path above Frenchman's Creek, eventually descending to continue alongside it through the woods. At the head of the creek you come to a definitive footpath. This is at the sign of the permissive path to Frenchman's Creek. Take the path on the right to Withan and Mudgeon past Frenchman's Pill cottage on the left, and across a footbridge over the river. Follow the waymarked route through the woods. When you get out of the woods, aim for the far left corner of the field and take the stile with the iron wheel gate on the left. Follow the boundary on the left and over the stiles past Withan Farm, from where you head in a westerly direction, until you reach a concrete-block stile to a farm lane where you turn left. Pass Mudgeon Farm on your right. When you reach a crossroads, turn right towards Mawgan. After a short distance, the path goes downhill.

Proceed uphill and you will join the road from St Martin where you turn right, passing the ancient settlement at Gear. Going downhill, you soon reach the narrow bridge over Mawgan Creek and on the next bend, you come to Bridge Farm. Turn left and proceed up the road. When you reach the main road, turn right. Just before the church turn left at the Gwarth-an-drea sign and left at the back of the bungalow called The Oaks. When you reach the road, turn right along Gweek Drive and follow this road until you meet a road on the left with a ford, and cross the bridge and follow the road to Gweek.

From Gweek, take the road opposite the Gweek Inn past the post office and take the footpath on the right through a wooden gate, just before light industrial units. The path runs parallel to a stream and it is not very clear. You join a bridleway at the ruins of a building and need to turn right, passing Kestle Dee farm. You will meet the road at Carwythenack Chase and need to take the Constantine / Port Navas road. Follow the field edge and cross the corner of the field to the stile by the signpost. Follow the road, crossing a stream and take the footpath on the left after the stream. Follow the field edge and go over the stile in the corner of the field behind the hut. Follow the road to Nancenoy and Polwheveral. You will now have to climb uphill.

Descend from the footpath junction towards Polwheveral. At the crossroads, turn right into the Port Navas road. After about 140 yards (128 m), take the left footpath into the corner of a field and cross the field to a stile left of the gate. Follow the field edge and cross the corner of the field to the stile by the signpost. Follow the road to Port Navas. We suggest you walk through Port Navas, exploring the creek and the quay. At Trenarth Bridge, by the post box, follow the Mawnan / Falmouth sign.

At the head of Port Navas Creek is a footpath on the left to Lower Penpol. Take the next footpath on the right, just past a turning to some houses. Cross the field to a stile left of a house. Continue right up the road past Budock Vean Golf and Country Club. Turn right at the road for Helford Passage. Turn right past Dring House. At the end of the road turn left onto a new definitive footpath before 'Ridifarne' and walk down to The Bar and turn left, following the coastal path to Helford Passage. You now reach the Ferry Boat Inn at Helford Passage, where the ferry from Helford would have put you down had it been operating.

Coast Path continues
At Helford Passage go along the beach eastwards to go up the steps at the end. At Durgan bear sharp right, when you reach the track, then bear left by the old school. Go up the road past a little grassy area with a seat on the right then DO NOT turn first right; it is the second turning you want.

At the next beach you come to Porth Saxon; you go in front of the boathouse, and the path is then at the back of the shore. At the following beach, Porthallack, the path in contrast stays in the fields to go on to the beach beyond a building.

The true coast path goes out round Rosemullion Head with its fine views, but there is a short cut across its neck. You come to the National Trust Nansidwell property and shortly into a big field; go downwards and across to join the bottom hedge. The exit is in the corner. There is another path better walked going ahead but it is the wrong path. The path does not go on the beach but bears left at the last moment.

You come out onto the road at Maenporth (refreshments in season). Turn right along the road, turning right again at the other end of the beach.

There follows a 1.5 mile (2.25 km) stretch past a golf course and around Pennance Point to the outskirts of Falmouth.

On reaching the road turn right for Swanpool, there walk across the back of the beach to continue on the coast path turning right at the first junction. At Gyllyngvase Beach turn right along the road; it will not be most people's favourite walking but it is quite rewarding looking back to where you have previously been.

When you get towards the end of the sea front passing the last big hotel, The Falmouth Hotel, do not go down right but continue on the pavement beside the road until you have passed the cul-de-sac notice, then you can bear right if you wish, away from the road. However presently you will need to cross the road for the safety of the pavement around Pendennis Point.

There is a path on the right from Pendennis Head towards the docks which you can take if you wish.

You come to a T junction where you turn right, there is then a town centre sign pointing left but that is the long way round for traffic so stay with us. Go ahead under the railway bridge. The road shortly bears left and there is a pub on the right which still proclaims it has hotel stables and a motor garage.

The road bears right passing a big car park and soon becomes a shopping street. Continue until Marks & Spencers, and the next turning on the right takes you to the ferry.

43 | Falmouth to Place House   OS E105 (T) Falmouth (Trains); (V) St Mawes

No Grading   Distance -   0   539.4   0   335.1

See also our Falmouth to Portloe Path Description.

In season you can cross by using two ferries, see details below. The only point to watch is that depending on conditions, the first ferry takes 20 to 30 minutes for the passage.

The ferry from Falmouth to St Mawes runs the whole year round except for winter Sundays. The scarcity of public transport in winter on Sundays combined with the fact that it is a long hike, makes us advise anyone arriving in Falmouth in winter on a Sunday to take it as a day off!

The ferry from St Mawes to Place only runs in season. If you are a purist there is a reasonable walking route round of 8-9 miles (13-14 km), two sections of which are very good walking indeed, see below for details. There are about a couple of buses a day from St Mawes to Gerrans, except on Sundays, or you could consider a taxi. If the ferry is not in service you can always ask. We have heard from walkers who have been lucky enough to get a lift from local boat owners.

Falmouth/St Mawes   All year round. Weather permitting.
St Mawes Ferry Co   Summer service every 1/2 hour, Winter service
75 The Beacon Falmouth TR11 2BD   every hour.
(01326) 313201 - Office   Summer Sundays departs Falmouth on the hour,
(01326) 313587   departs St Mawes 1/2 past the hour.

Winter service every hour but no sailings at 0915 and 1215 from Falmouth, and 0945, 1245 and 1545 from St Mawes. No Sunday service.

The St Mawes Ferry Co. is prepared to land pre-organized parties of 20 or more at Place House. To do this they would need prior knowledge to lay on an extra boat. This is also dependent on the state of the tide and weather.

St Mawes/Place House (St Anthony)   Seasonal
For information please write to: Daily - 1 May-30 September, 2001.
Mr R Balcombe   St Mawes - Place 1/2 hourly
Turks Folly, Drump Road   from 1000 to 1630 hrs. No 1300 ferry.
Redruth TR15 1PR   Place - St Mawes 1/2 hourly from
Tel: (01209) 214901   1015 to 1645 hrs. No 1315 ferry.

Walking route around the Percuil River (approx. 9 miles / 14 km)
At St Mawes, on leaving the ferry from Falmouth turn left along the road. As you approach the castle, take a minor road going left, the most prominent sign being 'St Mawes Castle car park'. If you look carefully there is also a small footpath sign amongst the clutter. Follow this minor road until you come to the National Trust's Newton Cliff, which you enter. The route follows a very scenic path along the Carrick Roads with superb views across to Falmouth and the far shore. Ignore two minor stiles on the left which lead down to small coves. You come out on a minor tarmac road to turn right. Continue along this road bearing left at the junction to pass in front of a boatyard. Immediately after passing the boatyard buildings the path bears a few yards to the right to proceed along the bank above the shore.

You come to the gate leading to the churchyard with a large sign 'Dogs on Leads Please Consecrated Ground'. Go through this gate keeping left all the way to pass the church on your right. Ignore the turning right marked 'way out' but instead keep left through a lych-gate and pass a house called Lanzeague. After its second gate the path bears right up the hill. You go through a metal gate where there is a public footpath sign 'St Just Lane' and continue uphill with views of the creek to your left. You go through another gate into a lane, in parts muddy in parts green, to finally exit onto the road.

Turn left and walk along the road for about 150 yards (135 m), ignore the first footpath on the right immediately past a house, but take the second on the right shortly afterwards. For the first field you have the hedge on the right. For the second and third it is on your left, then for the fourth it is again on your right. Take care in this fourth field, as there is a temptation as you enter to turn right; do not do this but go straight ahead to continue with the hedge on the right. Look for the sharp right turn through the hedge a little before you come to the end of the field. Descend the bank to the road, where you turn right and proceed down to meet the main A3078 at Trethem Mill.

Turn left - this is on a bridge crossing the creek - and immediately turn right up some stone steps and ascend the footpath through a wood. Coming out of the wood, cross the field on a bearing of 110. In the next field bear right on 140 and leave by a wooded track. At the top there is a stile; cross it and bear 137 diagonally across the field to a hedge and follow this to the road. Turn right down the road.

At the next junction follow the road curving round to the right past Polhendra Cottage. Here almost immediately turn left through the second gate, a metal one. There is a footpath sign if you look for it, but it is not readily apparent. Aim across on 123 to descend to the bottom of the hedge which you can see on the opposite side of the valley. Here you will find a bridge, cross it and proceed up, with the hedge on your left. At the top ascend some stone steps and cross the next two fields on 125. On reaching the road turn right into Gerrans and walk down to the church.

At the church take the left fork (not left turn) into Treloan Lane. You walk via Treloan and Rosteague, at each junction keeping straight ahead. At the house just beyond Rosteague you pass through a pedestrian gate and the path unexpectedly goes right, through a hedge gap, before continuing in the same direction but with the hedge on your left. You cross an open field to enter an enclosed lane eventually coming to the road at Porth Farm about 1.5 miles (2.4 km) from Gerrans.

The slightly quicker way is then to turn right along the road and left where there is a sign 'Footpath to Place by Percuil River' to cross a wooden bridge. The pleasanter alternative, a few yards longer, is to go ahead on the road to turn right through the gates of the Trust's Porth Farm then turn right to come to the same bridge.

Over the bridge the path turns right to follow Porth Creek and then the Percuil River, down to the low tide landing point for the ferry and soon on to Place itself. This last stretch of walking is very scenic.

---

44 | Place House to Portscatho (The Quay)   OS E105

Grading: Easy   Distance -   10.0   549.4   6.2   341.3

Timing: 2.75 hours

See also our Falmouth to Portloe Path Description.

The St Anthony Peninsula, thanks to the National Trust, offers a very good half-day circular walk. Most people will start at Porth Farm, walk to Place as already described, and then follow the coast path round St Anthony's Head and on to Towan Beach, here turning back inland to Porth Farm.

Some maps show a definitive right of way across the front of Place House; this route however is not really practical except at very low tides.

The Coast Path continues up the road at Place passing the gates of the house and shortly turn right to go behind the church. You get back to the creekside, soon to leave it again to go over behind Amsterdam Point. The path then is superb with wonderful views across the Carrick Roads. After the footbridge across the top of a one-time dam turn sharp right. Shortly turn even sharper left to go up steps and turn right again at the top. Look for the very little path forking right up to the topograph for the best viewpoint.

The path then proceeds forwards without problems to Portscatho; however, owing to the lie of the land you do not see the village until the very last moment and it always seems to take longer than you think it should.

45 | Portscatho to Portloe (Post Office)

OS E105 (V) Portscatho

Grading: Strenuous

Distance -   12.0   561.4   7.5   348.8

Timing: 3.75 hours

See also our Falmouth to Portloe Path Description.

You leave Portscatho going through a couple of small fields; if the tide is out you have a choice. You can start down the steps then turn right and go down to cross Porthcurnick Beach - this is slightly shorter. The reward for not turning for the beach but going up the steps opposite is that you then pass a seasonal refreshment hut.

If the tide is out it is easier to walk along Pendower Beach to Carne Beach. You can look forward to see if this is feasible as you walk down by the car park before Pendower Beach.

Having ascended Nare Head, it is possible to short cut it by veering left but, unless the weather is poor, do not do this or you will miss out on the rewarding views. Study the way the first arrow is pointing and follow its direction along the edge of the gorse. There is an unmarked path going right to the head itself. Shortly afterwards there is a post with an arrow pointing left here on a bearing of 120 degrees; if you look carefully you will see a small path going forward into the gorse - take this. This path gives the best views of Gull Rock offshore. It winds back to join the main track, where you turn right.

At the other end of the track about 200 yards (185 m) on, where it opens up, there are little ventilators; bear across right to pick up the coast again; do not stay on the track.

Another place you can go wrong is after the very steep descent off The Blouth where the path bears left and then right over a stile. There is a sign but it is badly sited so it is easy to miss and as a result a lot of people go wrong here.

At The Straythe there is a pleasant surprise for those who walked this way some years ago. A well engineered path zigzags up to replace the old uncomfortable and nearly vertical flight of steps. At the top the route is well signposted through the gardens, but you do need to turn right in the field when you get there.

There is a long descent into Portloe but at least you can see it, unlike Portscatho. Watch for the sharp left turn just as you draw nearly level with a green seat on your right. Then you want the second turning on the left to pass in front of the public toilets and so down to Portloe.

46 | Portloe to East Portholland (Car Park)

OS E105

Grading: Strenuous

Distance -   3.8   565.2   2.4   351.2

Timing: 1.25 hours

See also our Portloe to Mevagissey Path Description.

This stretch is rewarding and will give you enjoyment for your efforts.

From the quay at Portloe you can turn first right, scramble along and up some steps, to rejoin the Coast Path that way. However the true Coast Path goes up the road, turns right along another road, and then shortly leaves it down some wide steps past cottages. The official route does have the advantage that it passes the Post Office which serves cream teas.

A new path has been made in the landslip area just before West Portholland.

You can, if you wish, avoid the road walk from West to East Portholland by going forward behind the beach at West Portholland and walking along the sea wall between the two settlements. This is a little rocky at the beginning but should present no problems to any surefooted walker.

47 **East Portholland to Gorran Haven (Beach)**   **OS E105**

Grading: Moderate   Distance -   10.3   575.5   6.4   357.6

Timing: 3 hours

See also our Portloe to Mevagissey Path Description.

The path starts along a one time tarmac lane from East Portholland. Turn right at the end of this lane to descend a field and continue alongside the coast. There is a path forward but if you use it, you simply get a longer stretch of road to walk to get to Porthluney Cove.

There is a seasonal cafe behind the beach in front of Caerhays Castle. Note one point, on leaving the road you cross half the first field joining a rough track close to a projecting corner of waste land. The path does not stay on the track here but turns sharp right along the fence; the badly sited marker post is usually invisible in the long grass.

From Hemmick Beach via The Dodman to Gorran Haven, it is all good walking; there are wonderful views from The Dodman in the right conditions. You can look back on triumphs past and challenges still long to come! Just north of The Dodman Cross is an 18th Century coastguard watch-house which does prove useful shelter in heavy rain.

At Little Sand Cove there is an old path cutting the corner off Pen-a-Maen Point. We do not recommend it - you climb higher and will not have such good views.

You come into Gorran Haven on Foxhole Lane, turn right into Canton and just before the beach turn left into Church Street. Proceed up this; there is a footpath loop to the right if you want a brief and better look at the beach, and turn right at the top into Cliff Road.

48 **Gorran Haven to Mevagissey (Harbour)**   **OS E105 (V) Gorran Haven**

Grading: Easy   Distance -   5.7   581.2   3.5   361.1

Timing: 1.5 hours

See also our Portloe to Mevagissey Path Description.

This section starts happily enough but you are beginning to leave the most remote and least spoiled section of the South Cornish coast behind.

You go up past the old coastguard row and turn right again at the top, still Cliff Road. At its end Cliff Road turns left and you go over a stile into a field.

From Turbot Point you descend to Colona Beach passing the National Trust Bodrugan's Leap sign. Turn right to pass behind the beach, do not go left when the track bears left, but proceed ahead very shortly to cross the tarmac drive to continue ahead on a footpath across the grass. At its start you are heading in a straight line for Mevagissey harbour; later it veers a little left and you pick up a hedge on your right. Continue along this hedge until it goes up to join the road where you turn right.

At the end you will find the road is called Chapel Point Lane; turn right, bear left at the sea and follow the road round past the Rising Sun.

You bear right on entering Mevagissey on Polkirt Hill. You pass buildings on your right and then enter a park; proceed through this to the other end. Turn right down the first flight of public stone steps on the right to come out on the quay close to some public toilets.

Grading: Strenuous   Distance -   11.6   592.8   7.2   368.3

Timing: 4 hours

See also our Mevagissey to Fowey Path Description.

(It may be of interest to know that there is now a ferry service between Mevagissey and Fowey which runs from May until mid October, weather and sea conditions permitting. Timetables are available from Fowey TIC (see page 131) and information is usually available on 07977 203394).

In Mevagissey walk along the back of the harbour to turn right and then very shortly bear up left veering away from, and up above, the quayside. You come out into open playing fields, go across but aim for the extreme right end of the terrace of buildings you see opposite.

Continue along, avoiding the right turn down some steps. The path comes out again into a field and there is a descent to cross a bridge. Here, turn left. You descend from Penare Point to walk behind the ruins of Portgiskey. Ignore the next stile on the right but proceed, curving right up the hill, following the signs to join the road, where you turn right.

You come out on to the road close to the entrance of a massive caravan park. Here you have the choice of:

1. turning left to the main road B3273, then right towards St Austell and first right again signposted Pentewan and called West End, which is the official route, or;

2. turning right towards the sea, then left after the public toilets along the front, then go over a bridge across the St Austell River. You then make for a stone arch ahead, and turn right to go over a narrow wooden bridge.

This route avoids the shops at Pentewan, although there is a seasonal cafe on the campsite.

Do not leave Pentewan unrefreshed as you have a long tough section ahead.

You are then faced with another choice. You can either:

A. continue on the road through Pentewan, and take the road to the left to follow the official path (you will need to walk back from the harbour if you followed option 2 above).

B. take the Association's preferred route by turning right off the road into the harbour area just after the public toilets, and walking along the harbour to the end of the cottages where you will see a path on your left going up through gardens to link up with the Coast Path behind the cottages. (If you followed option 2 above, simply pass the winding gear, turn right immediately in front of the Pentewan Beach sign to join the path going up through the gardens.) The path through the gardens is signed as a public footpath and does not look like a public right of way, but it is!

Back on the Coast Path put this book away; you will need your energies for other things! However take it out again when you have crossed a wooden bridge in a sizeable wood.

Having crossed the bridge, you soon cross another small stream and come to a T-junction. The right turn will take you down to Hallane Mill Beach, a lovely spot for a picnic with a waterfall. The Coast Path turns left soon to turn right again to start ascending to Black Head, a superb diversionary viewpoint on a clear day. It was once a rifle range but was purchased by the National Trust, helped in a small way with a donation from this Association. If you wish to visit Black Head, turn right at the memorial stone to A L Rowse, the Cornish poet and historian: to continue, turn left.

The passage of the wood behind Ropehaven can give trouble if signing is not maintained. On entering the wood you turn right taking care on this rocky path which can be slippery when damp, then left at the seat. Avoid the right fork down to a cottage and turn sharp left at the top into a narrow walled lane. Turn right on to the narrow road. The path leaves it to go into a field just beyond the little car park/lay by. After the stile which follows the long climb to Silvermine Point, keep to the fence, and don't be tempted to follow the better defined track inland.

At Porthpean Beach the sign forward can be misleading - you do in fact go down on to the promenade to walk along past toilets and a seasonal cafe. Continue to the end; it does not look likely, but there is a steep set of steps at the end to get you back on track.

50 | Charlestown to Par (Polmear)   OS E107 (V) Charlestown

| Grading: Easy | Distance - | 7.0 | 599.8 | 4.3 | 372.6 |

Timing: 1.25 hours

See also our Mevagissey to Fowey Path Description.

The official path does not go across the dock gate at the mouth of the harbour, but provided the gate is closed most people will go that way.

You come up from the harbour keeping to the right of a house called Salamander. It is at first a tarmac track and then goes into fields. Later you come out beside a road, walk a few yards along it to turn right and then fork left.

After passing the Carlyon Bay Hotel you come out by a car park area; keep to the right of this to cross the road and continue alongside a golf course.

The clay processing industrial complex gets nearer, and you turn left just before a wall/wire netting fence. The path continues through the complex itself, giving you a detailed look at one of Cornwall's major industries. Avoid the escape route left under a low railway culvert, but continue ahead along what looks like a dead end to the road and turn right to go past the entrance to the clay works.

Continue north on the road and go under a railway viaduct to turn first right signposted A3082 Fowey, cross a level crossing and under another railway bridge. The road forks, and you should keep right to enter Par Green, which is a one-way system, and brings you into the town of Par. You pass The Good Shepherd Church on your right and Welcome Home Inn on your left. (If your journey ends at Par and you need the railway station, keep walking along Par Green until the turn on your left for Eastcliffe Road, which you follow until you reach the station.)

You can then take the second path off on the right, although the National Trail waymark indicates straight on along the road. To try and make this clearer, the beginning of the path has a low concrete wall and house No. 52 (Sandroy), on the right. It soon comes to a tidal stream; bear left to walk along it, cross a road and come out in a caravan site. Keep down the right hand side, to turn left and go along the seaward side of a blue roofed building. You pass a cafe, and finally come to Polmear, where you bear right to rejoin the official path.

If you miss all this you can simply walk along Par Green, then bear right at its end to get to Polmear by main road. It is less pleasant, gives less chance of refreshment but it gets you there just the same.

51 | Par to Fowey (Town Quay Ferry)   OS E107 (T) Par (Trains)

| Grading: Moderate | Distance - | 9.6 | 609.4 | 6.0 | 378.6 |

Timing: 3 hours

See also our Mevagissey to Fowey Path Description.

It is a fine walk out from Polmear via Polkerris around Gribbin Head to Menabilly and so on to Fowey. The availability of public transport from Par to Fowey makes this a very practical half day excursion with lovely views nearly all the way.

The path leaves the main road at Polmear just beside the eye-catching Rashleigh Cottages. At the first junction keep right and at the second turn right.

As you enter Polkerris you turn right. Go down to the beach and turn left, currently no sign, to proceed up the ramp and join a zigzag path to the top.

You should have no problem then until you enter the National Trust The Gribbin property through a field gateway. There is soon a junction; bear right and you come to a pedestrian gate.

65

The official route goes to the Daymark and then sets off downhill inland. (There is a better alternative seaward; bear right along the fence from the pedestrian gate to presently go through a second pedestrian gate and the way forward is then obvious passing through a little wood; when you come out proceed downhill to join the official route. If you want the best route but also wish to make a closer examination of the Daymark itself bear left and go and find out. When you have satisfied your curiosity, proceed due south and you will come to the second gate already mentioned.)

If you are walking between mid-June and mid-September, it is worth planning your walk to arrive at the Daymark on a Sunday. The Daymark, now owned by the National Trust, is open to the public on mid-season Sundays, and the views from the top are memorable. The Trust provides torches, and there are guides at the bottom and the top of the tower, so it is thoroughly recommended, provided you are not anxious or do not have a head for heights.

You come down towards Polridmouth Beach and walk around close behind it; the path becomes concrete and there are even concrete stepping stones. This does not sound delightful but this is a lovely little stretch by the house and lake. The path goes steeply up bearing right through woods at the other side.

Again there should be no navigational problems until you reach Allday's Fields (memorial stone on your left). You enter a wood; first right is a loop path out towards the castle and there is a steep path dropping to the beach which can be used as a short cut when the tide is out. On entering the wood the more direct route is to go ahead at the first junction and to turn left at the next. This takes you down an increasingly rock cut lane which has a very sharp elbow about two thirds of the way down.

The path comes out at Readymoney Cove and it is then all road to Fowey. However if you are continuing along the Coast Path, watch for the ferry point on your right before you get into the town. It is down steps just after Fowey Hotel's tea garden (although if you are walking in low season, you may find that the ferry is operating from the Town Quay in Fowey itself).

A guide book to the Saints' Way is available from Fowey TIC (see page 131).

52 Fowey to Polperro (Harbour)   OS E107 (T) Fowey; (V) Polruan

Grading: Strenuous   Distance -   11.5   620.9   7.1   385.7

Timing: 3.5 hours

See also our Fowey to Looe Path Description.

This section is very good value for money in two senses of the word. Firstly there is a fine path all the way from Polruan to Polperro with magnificent sea views. Secondly, it is probably the toughest stretch of walking on the South Cornwall coast. (Leaving Fowey, if you have time on your side, you can go via the higher vehicular ferry to Bodinnick and walk The Hall Walk to Polruan [4 miles / 6 km]).

Fowey/Polruan (River Fowey)	All year round at 5-10 min intervals.
Polruan Ferry Co. Ltd	1st May - 30th Sept. Daily 0715 - 2300 hrs
Toms Yard	except Saturday 0730 start, Sunday 0900 start.
East Street	1st Oct - 30th Apr. Daily 0715 - 1900 hrs.
Polruan-by-Fowey	except Saturday 0730 start, Sunday
Cornwall	1000 - 1700hrs. Closed Xmas Day
PL23 1PB	
Tel: 01726 870232	

In winter months when the weather deteriorates you will find that the ferry operates to and from the Town Quay at Fowey rather than from Whitehouse Quay lower down the harbour; there should be a sign up to this effect.

Landing from the ferry in Polruan, go along the quay and up Garrett Steps just beside The Lugger and at the top turn right along West Street and then left when you get to Battery Lane. The path comes out in a grassy area; keep with the wall on your left going round the corner. The path goes right, just after an earth bank and then you proceed ahead across another open area with a small ruin up on your left. It joins the road beside a school; continue ahead to turn sharp right just before the notice saying 'Furze Park'.

When you reach the National Trust money box on the path, take the right, downward path.

About 2 miles (3 km) after leaving Polruan there is a considerable hill behind Great Lantic Beach. You can go all the way to the top and turn right there. The route we recommend turns right about 30 yards (28 m) before the top, goes over a stile and drops down again. Ignore the first two turnings right as these are beach paths. Presently a wide path, the other route, joins from the left (there is a gate on your right). Shortly after that is another path right - this is a spectacular, seaward path, and makes you appreciate the rugged beauty of Pencarrow Head even more.

Although a definitive right of way is shown below the Watch House, at the moment the practical route is the broad path above it. Assuming you are on this path, ignore the stile on your right which goes directly to the house. Just after this is another loop path right but it has little in views to compensate for the extra effort. After this you can either take the right turn, or keep to the upper path and then join the lower one to follow the path around the back of a cove. When you come to Lansallos, turn inland for the Coast Path.

Later, as the first houses in Polperro come into view, there is a series of parallel paths all going to Polperro. You should take the rocky path on your right by an outcrop on your left, as you get a glimpse of some houses on the opposite cliff. This is the most seaward path and passes several seats and shelters to arrive at a rocky area overlooking the mouth of the harbour. From the rocky area turn left and the official route into Polperro is the first set of steps on the right.

53   Polperro to Looe (Bridge)   OS E107 (V) Polperro

Grading: Moderate	Distance -	8.0	628.9	5.0	390.7

Timing: 2.25 hours

See also our Fowey to Looe Path Description.

This next section is particularly well walked and the local bus company is sufficiently commercially minded to put up bus times for cliff walkers between Polperro and Looe actually on the path!

In Polperro you have to walk behind the harbour crossing the Roman Bridge to turn right. Leaving Polperro there is a loop path right called Reuben's Walk. If you take this turn left again just before the miniature lighthouse.

When you are about three quarters of the way up the hill, take the right fork at the junction of two well-defined paths; thanks to the National Trust, a wonderful new stone sign has replaced the former wooden signs which were previously vandalised.

Note the spectacularly sited War Memorial on Downend Point. A little way past this is another beach path right which you ignore.

There are seasonal refreshments at Talland.

After the beach cafe go up the tarmac track, turn left to pass the toilets, and then right. Turn right at the Smugglers Rest cafe into a small car park to rejoin the path.

The walk to West Looe is pleasant and quite easy. However, there are often copious amounts of horse manure on the stretch from Talland as far as Hendersick.

Due to continuing problems at Hendersick Farm, the National Trust has had to install a diversion behind Portnadler Beach, and it is important to follow the Trust's relevant route.

On entering Looe at Hannafore, you have a choice. You can either follow the official path along the road, passing flower beds and a seasonal cafe, or you can take the first right to walk alongside the beach, ascending the steps in front of a black barrier and turn right. Either route will bring you to a stretch of road with no pavement. This drops into a dip and watch for a battlemented look-out platform on your right. Just past this are steps down to the harbour area of the river; that is the best way to go. This has a double advantage: it keeps you away from the traffic and takes you past the seasonal ferry to East Looe: certainly if you are walking straight through, this is the best way to go.

The ferry runs between West and East Looe generally during the mid and high season. It is, however, dependent on both the weather and tide, and you may find it running off-season if the weather is exceptional.

If you are walking, simply keep to the quayside in West Looe, cross the bridge, and turn right into the main street, Fore Street, in East Looe.

54 | Looe to Portwrinkle (Quay)   OS E107 & E108 (T) Looe (Trains); (V) Downderry

Grading: Strenuous - Moderate in parts   Distance -   12.2   641.1   7.6   398.3

Timing: 4 hours

See also our Looe to Plymouth Path Description.

NOTE: Please read the excellent news at the end of this section. If the new COAST PATH is fully completed when you do this walk, the grading will definitely be strenuous.

You leave East Looe by turning up Castle Street, cross a minor crossroads and continue up the hill. The road peters out becoming a pleasant high level path above the sea.

The path becomes a road again and at the first junction bear right into Plaidy Lane. Pass Plaidy Beach on your right, and continue on the road until just after it has veered left. Here a steep tarmac path takes off right just beyond a big electric cable post.

At the top of the path you come to a road again to continue ahead for a while until the road bears left but the path goes forward again between houses. Go down steps, do not turn left or right but continue nearly opposite to go ahead.

The path comes down to Millendreath (seasonal refreshments): pass behind the beach to go up the cul-de-sac road the other side. The road becomes a path in a sunken lane, but 150 yards (135 m) after you reach the road again, turn right into the National Trust's Bodigga Cliff property, keeping to the left of the picnic tables. This beautiful place is now accessible for people of varying abilities, including wheelchair users.

The path comes out on the road above Seaton, and you turn right down what is Looe Hill. Go down to the bottom and turn right into Bridge Road. If time presses, the quickest route is along the road to Downderry.

Beach Route (tidal)
However, at most states of the tide, there is a better alternative. (If there has been flooding in Seaton, which you will have noticed at the Seaton Nature Reserve, and / or the tide is high, this beach route will be very difficult to negotiate, and it is therefore recommended that you take the road option instead.) Where the road starts to go uphill opposite the post office and general store, there is a wall on the seaward side. Behind this wall is the beginning of coastal defence works with a path on top. After a while you have to go down to the beach and make a choice. The first left turn by a stream will bring you into the centre of Downderry for shops, toilets and seasonal refreshments. The next will bring you to the Inn on the Shore. If you don't need any facilities, you should continue on to the next stream and turn left up some concrete steps; this latter option will lessen the amount of road walking, and there is a lot to come in the next section. You come up beside a school to turn right along a road, and to rejoin the official route.

Coast Path continues
Continue with the road as it bears sharply inland at a hairpin bend. Take the waymarked turn off right, next to a house called Downderry Lodge, ignoring the right turn immediately after you have taken this path. The path zigzags uphill to come eventually into a field.

By the time you read this, the long-awaited Coast Path should have been installed: this Association has been lobbying for over 15 years for its installation, so enjoy it - better late than never. The Association thanks those responsible, particularly Cornwall County Council and the Port Eliot Estate.

The new path will be easy to follow, so, when you reach the field, if there are new signs pointing you right, then go ahead and enjoy your walk.

If there are no such signs, we regret that you will have to follow the dull bypass route which goes forward through a few inland fields and then joins a road where you turn right. You then have a long tedious section on the road before turning right again just after a bungalow named 'The Bungalow' to go down to Portwrinkle to turn left.

Grading: Moderate

Distance -   21.4   662.5   13.3   411.6

Timing: 5.75 hours

See also our Looe to Plymouth Path Description.

The Coast Path takes the second path on the right, opposite the entrance to the golf club. It is currently well marked except right at the end of the course, where you need to aim for the pedestrian gate seen on top of a rise.

You come out to the road but the path for a while is just inside the hedge. This travesty of a path ends by the road junction to Torpoint where you have to come down to the road and turn right along it. All this agony is caused by some bureaucrat in the MOD who refuses to let you walk through the rifle range when not in use; if it can be done elsewhere, including on a tank firing range in Dorset, with good will it could here.

However, back to the road: you pass the Tregantle Fort entrance, then the road bears left and shortly you turn right, signposted Whitsand Bay etc. The road shortly bears left to lead you to a National Trust path.

There is then another long stretch of road, until you see notices for Whitsand Bay Holiday Park on the left and the Coast Path starts again on the right; at this point even sharper left is a seasonal cafe. The Coast Path is now well marked and a great improvement over the road, but it does involve two steep climbs.

The path continues to be well marked, and you should take the diversion onto the lovely Rame Head if time allows.

Continue along the tarmac avoiding the path turn off on the right. The road turns left with intermittent views ahead to Plymouth Sound Breakwater and presently, over a 0.25 mile (400 m) later, takes off into the wood right.

Traversing Cawsand/Kingsand the official and in fact easiest way is not straightforward and only some of it is signposted, so read the next paragraph carefully.

You enter Cawsand from Pier Lane, go across the square to pick up Garrett Street. As you come towards the end of this street look for the old Devon/Corn boundary mark on a house on your right. Then turn right in front of the Post Office. Soon you will approach a street called The Cleave. Just before you reach it, turn left. Then turn first right up what is Heavitree Road but you will not know this until you are a few yards up it. As you ascend you will presently see Lower Row on your left; here turn right and enter Mount Edgcumbe Country Park.

When you come out on to a road at Hooe Lodge turn right, but look in 20 yards (18 m) for the path leaving the road on the left. You continue along a section of the Earl's Drive. There was a major landslip here in 2001 and a substantial diversion has been installed where you used to go under the old stone arch: unfortunately, the arch was damaged in the slip and is unsafe. The diversion is permanent and quite well signposted - it will return you quickly to the original path. Follow the signs which direct you down to the foreshore, the Country Park Rangers have improved this area beyond recognition, and it is a shame to ascend once more.

You continue through a high deer gate; you come out by a classical summer house and you should keep along right to pick up a concrete driveway, and later right again when the drive goes left to walk inside of a hedge. You pass an old blockhouse on your left.

If you are not too pushed for time, a visit around the gardens of Mount Edgcumbe is worthwhile, and free. A charge will be made if you wish to visit the House.

The path comes out by The Orangery; go through an arch then go forward to turn right through the park gates to the ferry point for Plymouth.

(At Plymouth you can take the coast to coast walk to Lynmouth by using the Erme/Plym Trail, the Erme Valley Trail and the Two Moors Way. Guide books to all three routes are available from Ivybridge TIC (see page 131).)

Grading: Easy

Timing: 2.5 hours

Distance -   12.0   674.5   7.5   419.1

See also our Plymouth to Wembury Path Description.

The distance includes the walking route around to Mountbatten Point. If you use the Mountbatten Ferry service, then deduct approximately 5 miles (8 km).

Cremyll/Plymouth

Cremyll Ferry,
Cremyll Quay,
Cremyll,
Torpoint,
Cornwall. PL10 1HX
Tel: 01752 822105.
(Full timetable available - phone above no.)

All year round at 30 minute intervals, but no sailings at 0930, 1230 and 1530 from Mount Edgcumbe, and 0945, 1245 and 1545 from Plymouth.
Summer service from 1st May to 18th Sept.
From Mt Edgcumbe Weekdays 0650 to 2015
Saturdays 0815 to 2100, Sundays 0900 to 2100
From Plymouth Weekdays 0715 to 2030
Saturdays 0845 to 2115, Sundays 0915 to 2115
Winter service from 19th September to 30th April
From Mt Edgcumbe Weekdays 0650 to 1815,
Saturdays 0815 to 1830, Sundays 1000 to 1700
From Plymouth Weekdays 0715 to 1830,
Saturdays 0845 to 1845, Sundays 1015 to 1715
Closed Xmas, Boxing & New Year's Days

Plymouth's new Waterfront Walk has been installed. From stepping ashore at Admirals Hard, watch out for a variety of information plaques and pieces of artwork all relating to Plymouth's history.

On landing at Admirals Hard, walk up the road and turn second right into Cremyll Street, and continue to the massive gates of the Royal William Yard. Pass them on your right and continue on out to Firestone Bay. At the sea wall you have a fine view to Drake's Island and beyond towards Wembury. A slight excursion could be made by turning right to walk out to Western King's Point and Devil's Point, for River Tamar views, but you will have to return.

From the sea wall turn inland to walk into Durnford Street, continue along it and walk past the Royal Marine Barracks, turning right immediately after them. This will bring you into Millbay Road where you continue, passing the Dock Gates (east). Then you turn right into West Hoe Road. Keep to this road. You are now in the West Hoe area and the streets surrounding you have numerous B & B establishments. Fork right into Great Western Road.

As you approach a terrace of three storey small hotels, watch out for a path on your right known as Rusty Anchor. This is a slight diversion from the main road and provides a shore line walk.

On regaining the main road, turn right and continue along the Hoe foreshore. You stay on this promenade all the way around to The Barbican and Sutton Harbour. However, you could achieve grand views over Plymouth Sound by climbing steps opposite the former swimming pool up to the lighthouse, Smeaton's Tower, and passing that to cross The Hoe to have a look at Sir Francis Drake, still scanning the English Channel for the Armada.

Retrace your steps and continue your shore line walk to The Barbican. A small jetty on your right is of historic significance in that it is the site of the Mayflower Steps; of great interest to our US members.

Whatever you decide upon, ferry or the walking route, it is well worth exploring the ancient Barbican area before carrying on.

Sutton Harbour / Mountbatten

Mountbatten Ferry
07930 838614

All year round. Runs 15 and 45 minutes past the hour from Sutton Harbour, and on the hour and 30 minutes past from Mountbatten Point. Ferry starts at 0745 from Sutton Harbour on weekdays, and from 0900 at weekends. Last ferry departs Mountbatten at 1815 in winter.

In the unlikely event of the ferry not operating to Mountbatten Point, this is your walking Route from Sutton Harbour to Mountbatten Point. It is well marked with Plymouth's innovative signs and symbols.

Lock gates have now been installed at Sutton Harbour, so walk on across them into Teat's Hill Road. As you progress along Teat's Hill Road you will arrive at Breakwater Hill. Turn right here, but do not walk into the scrap yard unless you want to view vehicles being broken up. Carry on up the hill for a limestone, cliff top walk with views over the Cattewater. At a fork in the lane bear left and you will descend to the area of Cattedown Wharf. We will now just supply directions - continue on past warehouses into Maxwell Road, a road will take you direct to Laira Bridge which you take to cross the River Plym. You now have pavements to walk upon. At the first roundabout turn right into Oreston Road.

After a small roundabout, keep on to the top of the road, bear right, then when you reach Rollis Park Road, turn right to descend to Oreston Quay. You are beside the water only for a couple of hundred yards, and at Plymstock Road, you turn left. Start climbing away from the estuary and at Lower Saltram, turn right and carry straight on to Radford Lake.

The 'castle' through which you walk was once the lodge to a large house, now no more. Turning right after the causeway brings you to a path alongside the southern shore of Hooe Lake. You will join a narrow road which leads to Hooe Lake Road.

Walk straight across the grassy area keeping to the shore and turn right along Barton Road, and by staying with this road you will come into Turnchapel. Continue on up St. John's Road to a car park on your right. In the corner is a signed route to Mountbatten Point.

NTG - Does not supply walking instructions for this section of the Coast Path.

57 | Mountbatten Point to Wembury (Warren Point Ferry)   OS E108 & OL20

Grading: Easy		Distance -	11.8	686.3	7.3	426.4

Timing: 3 hours

See also our Plymouth to Wembury Path Description.

Due to the praiseworthy activities of Plymouth City Council you are about to step out onto welcome Coast Path realignments. Those who have walked this section before will be amazed at the difference and those who have been Association members for a while will realise that our efforts have been successful.

The path goes around Mountbatten Point then runs south climbing to Jennycliff.

Keep to the cliff edge and continue south, that is to the end of the grassy area where you will find a signed path entering woodlands.

This up and down new path is a delight and well below the dangerous road that we once had to walk. Within a 0.25 mile (400 m) this new path links in with the original Coast Path. Turn right for a scenic uncomplicated path to Fort Bovisand, one of the great forts that once defended Plymouth.

Those who have been this way before should now pause to reflect. Since Mountbatten Point you have not had to set foot upon a vehicular road! We congratulate all responsible for this improvement.

On the descent to a road the path can be seen ahead between hundreds of chalet/huts and the sea. At Heybrook Bay when you reach the road, turn right.

The path passes in front of HMS Cambridge, the one-time gunnery school.

Now follows a low cliff top walk to Wembury Beach. The path passes seaward of the church and climbs to a level path that leads into the estuary of the River Yealm. At a small house, The Rocket House, once used for the storage of life saving apparatus, the official path takes off downhill diagonally towards the river and the ferry point. We suggest you walk down to the ferry point, even if the ferry is not running or you do not intend to use it, because you can take advantage of a scenic short circular walk back to the Rocket House. Once the ferry steps have been reached, carry on for a few yards then take a wooden stepped path on the left that climbs to good views over Newton Ferrers and Noss Mayo.

NTG - Map (page 83) the coast path now runs out and around Mountbatten Point and is now 'off road' at Staddon Heights Farm.

58 | Wembury (Warren Point) to Bigbury-on-Sea (Car Park)   OS OL20

Grading: Starts easy then strenuous   Distance -   21.8   708.1   13.5   439.9

Timing: 5.75 hours

See also our Wembury (Warren Point) to Bigbury-on-Sea Path Description.

The first obstacle is crossing the River Yealm

Wembury (Warren Point) to Noss Mayo Ferry.
River Yealm

Bill Gregor,   Seasonal all week, on demand.
1 Underhaye,   Easter until end September
Yealmpton   1000 - 1100 and 1500 - 1600 hrs.
PL8 2JR.
Tel: 01752 880079

During fine weather and school holidays the ferry is operational between 1000 and 1600 daily - but please phone first. Mr Gregor is often there outside normal operating hours. There is a signal board to summon the ferryman by the steps at Warren Point or at the slipway at Noss Mayo. We suggest you might also telephone ahead to Mr Gregor to give him an idea of your estimated time of arrival.

If there is no ferry then this means a walk back to the Rocket House to follow the path described below into Knighton. There is an hourly bus service (number 48) to Plymstock and Plymouth where there is available an infrequent service to Noss Mayo (number 94). For a quicker conveyance around the estuary there are reasonably priced taxis available:-

Wembury Cabs - John Pitcher (01752 862151) and

Tim's Taxis - Tim Craig (01752 830225)

Walking route around the River Yealm.
From the Rocket House the track leads into a road. At Wembury House a stile leads to a field and to the footpath junction. The path you want is the one to the right which runs alongside a high wall. Follow it to the end of the wall where it goes through two successive kissing gates. It then bears left approximately 330° across fields towards Knighton. As you leave the fields it goes down a few steps. Turn left and then first right. This will bring you out onto the road. Turn left and the bus stop is a little further along on the other side of the road just before the pub. The distance from ferry point to bus stop is 1.5 miles (2.5 km). Before reaching the bus stop you will pass a telephone box where you can call a taxi if you want.

Go across to a minor road opposite to descend and turn left and then right at the next road junction. Continue along the road for about 0.5 mile (800 m) ignoring all turnings and footpaths. At a major road turn left for a few yards to turn right on a footpath just by a bus stop. This is now a waymarked route, the Erme-Plym Trail. Stay with it down to Cofflete Creek and up the other side until you reach the main A379 road. Turn right and a mile of main road walking follows, the best pavement is at first on the left, then switches to the right leaving Brixton, then for a long stretch there is none at all but it restarts on the left. (There is a safer but longer alternative starting at Brixton Church, see below). Turn right down the road signed Newton Ferrers 3 miles. Go down to Puslinch Bridge and bear right up the hill. Nearly at the top, a footpath goes right cutting the corner to Wrescombe. Emerging onto the road turn right to continue along to The Butts and down the main road to Newton Ferrers. If you arrive within approximately two hours of low tide you can bear right down Yealm Road and turn down Newton Hill, to cross a tidal causeway to Noss Mayo and another across the inlet at Noss. If you are not so fortunate turn left down the road to Bridgend and Noss Mayo, being sure to turn first right as you enter Noss. Here those who have come around will have a picturesque riverside walk out to where those who have been fortunate enough with the ferry will disembark.

Alternative route - Brixton to Puslinch Bridge
At Brixton Church go up Old Road and follow the waymarked Erme-Plym Trail signs until you arrive on a minor road in the outskirts of Yealmpton. Here turn right and continue down the road ignoring the footpath left turn of the Erme-Plym Trail. At the main A379 road, cross over turning left and immediately right into Stray Park. At the bottom bear right along a tarmac footpath. This comes to a road; turn left along a stony track. At the footpath sign continue ahead to pass the entrance to Kitley Caves. The path eventually emerges in a car park. Leave this and turn left on the road to reach Puslinch Bridge. From here on the route is as described above.

Coast Path continues
From the ferry, the Erme Estuary is about 9 miles (14 km) ahead. You are the best judge of how long that will take you to get there for low tide, so plan your Noss Mayo departure accordingly. The well-marked path climbs through woodlands to pick up Lord Revelstoke's nine- mile drive, made for the carriages of his guests at Membland Hall, since demolished.

At Battery Cottage, just as you are leaving the woodlands, look out for a path going off to the right. You can take this down to Cellars Beach, for a swim maybe. It continues on around the back of the beach then climbs to rejoin the Coast Path at Brakehill Plantation where you turn right onto Lord Revelstoke's drive.

There is a definitive seaward path at Stoke Down at 560460 just after passing a single stone gate post on the left. Use this if you wish to visit the historic Church of St Peter the Poor Fisherman; this will mean an uphill road walk to regain the Coast Path. If you do not divert then the path crosses the Stoke Beach road to continue along, passing the ruined 'Tea House'.

You are now in for a very steep descent and further on a steep climb up to St Anchorite's Rock and you pass Bugle Hole. The section then to Mothecombe Beach provides superb views to the Erme estuary. It has been fairly described as England's most unspoilt river estuary: we certainly believe it to be the most attractive. At the beach do not turn inland but take the seaward path in the woods at Owen's Hill.

River Erme   No ferry

Low water is at about the same time as the Devonport Tide Table shown here.

It is usually possible to paddle across the river 1 hour each side of low water along the old ford. Great care should be taken because heavy rains or seas can make the crossing dangerous. On modern maps the old ford is not shown but this in fact ran from Ordnance map ref. 614 476 to map ref. 620 478. In other words, the old ford connected the road by the row of coastguard cottages with the end of the inland road to Wonwell Beach from Kingston.

Should you arrive at the River Erme at a time that promises a very long wait for low tide to enable you to wade across then there is an inland alternative. This alternative is of about 7 miles (11 km) with fairly steep up and down country lanes. You are the best judge of your rate of travel so the decision to wait for the tide or continue walking is yours.

Walking route around the River Erme
If you follow the riverside paths shown on OS map OL20 you will be trespassing on a private estate so follow the narrow country lanes to Holbeton village. Then continue on a northerly route to Ford and Hole Farm. Soon after passing Hole Farm take off on a public footpath on your right. From here to the main A379 road is about 0.75 mile (1.2 km). Turn right to cross the River Erme at Sequer's Bridge. Stay on the A379 for about 0.5 mile (0.75 km) but take care as this is an extremely busy road. You will see a road on your right signposted to Orcheton. Follow this road south towards the village of Kingston but before you reach that village you will see road signs to Wonwell Beach. Just before the slipway on to the sands you have a choice. If the tide now permits you can continue south along the beach or take to the waymarked Coast Path in the woodlands on your left.

Coast Path continues
Beyond the Erme the walking becomes tougher but the all round views will compensate for the effort. The path passes Challaborough with its cafe and caravans to Bigbury-on-Sea, where the Bay Cafe is open all day and the only establishment for evening meals.

Burgh Island can be visited by walking across the sands or by a 'sea tractor' if the tide is in. The pub is very old, the hotel is fascinating art deco modern and the hut at the top of the island stands on the site of a chapel. This hut was used by the 'huers' - pilchard fishermen on the lookout for shoals of fish.

| Grading: Moderate | Distance - | 9.2 | 717.3 | 5.7 | 445.6 |

Timing: 2.75 hours

See also our Bigbury-on-Sea to Salcombe Path Description.

There are riverside footpaths along both west and east banks of the River Avon to Aveton Gifford. This makes the inland walking route from Bigbury-on-Sea to Bantham and vice versa about 9 miles (14.5 km) in total. The OS OL20 map shows the riverside paths. What you have to watch is that the road between the two words 'Ford' is tidal and therefore is at times submerged. This route is described below.

Coast Path continues

The official route turns right at the bottom of the road on to what is called Clematon Hill at the western side of the mouth of the River Avon.There are good views here across the estuary but unfortunately you have to walk up the busy road to Mount Folly Farm afterwards. However, again there is compensation because the views southward across the estuary just after the farm are particularly spectacular.

Bigbury/Bantham (River Avon)	Seasonal - Monday to Saturday.
Neill Schroeter, Harbourmaster	from 9th April - 8th Sept.
Marsh Cottage, Fore Street,	1000 - 1100 hrs and 1500 - 1600 hrs.
Aveton Gifford, Devon TQ7 4LR	Sundays if pre-booked party of 10 or more.
Tel: 01548 561196	

The ferryman is generally around, and can be called by waving. Low water is about the same time as the Devonport Tide Table. It is possible at low tide, when not rough, or the river is not in flood, to wade the river. However, we strongly stress we are not advising this as a cheap method of avoiding the ferry crossing. When the ferry is working, you are strongly advised to use it because wading is not easy and you may get a lot wetter than you expect. You will most likely be up to your thighs in water and in no circumstances should the crossing be attempted if conditions are wrong. The two guide points are just below the ferry crossing. On the true right bank - the western side - there is a well defined hedge running north and south with pine trees. On the left bank - the eastern side - there is a castellated building with battlements and a little flag pole in the middle. However, if crossing from the true right to the left - in other words from west to east - take off at the hedge and wade towards the castle-like building. If going the other way, vice versa. Please note it is important that you do wade at this point. The river looks shallow in a number of other places but there are deeper channels and indeed soft sand patches which can make it extremely difficult. Further towards the sea, there is a considerable tidal ebb which can be exceedingly dangerous.

PLEASE NOTE WHEN THE FERRY IS NOT OPERATING A RECOMMENDED WAY TO REACH BANTHAM IS BY REASONABLY PRICED TAXIS:

Acorn Taxis (Telephone: 01548 531010 : Mobile: 07967 023336 / 7)

Arrow Cars - Mr Kemp - (Telephone: 01548 856120)

Phoenix Taxis (Telephone: 01548 852906).

It should always be borne in mind that the depth of water at low tide and consequently safe passage across is affected by natural conditions inasmuch that strong south west or westerly winds tend to bank up water in the English Channel and, therefore, there will be a greater depth of water than expected. This will also happen if there is a lot of rain in the catchment areas of the rivers, with consequently more water coming down. Caution: although we know several who have waded the River Avon we do not recommend it; great care is required, especially by those with backpacks.

VERY IMPORTANT - PLEASE TAKE NOTE

EVEN AT DEAD LOW WATER WE STRESS THAT YOU MUST CONSIDER VERY SERIOUSLY WHETHER YOU SHOULD WADE THIS RIVER. IT IS VERY DIFFICULT AND CAN BE DANGEROUS EVEN FOR TALL AND STRONG ADULTS. MANY OF OUR MEMBERS, INCLUDING YOUR SECRETARY WILL NOT VENTURE ACROSS. THEIR OPINION BEING - 'WHEN THE FERRY IS NOT RUNNING THEN THE *ONLY* ALTERNATIVE IS TO GO ROUND'.

Inland Walking Route - approx. 7 miles (12 km)

Much of this route has been waymarked 'Avon Estuary Walk' with a heron motif in blue and white.

When the tide is not low (and we urge you to read again our advice about wading) and the ferry is not available, the only way to the other side is an inland walk to Aveton Gifford and around. This is a pleasant 7 mile (12 km) diversion as it is mostly along country paths. Walking through agricultural land in deep country makes a change from the coast. The paths are shown on OS OL20 and are quite well marked but they are little used and are not always easy to follow. Allow plenty of time for some heavy walking, for straying off route or for a possible delay at the tidal road near Aveton Gifford.

Disregard the coast path where it turns right through Mount Folly Farm and descends to the ferry point, but proceed towards Bigbury for 60 yards (55 m) to the next footpath sign. Turn right into the field over a stone stile and walk along the field edge. Over a wooden stile will bring you onto the golf course where, after a short distance, you meet a surfaced track. Go northwards along the track towards the clubhouse for 200 yards (185 m), turning right at an entrance between two huts going down a track to Hexdown Farm. Pass left of the farmhouse to bear immediately right and then left. Bear right before the next gate to continue downhill with the boundary on your left. Proceed along a track through a timber gate. Follow the footpath sign slightly left along a tarmac drive, into woodland, then through Lincombe and on to the B3392 on a corner. Proceed northwards towards Bigbury for 350 yards (320 m) (be careful of the traffic) and turn right at the footpath sign to Aveton Gifford (via tidal road). Cross the field to a post and wire fence and enter the top of Doctor's Wood. Re-emerge into a field and cross due east to a wooden stile. Proceed along a high level path (beautiful views) then walk downhill to the tidal road which will bring you to Aveton Gifford. There is a viable alternative if the tide is over the road by walking north-westward to Foxhole then north-eastward to Waterhead and Aveton Gifford. The whole path is adequately waymarked.

Cross the Avon on the roadbridge (A379) towards Kingsbridge, and turn right at the end of the bridge into a cul-de-sac named Bridge End. Continue to a gate at a signpost, and straight on to a metalled road, where you turn right at a signpost.

Bear left at the road fork, following the footpath sign to a gate; turn right here and follow a fence on the right, and through another gate into a field.

Turn half right down to the bottom of the valley, and bear right to a gate with a waymark 'to Stiddicombe Creek'. Cross this and enter the wood on the right. Work steadily uphill to the top corner and follow the waymark signs along the top of the field with a hedge on the left (watch for herons by the river) to a stile by a gate; over another stile and continue. Bear right and cross a farm track to a gate between walls. Cross the stream ahead with stepping stones, and along to a stile and waymark signs, where you turn right and go straight on to Bantham, where you turn right and go through the village where you will see the ferry sign; here you would have stepped ashore had it been operating. The coast path is straight on towards the sea. Some of this walk is shown in the National Trail Guide.

Coast Path continues

You should take great care where the path proceeds along the seaward boundary of the Thurlestone Golf Course; watch out for golfers and where they hit the ball. We have had a report of a walker on this section who was hit in the mouth by a golf ball at close range, with resulting horrific damage to teeth and lips.

---

60 | Hope Cove, Inner Hope to Salcombe (Ferry)   OS OL20 (V) Hope Cove

Grading: Strenuous		Distance -	12.9	730.2	8.0	453.6

Timing: 4 hours

See also our Bigbury-on-Sea to Salcombe Path Description.

Excellent coastal walking, some of the finest in South Devon. Before leaving Inner Hope you ought to walk along the inland road to look at The Square and its attractive thatched cottages. It is well marked out to Bolt Tail where the remains of an Iron Age fort are marked by a dry stone wall and the remains of a ditch.

The path is obvious to Bolberry Down (refreshments available - Port Light Hotel) and on to a viewpoint overlooking Soar Mill Cove. There is a steep descent to the cove but the climb out is easier. We have heard of walkers going wrong as they near the splendid rocky Bolt Head. The correct route is the coast route; do not divert inland anywhere until the headland is reached. The path then runs due north into and around Starehole Bay.

From the bay the path joins the Courtenay Way which was cut out under rocky pinnacles. The way ahead is through woodlands to the roadway below the National Trust's Overbecks House and Youth Hostel. Follow the road to South Sands where, in season, a ferry can be taken to the main ferry point in Salcombe. If it is not running or you are a purist, the way ahead to the town and ferry for East Portlemouth is along the most seaward roads ahead.

OS - Outdoor Leisure Map 20. The Coast Path runs out onto Bolt Head. This is not shown on the map.

61 | Salcombe to Torcross (Car Park)   OS OL20 (T) Salcombe; (V) Beesands

Grading: Strenuous   Distance -   20.8   751.0   12.9   466.5

Timing: 6.75 hours

See also our Salcombe to Torcross Path Description.

This is first class walking, some of the best of the whole Coast Path.

Salcombe to East Portlemouth Ferry   All year round.
The Salcombe Ferry,   Winter - $1/2$ hourly between 0800 - 1730 hrs.
Somerset House,   Summer - Continuous service 0800 - 1900 hrs.
Devon Road,   0830 hrs start weekends and bank holidays.
Salcombe   Check times before travelling.
Devon TQ8 8HQ
Tel: (01548)842061/842364

Having crossed the estuary the path goes off to the right along the narrow road. Just after the National Trust car park at Mill Bay the path now goes uphill on the left through the trees. Refreshments are available at the Gara Rock Hotel if you want to climb the hill from the path.

The official route is to the very end of Prawle Point, to the Coastguard lookout. It is hoped that the National Trust will mark a path out to the point along the western side of the headland. The path is there and it is a better route than the one on the top. The official route is back inland again but near to the lookout on the east side of the point is a path descending a valley; this is the better one. Prawle Point is National Trust property and there is a true coast path along the top of low cliffs around Copstone Cove to link in with the official route at Western Cove.

It is easy walking for a while along the edges of fields on what is a 'raised' beach. The path then becomes rocky and up and down prior to Lannacombe Beach. About 0.5 mile (800 m) before Lannacombe, try to find time to take the new path that the National Trust has cut to the right, signposted to the previously hidden Woodcombe Sand beach. Until now the beach, a peaceful isolated spot, could only be reached through the grounds of Woodcombe House, and many people didn't even know it was there. The path twists and drops, and you have to come back the same way, but it is only about 100 yards (90 m) and well worth the effort.

The path is straightforward to Start Point and on to Torcross and has recently been rerouted following the purchase of land between Hallsands and Beesands by the National Trust - this is a distinct improvement. It is not currently possible to visit the old deserted village at Hallsands, and the latest news is that it is deemed to be unsafe. You can, however, get a glimpse of the ruins by taking the path to the village as far as the closure notice, which will not take long and is a very moving experience.

62 | Torcross to Dartmouth (Lower Ferry)   OS OL20 (V) Torcross; (V) Strete; (V) Stoke Fleming

Grading: Moderate   Distance -   **16.4   767.4   10.2   476.7**

Timing: 4.75 hours

See also our Torcross to Dartmouth Path Description.

The Coast Path runs along the length of the shingle bank. You can walk either side of the road; the top of the beach for sea views or alongside the Ley for bird watching.

There is no true coast path from Strete Gate to Warren Point and virtually the whole route is inland and some on a busy main road. This is reckoned to be the worst section of the whole of the South West Coast Path and the Association continues its efforts to obtain an enormous improvement. WE CANNOT OVEREMPHASISE THE NEED FOR EXTREME CAUTION ON THIS SECTION, SOME OF WHICH IS ON DANGEROUS, BUSY ROADS.

If you intend to avoid the busy main road through Strete, then as you approach the village, look for Hynetown Road on your left and turn into this road to follow the official path to rejoin the main road on the other side of the village. After this follow the main road for about 200 yards (185 m) and then take care to fork left, signposted 'Southwood' - there is no coast path sign here. Immediately before the entrance to Blackpool Sands you must turn left by the cottages.

Follow the inland signed route to Stoke Fleming and the rest of the signs along this poor route. You have about another 2.5 miles (4 km) to go before you regain the Coast Path proper.

As you stand on the National Trust's Warren Point this is another occasion to pause and reflect. The beautiful path you see ahead of you towards the River Dart estuary could easily be continued behind you nearly all the way back to Slapton Sands, if it were not for landowners who do not like you.

However, we are a step nearer to achieving the installation of a true coast path along the lines of the route this association has been lobbying for many years. The Countryside Agency Board has accepted the review by the South West Coast Path Team.

Dartmouth Castle commands the mouth of the River Dart and should be visited, time permitting. In season there is a regular ferry from the castle to Dartmouth and this can be utilised for a pleasant river trip, instead of walking down the road.

63 | Dartmouth to Brixham   OS OL20 (T) Dartmouth; (V) Kingswear (Trains)
(King William of Orange Statue)

Grading: Strenuous   Distance -   **17.3   784.7   10.8   487.5**

Timing: 5.75 hours

See also our Dartmouth to Brixham Path Description.

Walkers will probably use the lower ferry to cross the River Dart but there are two other regular ferries which also run all year round. Nearby is the passenger ferry, which lands by the steam railway station, and which gives a more comfortable crossing, and if these two are not running then further up the river is the higher ferry taking pedestrians and vehicles. If you use the higher ferry you will then need to turn right along the railway line to the road, then turn right again and descend the hill to join the Coast Path by the lower ferry slipway.

Dartmouth/Kingswear   All year round, continuous
South Hams District Council, Lower Ferry,   between 0700 and 2300 hrs.
Lower Ferry Office, The Square,   Sundays start 0800 hrs.
Kingswear TQ6 OAA
Tel: (01803) 752342

On landing at Kingswear, by the lower ferry, pass through an arch on the right. Ascend Alma Steps then turn right along Beacon Road. In 1.25 miles (2 km) turn right down steps at Warren Woods.

When you reach the old Battery Buildings at Froward Point do divert inland to see The Daymark navigation tower nearby if time permits but then return to the Coast Path to continue. The sign here is 8.75 miles (14 km) to Brixham and the path descends steeply going right from the back corner of the derelict look out building and then passes through the World War II gun and searchlight positions. Next at Pudcombe Cove you can obtain access to the National Trust gardens at Coleton Fishacre if they are open.

Walking on above Pudcombe Cove and Ivy Cove to Scabbacombe Head, you will see the Scabbacombe Sands, Long Sands, Man Sands, Southdown Cliff and Sharkham Point before reaching St Mary's Bay. Taken together, the strenuous grading of this section is well justified.

Now you have a pleasant walk to Berry Head Country Park, a Nature Reserve with much of interest - do spend time there if you can. The Northern Fort, one of the two Napoleonic Forts, contains the Berry Head lighthouse; next to it, the old Artillery Store houses an exhibition centre explaining 400 million years of Berry Head history, and the old guardhouse is now a cafe, open in the season and sometimes out of season as well.

Having left Berry Head and descending Berry Head Road, when you are level with the Breakwater descend the steps to the new promenade which follows the water's edge past the new marina to the inner harbour.

---

64 | Brixham to Torquay Harbour   OS OL20 (T) Brixham; (T) Paignton (Trains)

Grading: Moderate   Distance -   13.5   798.2   8.4   495.9

Timing: 4 hours

See also our Brixham to Shaldon Path Description.

The path goes along the back of Broadsands, along the back of Goodrington Sands beach, around Roundham Head, along Paignton and Preston sea fronts and along the promenade at Torquay.

From Brixham to Elbury Cove the path is fair though not as scenic as one might hope. Thereafter it becomes more urbanised with the poorest section from Hollicombe to Torquay Harbour where you usually have quite heavy traffic nearby. Remember, in case of need, there is a very frequent bus service from Brixham to Torquay via Paignton! There is also a regular Brixham/Torquay seasonal ferry service.

When departing from Brixham leave by the new path running along the harbour, signposted Coastal Footpath to Oxen Cove and Freshwater Car Park. At the car park continue on past the Zeneca Brixham Environmental Laboratory and on to the Battery Gardens where you follow the lower path to Fishcombe Cove. Ascend from the cove and at the road junction turn right, signpost Public Footpath to Churston Ferrers.

At the far end of Elbury Cove ignore the more obvious path going inland and leave the beach by ascending the steps. Take care at Broadsands beach that you do not follow the path up the cliff at the eastern end, but turn left up the minor road, pass under the railway viaduct and then turn immediately right where the Coast Path is signposted.

At Goodrington turn right under a railway bridge, follow the promenade round and just before the end a zigzag path takes you up, through ornamental gardens on to Roundham Head.

At Hollicombe Head you can turn right and go through the delightful park that was once the gas works. Bear left to emerge through the main gate onto the road. Then turn right for Torquay.

CP - At Goodrington South Sands the path crosses back under the railway line. There is no road walking until Paignton Harbour.

65 | Torquay Harbour to Shaldon (Ferry)

Grading: Strenuous Distance - 17.3 815.5 10.8 506.7

Timing: 5.75 hours

See also our Brixham to Shaldon Path Description.

You walk on round Torquay Inner Harbour, turning left up Beacon Hill and soon reach The Imperial Hotel. Turn in right here to pass in front of the main entrance to the hotel and then follow the scenic path to the grassy plateau of Daddyhole Plain, which you cross to find the path descending to Meadfoot Beach.

At the far end of Meadfoot Beach turn right through a small car park and ascend to Marine Drive where you turn right. There is some subsidence on this road but it does not affect pedestrians. Shortly, turn right at a signpost for the Coast Path, going towards Thatcher Point. However, at present, you will have to return on the same path as the footpath is closed between Thatcher Point and Thatcher Pines; this is because of a cliff fall which the path managers have yet to resolve. At the road turn right and shortly find a path above the left hand side of the road, and at the end of this cross the road and take the Bishop's Walk path signposted to Anstey's Cove.

As you join the road by the car park above Anstey's Cove you can, time and energy permitting, take the steep path down to the picturesque cove; however, you'll have to return the same way, as following repeated rock falls the adjacent Redgate Beach has been sealed off indefinitely by Torbay Borough Council, and it's no longer possible to cross the two beaches and regain the official route by the path up the cliffs. Instead, about 50 yards (46 m) beyond the turning down to Anstey's, take the path through the woods to the right signposted 'To Babbacombe & St Marychurch over the Downs', which takes you up to Walls Hill.

From Walls Hill the path will take you to the road descending to Babbacombe Beach, at the far end of which you traverse a wooden bridge structure to Oddicombe beach, where the path bears upwards just before the lower station of the Babbacombe Cliff Railway. Shortly you pass under the railway and then take care to turn right downwards at the start of a pleasant path leading to a grassy picnic area where you bear left uphill to join the track to Watcombe.

At the valley road linking the main Torquay/Teignmouth Road to Watcombe Beach, turn left and immediately right, signposted Maidencombe 0.75 mile (1 km) and follow a wooded path until you reach a path junction, where the signposting shows the inland route as the coast path and the more coastal path as an alternative path. We suggest you take the new more coastal path, which in time will become the official route, and then from the car park at Maidencombe go a few yards up the road and turn right, unless you wish to obtain refreshment in the village.

From here there are some quite stiff gradients until you reach the road at Labrador where you turn right and in a few yards leave the pavement to take a sunken path on your right and shortly enter a field on your right via a stile by a field gate.

You will get superb views now as you descend along the coastal side of the field system, then take the path round The Ness to Shaldon.

66 | Shaldon to Exmouth (Ferry)

Grading: Easy Distance - 12.7 828.2 7.9 514.6

Timing: 3 hours

See also our Shaldon to Sidmouth Path Description.

The above figures relate to the distance involved when the Starcross ferry is operating. If not, the walking route around the Exe is described below, and you should add approximately 10.6 miles (17 km).

This is a section where you may have problems depending on the time of year and state of the tide.

There is no ferry at winter weekends. Your walking route around is to continue along riverside roads from the ferry point and cross Shaldon Bridge. Immediately after crossing the railway line, exit from the bridge into Milford Park. Walk beside the railway line, through Bitton Sports Ground into Park Hill, cross into Bitton Avenue at Clay Lane then turn right into Willow Street. At the end bear left then right which will bring you into Quay Road, into Osmond Street and then straight on to Harbour Beach and the ferry. Keep going on out onto 'The Point', turn north east and once more you are upon the Coast Path.

Shaldon/Teignmouth (River Teign)	All year round. (except Xmas Day)
The Teign Ferry Ltd.	20 minute intervals.
Little Coombe, 18 Haldon Avenue,	Weekdays 0800 hrs - sunset
Teignmouth. TQ14 8JZ	Weekends 1000 hrs - sunset
Tel: 01626 873060 Fax: 01626 872996	All times are dependent on the
E-mail: teignferry@eclipse.co.uk	weather.

Coast Path continues

After crossing from Shaldon by ferry, follow the promenade past the pier and shortly you reach Eastcliff Walk forking up on your left and there you must make your first decision. The true route is ahead along the sea wall but at certain states of the high tide and particularly in bad weather it may be impossible after a 2 mile (3.2 km) walk to pass under the railway line at the end of the wall, and if this appears likely a detour is needed. You should ascend Eastcliff Walk which soon becomes a track and will eventually lead you to the A379 where you turn right and rejoin the Coast Path at the top of Smugglers Lane.

If conditions look right, enjoy the walk along the sea wall and at the end pass under the railway line and ascend Smugglers Lane to the A379. Now you have a short walk on this busy main road, although there is a footpath on the left hand side, and after about 150 yards (135 m) turn right into Windward Lane, then immediately left and take the path over a stile on your left. After a field section you are back on the road but immediately follow the Old Teignmouth Road on your right, until you reach the main road yet again, turn right and shortly by some railings turn right and follow the path which soon zigzags down to the boat cove and follow the sea wall to Dawlish Station.

From here it is possible at low tide to walk along the sea wall to Dawlish Warren, then at the start of the new promenade cross the railway by a footbridge to join the inland path and reach the main road. If the tide is high you must take the alternative route by turning left opposite the Railway Station and in 30 yards (27 m) turning right through an arch and ascending the steps. Continue forward, passing a new housing development on your left, and after passing through another two arches, you emerge onto the A379 road and continue forward. Shortly after passing the new Rockstone Flats turn right on the road signposted Dawlish Warren 0.75 mile (1 km) and immediately take the coastal footpath signed on your right to follow the Ladies Mile to Dawlish Warren. (You can in fact take a footpath immediately before the Rockstone Flats, although this is not signposted, then take the left fork to join the Coast Path.)

There is no official path along the Warren but if time and energy permit you can enjoy a circular walk round this sandy Nature Reserve.

You are now faced with crossing the River Exe and in the summer months there is a ferry from Starcross to Exmouth reached by walking along the road from Dawlish Warren. However this is a busy road and you can if you wish catch one of the frequent buses to Starcross.

Starcross/Exmouth (River Exe)	April - end October.
Mr B Rackley,	Hourly, 7 days a week.
Starcross Pier & Pleasure Company	From Starcross Pier
26 Marine Parade,	on the hour from 1000 hrs.
Dawlish.	From Exmouth, Ferry Steps.
Tel: (01626) 862452	on the half-hour from 1030 hrs.

Alternative routes around the River Exe

1. You can catch a train at Dawlish Warren changing at Exeter and going back down to Exmouth.

2. You can do the same thing using the frequent bus services, changing over routes at either Countess Wear or in Exeter.

3. You can use the all year round ferry at Topsham to cross the River Exe. From Starcross continue by road to Powderham Church where a footpath follows the river and then

the canal to a bridge across the canal where the ferry then crosses the river. (This ferry is dependent on tide and weather and does not operate at lunchtime or on a Tuesday.) If you use this route add 10.6 miles (17 km) to your walk.

Topsham Ferry (River Exe)
Exeter City Council Canals & Rivers Dept.
Tel: (01392) 274306 (Office)
Tel: (0780) 120 3338 (Site)

All year round on request.
Apr. - Sept. Daily except Tuesdays, from 1100 to 1700 hrs. Oct - Mar. Saturdays, Sundays and Bank Holidays 1100 to 1700 hrs or sunset.

Once across the river you have to get to Exmouth and we are inclined to suggest the frequent bus service, but failing this the walk as far as Lympstone will be on the road except for a small footpath section between Clyst Bridge and Ebford. From Lympstone there is a riverside path to Exmouth, now part of the East Devon Way - look for the mauve markers featuring a foxglove.

4. **Exe Water Taxis** (1st April to 3rd September. Runs daily from 10am to 5pm, weather permitting) will pick up passengers and take them to Exmouth. Please telephone 07970 918418 before relying on this service.

67 | Exmouth to Budleigh Salterton (River Otter Car Park)   OS E115 (T) Exmouth (Trains)

| Grading: Moderate | Distance - | 9.9 | 838.1 | 6.2 | 520.8 |

Timing: 3 hours

See also our Shaldon to Sidmouth Path Description.

No real problems here for walkers but keep inland of the range at Straight Point.

68 | Budleigh Salterton to Sidmouth (River Sid)   OS E115 (T) Budleigh Salterton

| Grading: Moderate then strenuous | Distance - | 11.1 | 849.2 | 6.9 | 527.7 |

Timing: 3.5 hours

See also our Shaldon to Sidmouth Path Description.

The start is along a raised path inland to the River Otter Bridge at South Farm, then a riverside path back to the coast.

The path around High Peak is well marked but it does not unfortunately go over the top as you, and many others in the past, obviously expected. If you do battle your way to the top you will certainly not be disappointed with the views. The path on the top of Peak Hill immediately west of Sidmouth has been improved to give better seaward views.

The descent from Peak Hill towards Sidmouth takes you down through a wood and out on to the road. Turn right and keep to the right hand side of the road to pass through two kissing gates, then bear right through a gap in the hedge on to parkland for the descent into Sidmouth. At the bottom of the lawn, make your way onto the zigzag path which leads down between beach huts onto the small esplanade. Turn left and continue at sea level on the Clifton Walkway to the main esplanade.

69 | Sidmouth to Seaton (River Axe)   OS E115 & E116 (T) Sidmouth

| Grading: Severe then strenuous | Distance - | 16.7 | 865.9 | 10.4 | 538.1 |

Timing: 5.5 hours

See also our Sidmouth to Lyme Regis Path Description.

Please note that there are a number of quite considerable ascents and descents on this section, so do not judge the effort required purely on the distance. There are one or two places in this stretch where it is easy to come off the route but one is not likely to come to any severe harm.Landslips have caused diversions on this stretch, but the temporary route and the proposed alignments are well signed, and for the most part, enjoyable.

On leaving Sidmouth, dramatic cliff falls are the cause of a diversion, which is well marked.

After Branscombe Mouth there are alternative paths. The one over Hooken Cliffs gives superb views and is probably easier to walk. The undercliff path, apart from the beginning among the caravans is scenically better and we would recommend this if the weather is good. You have the interesting undercliff itself, the massive cliffs to the left, interesting rock formations ahead, and good views to seaward. At most states of the tide it is possible to walk along the beach from Seaton Hole to Seaton, avoiding some road work.

WATCH THE TIDE - YOU CAN GET CUT OFF

CP - Between Weston Cliff and Branscombe Mouth, the path is nearer the coast than the map suggests.

NTG - From Branscombe Mouth to Beer Head the map does not show the path along the top of Hooken Cliffs, only through Under Hooken. It is mentioned in the text, and both routes are official.

---

70 Seaton to Lyme Regis (Town Car Park)   OS E116 (T) Seaton

Grading: Moderate   Distance -   11.0   876.9   6.8   544.9

Timing: 3.25 hours

See also our Sidmouth to Lyme Regis Path Description.

You leave Seaton across its concrete bridge over the River Axe and have to turn inland. Go up the road to the golf course, then walk due east across the fairway into a lane, which you go along, turning to the coast in less than 0.25 mile (400 m).

The section through the Landslip is in a National Nature Reserve and can be very rewarding to some but extremely frustrating to others. Views are extremely limited and the path in places puts on a fair imitation of a corkscrew or helter-skelter; you are unlikely to get lost but most unlikely to know where you are. Suggested times to walk the Landslip range from 1.5 hours to 4 hours, but we are told that the standard time is about 3 hours.

The path into Lyme Regis has now been improved and you can take a path directly down to The Cobb without having to come into the car park, and then down the road.

DORSET
From Lyme to Studland the geology is such that the cliffs are very vulnerable to slippage. During the very wet winter of 2000/01 a number of considerable cliff falls and landslips occurred on the Dorset section. These resulted in some major temporary diversions having to be put in place. We have no clear information on when solutions will be found and the various sections of the Coast Path reinstated. In this year's edition we have included the details of both the coastal route and the temporary diversions which we hope may be removed by the time you walk the path. The diversions described start at the points in the text marked by a bold letter 'D' and a number e.g. (**D2**). However at the time of writing we still do not know what further damage could occur during the winter of 2001/02 so you will need to be on the lookout for possible diversions not mentioned in the Guide. When walking the Path the best advice we can give is to follow the signed route and any official notices or signs. For up to date details of temporary diversions you should visit the Association's website.

71 | Lyme Regis to Charmouth (River Char)   OS E116 (T) Lyme Regis

Grading: Moderate   Distance -   **4.4   881.3   2.7   547.6**

Timing: 1.25 hours

See also our Lyme Regis to Abbotsbury Path Description.

From Lyme Regis town centre take Church Street and Charmouth Road (A3052) until you reach
Lyme Regis Football Club on the right, beyond which you will find a stile at the corner of a lane
and take the footpath across fields to a lane where you turn left (yes west!) for 100 yards (90 m).
At a finger post sign turn right up through the wood and near the top **[D1]** turn right onto the
path that runs between the cliff edge and the golf course. Take the track downhill to Charmouth
and at the first junction (with Old Lyme Hill) turn sharp right and follow the signposted route
back to the cliff edge **[D2]**.

Alternatively at the end of the new promenade at Lyme Regis you may choose to walk along the
firm sand on the beach to Charmouth, if the tide is well out. DO NOT attempt to walk upon the
surface of the grey mud slide, and be aware of the state of the tide before starting out.

D1. Diversion 1 - Lyme Regis Golf Course. The diversion starts at the path junction in the wood
at GR 3456 9330. Turn west on a path for 130 yards (120m) to a junction with a road named
Timber Hill. Turn north on this road passing the golf course club house to join the A3052 road.
Continue north on this road for about 110 yards (100m) and turn eastwards onto a public
footpath (signposted to Fern Hill) across the golf course and bear north-east down through
woods to rejoin the A3052 road. Turn south east down this road for some 550 yards (500m) to
the roundabout with the main A35 road. Take the right hand fork, which is the local road into
Charmouth, and follow it south-south-east downhill into the village for about 760 yards (700m)
to the second road junction. Here turn right into Higher Sea Lane (which later becomes a
footpath) and proceed south-east for about 650 yards (600m) to rejoin the Coast Path at GR
3640 9305.

D2. Diversion 2 - Charmouth (Raffey's Ledge). If Diversion 1 has been lifted there is still the
possibility of a further diversion on this section. From the end of the track (GR 3580 9345) at
the west end of the road called Old Lyme Hill continue north-eastwards on the road to reach
the main road through the village. Turn right down this road and in 110 yards (100m) turn right
into Higher Sea Lane (which later becomes a footpath) and proceed south-east for about 650
yards (600m) to rejoin the Coast Path at GR 3640 9305.

72 | Charmouth to West Bay (Bridport Arms)   OS E116 1 mile to (V) Charmouth

Grading: Strenuous   Distance -   **11.2   892.5   7.0   554.6**

Timing: 3.75 hours

See also our Lyme Regis to Abbotsbury Path Description.

This is a section of interesting walking with spectacular views from Golden Cap, the highest
mainland point on the south coast of England, and later from Thorncombe Beacon. However, be
warned, your good views are not obtained without effort! **[D3]**

When you get to what looks like the top of Golden Cap you have to turn left and go a little higher
to the trig. point to find your way down, which starts at the north end before later bearing east
again. **[D4]** There is a car park and a pub at Seatown.

D3. Diversion 3 - Charmouth (Stonebarrow). From Lower Sea Lane west of the footbridge over
the River Char at GR 3652 9320 turn north east along a tarmac lane called River Way and at the
end continue along a gravel footpath to reach Bridge Road. Carry on northwards up this road
to the junction with the main village road, The Street. Turn eastwards along The Street to
Newlands Bridge and fork right into Stonebarrow Lane. Continue up this narrow lane for
nearly three quarters of a mile (1150 m) taking care of the traffic. At the top of this lane a car
park is reached. Immediately turn sharp right to find a three directional signpost. The direction
you need to follow is the one without an arm on the signpost. Take a grassy track south-
eastwards towards Westhay Farm (the start of this path tends to get slightly obscured by

bushes). After the track has started to descend in about 190 yards (170 m) turn south west through a barrier onto a footpath for another 190 yards (170 m) to rejoin the Coast Path at GR 3803 9301.

D4. Diversion 4 - Seatown. A minor diversion occurs on the western approach to Seatown. At the path junction at GR 4158 9197 following the signed diversion north-east and then easterly down to a road (Sea Hill Lane). Here turn southwards down the road to rejoin the Coast Path at GR 4199 9175.

73   West Bay to Abbotsbury (Swannery Car Park)   OS OL15 (V) West Bay; (V) Abbotsbury

Grading: Moderate   **Distance -**   **15.2**   **907.7**   **9.4**   **564.0**

Timing: 4.25 hours

See also our Lyme Regis to Abbotsbury Path Description.

SEE SECTION 80 FOR DETAILS OF THE ALTERNATIVE INLAND COAST PATH FROM WEST BEXINGTON TO OSMINGTON MILLS.

WARNING: If you intend to walk the whole length of Chesil Bank rather than going to Abbotsbury and along the edge of the Fleet (Section 74), you should telephone Major Hazard on 01305 783456 ext. 8132, to check whether the bank is safe to walk. There may be some firing at Chickerell Rifle Range and it is not unknown for the odd bullet to mis-target, and travel as far as the Bank. As a result, walkers will be sent back despite having walked half this gruelling hike.

After you have walked round the back of West Bay harbour, pass to the right of St. John's Church and ahead to the West Bay Hotel, opposite which is the coast path sign pointing across to the foot of surprisingly steep cliffs.

Watch out for the inland loop at Burton Freshwater which is still shown on current OS maps. This has been changed and an improved route running between the caravan park and the beach has been installed and is well signed.

At Burton Beach, just east of the hotel, there is a cafe / toilet (open all year).

At Burton Mere, unless you are particularly interested in maritime flowers, the definitive route goes inland of the Mere, rather than going along the seaward side: you will get quite enough pebbles later.

There is a fair weather cafe and all year round toilets at West Bexington, and seasonal snack wagons in the car park where the road turns inland past Abbotsbury Gardens. Walkers, however, should continue on the beach for another 200 yards (185 m).

There are refreshments, shops and B & B's in Abbotsbury. If you have time, the climb up to St Catherine's Chapel is worth the effort.

There is an alternative path to the south of Chapel Hill avoiding Abbotsbury village.

74   Abbotsbury to Ferry Bridge (Wyke Regis)   OS OL15 (T) Weymouth

Grading: Easy. Chesil Beach: Strenuous   **Distance -**   **17.5**   **925.2**   **10.9**   **574.9**

Timing: 4 hours (Official Route)

See also our Abbotsbury to Weymouth Path Description.

The Coast Path does not actually go into Abbotsbury. However if you visited the village the best route back to the coast is to leave by the path that you entered the village. That is the path going south from the B3157 (West Street) adjacent to Chapel Lane Stores. At a path junction in 220 yards (200 m) continue south to Nunnery Grove to rejoin the Coast Path.

The Coast Path now goes inland but is well marked and enjoyable to walk; part of it goes along a ridge and has some good views. You do not get back to the shores of the Fleet until Rodden Hive.

On the outskirts of Abbotsbury after Horsepool Farm keep going up the ridge; beguiling, much better tracks go round the hill to the right, but they will not bring you to the stile you need at the top. In about 1 mile (1500 m) turn south off to the ridge and turn sharp left after Hodder's Coppice. A track goes forward, but this is NOT the one you want. After you have crossed a minor road, the official path follows the field headland east and then south to the north east corner of Wyke Wood as signposted, and not in a direct line as shown on some maps. Take particular care as you approach Rodden Hive - the path suddenly dives through a hedge on your left. There is an apparent track and even a marker post which might make you think that the path goes to the right of the stream, but it does not.

At Tidmoor Point, follow the red and white posts unless you have to divert as firing on the range is in progress across the definitive right of way. A deviation has been made inland at Wyke Regis around a Service Establishment.

An alternative for the tough walker who wishes to stay on the coast is to use the Chesil Beach; you can do this by going onto the beach where the path turns inland at Abbotsbury but note you cannot 'get off' again until you reach the causeway from Wyke Regis to Portland. This is only a walk for the fit and not one to be attempted at times of severe gale! Please note that the Chesil Bank is closed to visitors from 1st May-31st August for the Schedule 1 bird nesting season. During the nesting season please keep to the seaward side of the beach so as not to interfere with nesting birds.

---

75 The Isle of Portland   OS OL15 (T) Portland

Grading: Moderate   Distance -   21.3   946.5   13.2   588.1

Timing: 6 hours

See also our Isle of Portland Path Description.

The total distance includes walking Portland Beach Road (A354) twice (there and back).

A circuit of the Isle of Portland is well worth the extra effort. It is a fine walk, with much of interest along the rugged coast, which can be spectacular in rough weather. The Island and Royal Manor of Portland still quarries its famous limestone, still 'hosts' H. M. Prison Services, but is replacing the Ministry of Defence with new port and tourism facilites, so you may be lucky enough to find a new route around the North East section.

From Ferry Bridge you have a number of choices, none of them of much merit, for the first 2 miles (3 km). Using the footway beside the busy A354 road; crossing over the car park beyond the Chesil Beach Centre to slog along the pebbles of Chesil Beach; or catching a bus to the roundabout at the south end of the causeway to alight at the Royal Victoria Lodge. Fourth, and probably best, is to cross the bridge to beyond the boatyard and on the eastern bank, walk along the raised bed of the old railway to near the end of the causeway, before returning to the A354 road. You come to Fortuneswell where you need to cross the road and follow signs for the Chesil Beach Gallery, turning left before the public toilets. Continue past the Cove House Inn and bear right up onto the promenade. Towards the end of this and just before the 'grassy walls', bear left and immediately left again up a zigzag path; then right past the school and up the steep path in the grass incline to the steps to the terraced path that was the old A354 road.

Bear off right onto the coast path running between old quarry banks and the cliff face. 3 miles (5 km) of spectacular and airy cliff top walking brings you to Portland Bill with the Pulpit Rock and lighthouse (refreshments). Continue around the end of the low headland and pass to the seaward of wooden chalets to follow a winding path along the top of low cliffs to join a road above Freshwater Bay after about 1.5 miles (2.5 km).

Turn right up the road for 600 yards (550 m), past Cheyne Weares Car Park to a finger post on the right. Follow the zigzag path down into the rugged undercliff area, and follow the waymarks through the disused quarry workings down to Church Ope Cove.

From this point there is the choice of two routes. Dorset County Council has signed and waymarked a route that rises to run along the cliffs to the prison road, then through disused quarries before returning to the west side of the 'island' where the A354 road reaches the top of the hill. The route then retraces its outward route to Fortuneswell. However we think our preferred route is better and is recommended until such time as a designated route is agreed for Portland. Our route is described in the next three paragraphs.

Before the 'West Cliff' and 'Coast Path' signs, turn right through a gap in the hedge with a 'Crown Estate' sign on to the undercliff path. Continue to seaward along the rugged path to Durdle Pier and bear up left to turn right onto a wide firm path (old track bed of the former Weymouth to Easton railway line). Continue along the track to just before a 'rockfall' sign, where it is necessary to turn left over a bank to follow a rocky path that climbs up the cliffs to an isolated chimney seen above on the skyline. A word of warning here - although the track continues northwards and appears to be well used, do not be tempted to continue as the way forward is eventually blocked by the perimeter security fence of the former MOD Establishments and there is no other route up the high cliffs.

Our preferred route is to turn sharp right at the chimney to go along a prison road, and follow a tarmac road northwards through a gap in a high wall. At the next road turn right and bear downhill toward the gates of the former MOD establishment, but shortly go left at a fork through a barrier gate. Continue forward to a left hand bend, and carry on ahead on a grassy path towards a large pinnacle of rock after which, at the 'rock falls' sign, bear left steeply up on to the higher escarpment heading for a large communications mast. At the high wire perimeter fence turn left and follow the fence along and then around to the north to the entrance of the Verne Prison. Take a path through a little gap to the left of the entrance, passing beside railings and down steep steps. Bear right along a path that traverses under the grassy banks and by a waymark post, bear left down to a hairpin bend in the road.

Turn left and past house number 90 to take a footpath down left. Emerging onto a road bear left, and take the path beside a 'No Entry' sign to Ventnor Road. Walk down to Fortuneswell Road, and cross the road to a path through a park and turn right onto the road to the roundabout by the Royal Victoria Lodge. From here retrace your steps for 2 miles (3 km) to Ferry Bridge.

76 Ferry Bridge to Lulworth Cove (Visitor Centre) OS OL15 (T) Weymouth (Trains)

Grading: This section runs the gamut from easy to moderate to strenuous. Distance - 22.7 969.2 14.1 602.2

Timing: 6.25 hours

See also our Weymouth to Lulworth Cove Path Description.

SEE SECTION 80 FOR DETAILS OF THE ALTERNATIVE INLAND COAST PATH FROM WEST BEXINGTON TO OSMINGTON MILLS.

A footpath sign shows you where to continue on to Weymouth, but leave the old railway line at the north end of the shallow cutting to get back to the Coast Path.

Pass the sailing centre and continue into Old Castle Road; opposite Castle Cove Sailing Club bear right onto a tarmac footpath known as Underbarn Walk. [D5]. Continue on the path close to the coast to Nothe Fort and bear sharp left down to the harbourside which is followed to the Town Bridge, which is crossed and the opposite side of the harbour is followed back to the Pavilion Complex. Here bear left to join The Esplanade. In summer a little ferry may run across the harbour to shorten the route.

Weymouth Harbour
Weymouth & Portland Borough Council,   April to October daily.
Harbour Master's Office,
Municipal Offices, North Quay,
Weymouth, DT4 8TA
(01305 206423 or 01305 206278) Ask for Borough Engineer's Department.

Leave Weymouth along the new promenade and at Overcombe, go up to the minor road to Bowleaze Cove. However, after passing the Spyglass Inn it is best to cross the grass public open space and follow the cliff edge to the Beachside Centre. Beyond the holiday camp, the path leads to a stile at the eastern end of the establishment shown as Short Lake House on maps [D6], and it is important that you follow the sign. It does in fact point in the right direction; compass carriers check it - it's about 72 degrees. You go up over the hill apparently going inland - you do not follow the cliff edge.

On the downhill approach to Osmington Mills the route avoiding the landslide bears away from the cliff edge over a stile and down the right hand side of a field. At the bottom it joins the inland Route just before it crosses two stiles to meet the narrow road that is followed down to the coast.

At Ringstead you are taken slightly inland, because the path shown on maps seaward of the houses does not exist. At the old coastguard cottages at White Nothe, be careful to take the left fork of the two yellow arrows, that being the correct route. From White Nothe onwards you will find that there are some quite severe gradients to be traversed before you reach Lulworth. West of Lulworth Cove the newly stone-pitched path will lead you down through the car park and past the Heritage Centre and onto a tarmac road to the cove.

However, some people turn even further inland than they need. Some signposts indicate 'Youth Hostel-Coast Path' and contain the acorn emblem. These signs are intended to indicate the route to the Youth Hostel at West Lulworth and are not the continuation of the Coast Path.

Those who wish to arrive at Lulworth by a quieter non-car park route should, on Hambury Tout, turn right and take the old path down on the right hand side of the fence. This links with the beach path to St Oswald's Bay; on reaching this turn left. Presently it comes to a tarmac road which you can follow into Lulworth.

D5. Diversion 5 - Weymouth (Underbarn) From the west end of the Underbarn Walk (GR 6752 7763) continue north east up Old Castle Road and in some 260 yards (240 m) turn right into Belle Vue Road. Continue for about 600 yards (560 m) to a crossroads and turn right into Redcliff View. At the end of this road a path leads across a grassed area back onto the Coast Path at GR 6815 7814. **Westbound** walkers should turn sharp right after the Wyke Regis Coastguard Station and turn westwards on the northern leg of Redcliff View to then follow the eastbound diversion in reverse.

D6. Diversion 6 - Osmington (Black Head). From the stile at the eastern end of the holiday centre at GR 7225 8208 turn left and head north east up the side of the field for 110 yards (100 m) to a stile on the left. Cross the stile and turn right up the lane for some 660 yards (720 m) to the main A353 road. Turn right and continue eastwards for some 580 yards (530 m) to a point just beyond Craig's Farm Dairy. Here at a signpost, stile and footbridge turn right to join the Inland Route which heads south-south-east across fields to rejoin the Coast Path proper on the northern outskirts of Osmington Mills at GR 7351 8207. (See page 91 for further details of the latter part of this route.)
NOTE: Progress is being made to reinstate a Coast Path around the landslip at this location thus avoiding the long diversion. It is hoped that at least a signed permissive path will be open soon pending the official creation of a new section of Coast Path.

77 | Lulworth Cove to Kimmeridge, Gaulter Gap (Beach car park) OS OL15 (V) Lulworth

Grading: Severe   Distance -   11.8   981.0   7.3   609.5

Timing: 4 hours

See also our Lulworth to Kimmeridge Path Description.

The coastal path through the Army ranges is open at the times shown below, and is a very fine walk indeed, but a tough one. If closed, two alternative routes are shown opposite.

The path behind the beach cafe has been reopened. Higher up follow a short signed alternative to avoid an eroded area close to the cliff edge. Tide permitting, the beach route is the better option. At most states of the tide, it is perfectly possible to walk along the pebble beach at Lulworth Cove, going up the path which rises diagonally on the far side of the beach. At the top of the steep ascent off the beach, the best route proceeds seawards and there the path turns south eastwards along the coast to the beginning of the Army Ranges, just by the Fossil Forest.

If time is of the essence, when you have crossed the beach and gone up the path, do not turn right but go straight ahead. This way you will come to the Bindon Gate into the ranges, and you can go ahead here, arriving at the coast again at Mupe Bay - shorter, but less scenic.

The village of Tyneham, church, school and historical information are worth going inland 0.5 mile (800 m) to see, between 1000 - 1600 hrs.

RAC Gunnery School Lulworth Ranges: No Firing and Firing Periods

1. *NON FIRING PERIOD.* The Range Walks will be open to the public during the following holiday periods, all dates are inclusive.:

EASTER 2002	29 MAR - 7 APR 2002
BANK HOLIDAY 2002	4 MAY - 6 MAY 2002
SPRING 2002	1 JUN - 9 JUN 2002
SUMMER 2002	27 JUL - 1 SEP 2002
CHRISTMAS/NEW YEAR 2002/2003	21 DEC 2002 - 1 JAN 2003

2. *FIRING PERIODS.* The Range Walks are normally open to the public every Saturday and Sunday except for some weekends in the year. For 2002 they have reserved the following 6 weekends for firing:

FIRST WEEKEND	2 - 3 FEB 2002
SECOND	9 - 10 MAR 2002
THIRD	11 - 12 MAY 2002
FOURTH	22 - 23 JUN 2002
FIFTH	12 - 13 OCT 2002
SIXTH	23 - 24 NOV 2002

3. Experience has shown that it is sometimes possible to avoid firing on some of these reserved weekends and if this is the case, the Range Walks will be opened. Should this occur in 2001 we will make every effort to publicise the fact.

4. Tyneham Church and the School are normally open for viewing 1000 hrs-1600 hrs when the walks are open.

5. Information is also available by ringing 01929 404819, which is a 24 hour answering service

Alternative Route when Lulworth Range Coast Path is unavailable: Lulworth Cove to Kimmeridge, Gaulter Gap.

Option 1 - approx. 13.5 miles (22 km) on a safer, quieter but more strenuous route using mainly rights of way, and permissive paths through Lulworth Park (pre-plotting of given grid refs. onto a map will assist navigation).

Leave the Cove and take the 2nd road on the left (825807).100 yards (90 m) on the right, a footpath leads north for 0.75 mile (1.2 km); turn right (east) and after 100 yards (90 m) turn left (north) to pass Belhuish Coppice and Belhuish Farm, and then across the B3071 at 835832.

At 844(5)828 eastern boundary of Burngate Wood, use the permissive (blue) path north-east past Park Lodge, and go across the road (855832) onto a bridleway.

(The permissive red path across the stile, just up on the left, loops around the lake - if you're ready for a peaceful stop - and meets this bridleway further up at 861(5)834.)

Continue NE along the bridleway to 865839 where it veers north, and later north-east through the Highwood to meet the road at 872862. On the road walk east, fork right (signposted Stoborough) at 882855; over the crossroads at 886855 east for further 1.5 miles (2.4 km) along Holme Lane to walk east 912855.

(*) Turn right just before a railway bridge onto Dorey Farm bridleway at 912855. After 1.25 miles (2 km) turn right onto Creech Road leading south-southwest towards the Purbeck Ridge. After another 1.5 miles (2.4 km) of road, walk up a steep gradient to a viewpoint car park. Beyond the car park 902815 take the left road that turns back and down over the ridge to Corfe. (A short cut bridleway 905817 zigzags down to meet the same road.) As the road levels out at a left hand bend 907812, take the bridleway ahead that leads out south through Steeple Leaze Farm.

200 yards (185 m) south of the farm, a footpath leads south crossing another ridge bridleway, down a steep path, and across a field to Higher Stonehips, and on to Gaulter Gap, the easterly point of the range walks.

Option 2 - approx. 12 miles (19 km).

This route is mainly road walking, and care is needed on narrow bends. Leave the Cove to West Lulworth on the B3070, and then turn right to East Lulworth at 835816 to continue on the B3070. After 3 miles (5 km), turn right (east) at grid reference 886855 along Holme Lane, and then continue from * above, at 912855.

78 | Kimmeridge, Gaulter Gap to Swanage (The Pier)   OS OL15

| Grading: Severe and then moderate | Distance - | 21.4 | 1002.4 | 13.3 | 622.8 |

Timing: 7.25 hours

See also our Kimmeridge to South Haven Point Path Description.

From Gaulter Gap, Kimmeridge, the path is straightforward although care may be needed where small sections have slipped, cracked or may be close to the cliff top; after descending Hounstout the official route tunrs inland to avoid dangerous wet and unstable ground on what appears to be the direct route to St Aldhelm's Head. Take care to follow the signed and waymarked route even though it seems to be heading in the wrong direction to go inland to Hill Bottom cottages where the path turns south again, and beyond the gate climbs left up to a high level route which is well signposted. The climb up West Hill is away from the views, but as you gain height along Emmett's Hill, the views back along the Dorset coast are very good. The Royal Marines memorial is just to the left of the path.

From St Aldhelm's Head, there is fine high level walking all the way to Durlston Head, but not much accommodation along this stretch.

There is only minimal signing in the Durlston Country Park. However, you keep on the low level path all the way round Durlston Head but as you come up on the north side of it you take the second turning right, not the first which is a dead end into a quarry. [D7]

The section of the Coast Path through Swanage is not well signed. You are unlikely to go far wrong, and will soon be walking along the sea front promenade.

CP - the map suggests that the Coast Path enters Worth Matravers; it does not, but turns sharply through the word 'Farm' of Renscombe Farm.

D7. Diversion 7 - Swanage (Durlston Bay). After leaving Durlston Castle at GR 0335 7728 follow the broad stony coastal path north through the woods above Durlston Bay for some 760 yards (700 m) to reach a barrier and sign. Turn left on a good path for some 125 yards (115 m) to reach Durlston Road at a kissing gate. Turn right and in about 185 yards (170 m) turn right again into Belle Vue Road. Just before a block of flats called Durlston Cliff the coast path proper joins the road at GR 0342 7811 which is followed north eastwards to the grassed open space leading down to Peveril Point.

79 | Swanage to Sandbanks (South Haven Point) OS OL15 (T) Swanage; (V) Studland

| Grading: Moderate | Distance - | 12.2 | 1014.6 | 7.6 | 630.4 |

Timing: 3.5 hours

See also our Kimmeridge to South Haven Point Path Description.

At the telephone box at the north end of Swanage Sea Front, tide permitting, you may prefer to keep along the pedestrian promenade to the end and then walk 200 yards (185 m) along the beach turning up some steps to the official route. At high tide you have to leave the seafront on the main road (Ulwell Road) and where it bears left into a one-way system continue ahead into Redcliffe Road. At the sub post office turn sharp right into Ballard Way and at the end do not be put off by the signs 'Ballard Private Estate'. Carry forward into the chalet estate and follow signs for the coast path to emerge on to a grassed area on the cliff edge.

From Ballard Down the path is obvious all the way to Handfast Point and the much photographed rocks of Old Harry.

When you reach a road junction by a public toilet, turn right. You will then pass two footpaths to the right but do not take either of them. Carry on up the road passing the Bankes Arms pub. After passing the Manor House Hotel, take the track / road down to the beach, and go left at the beach. When the tide is out, this is firm, but when it is in more effort will be required.

Further up the beach, maybe we should mention there is a naturist beach, so you must not be put off if you find that on this last lap that you are the only one wearing clothes! The National Trust has also provided an alternative route, The Heather Walk, through the dunes, and this is marked by yellow topped posts.

Despite any notices you may see, dogs on leads may accompany Coast Path walkers along the shore line, but be sure to clean up after your dog if necessary.

Studland/Sandbanks (Mouth of Poole Harbour) Bournemouth-Swanage Motor Road & Ferry Company, Shell Bay, Studland. BH19 3BA. Tel: 01929 450203.	All year round. Daily every 20 mins. Sandbanks 0700 - 2300 hrs Shell Bay 0710 - 2310 hrs Closed for 2 - 3 weeks in November 2002 for refit (phone for info).

Wainwright at the end of his work on the Pennine Way said it all, and said it better, of a shorter path. Ward & Mason in the old Letts Guide simply say 'That's it'. We will add whether you have been lucky enough to walk the whole way from Minehead at one go, or simply, as most of us have, in bits and pieces over a period, nonetheless you will be glad you walked and have just finished Britain's longest and finest footpath. It's a longer step than most take in their lifetime!

80 Alternative Inland Coast Path: West Bexington to Osmington Mills OS OL15

Grading: Moderate   **Distance - 27.0   16.8**

See also our alternative Inland Route Path Description.

Although this is certainly not a coastal path it is an enjoyable walk along a well-marked path with good views seaward from the ridges. Because it is inland a more detailed route is given. When walking this section bear in mind that we found no place for obtaining refreshments between the start of the walk, where there is a cafe, and the village of Osmington.

At West Bexington car park turn inland up the road signposted 'Inland Route - Coast Path', and where the road turns left, continue forward up a stony track, signposted 'Hardy Monument $5^1/_2$ miles'. At top of the hill the footpath briefly joins the main road but you immediately leave again over the stile on the right through the field, signposted 'Hardy Monument 5 miles'. Take care, as the way across this field is not clear and should, at first, keep parallel to the road and then you bear right to a waymarked post. After you have crossed the wall, you can start to bear upwards to the left to the further signpost near the road, marked with the acorn symbol and the words 'Inland Route'. After about 300 yards (275 m) continuing through the field and by the corner of a wall there is a further signpost 'Hardy Monument $4^1/_2$, Osmington Mills 15'. Continue forward, very shortly emerging on to the B3157 road which you cross and leave through a gate, signposted 'Hardy Monument $4^1/_2$'.

You now approach Abbotsbury Castle and where the path in front divides, take the upper right-hand fork along the top of the south side of the Fort past the trig point, from where you can get superb views in all directions, and you should be able to see the Hardy Monument clearly in the distance. Proceed eastwards and cross the minor road now and go forward, signposted 'Hardy Monument 4'. Proceed in an approximate easterly direction along the ridge of Wears Hill and the crest of White Hill for about 2 miles (3.2 km) following the signposts and waymarks. However be careful not to follow signs with the acorn symbol incorrectly shown that indicate routes down to the village of Abbotsbury lying in the valley below, with the old chapel clearly visible. At the east end of White Hill bear north-east as signposted and leave in the inland corner through a gate on to a minor road. Turn left along the road for approximately 50 yards (46 m) and then turn right, signposted 'Inland Route - Hardy Monument 2'.

Follow the bridleway marked with blue arrows along the wire fence above the scrub to a path junction; where the bridleway carries on forward take the yellow waymarked footpath to the left and cross a stile. At the far side of the field the track then leads approximately 50 yards (46 m) to a further gate with a stile and waymark. Immediately adjacent to this gate is a stone circle which is an ancient monument and there is a sign to this effect. You now continue forward, leaving a small wood to the left, to reach the road from Portisham to Winterbourne Steepleton.

Turn left along the road for approximately 60 yards (55 m) and then turn right into a field over a stile, signposted `Hardy Monument $1\frac{1}{2}$ - Osmington Mills 13'. On the far side of the field proceed forward, signpost `Hardy Monument 1'. At this point there is a signpost forking right to Hellstone only, with a return possible on a different path.

At Blackdown Barn turn left to climb up through the woods, signposted `Hardy Monument $\frac{1}{2}$'. At the monument you will find a small signpost 'Inland Route - Osmington Mills 11 miles' with a blue arrow indicating the way forward. Cross the road to a further signpost with the acorn symbol and now descend through the bracken. You shortly reach the road again, turn left and in a few yards ignore the signpost on the right, cutting back indicating 'Bridleway to Coast Path' and continue forward, (signposted 'Coast Path East') and in another 100 yards (90 m) turn right, signposted `Inland Route to Courton Hill' on one side of the sign and `Osmington 12 - Courton Hill 2' on the other. Now there is a good ridgeway path without navigational problems for some 3 miles (4.8 km) and good views to seaward in the distance. After passing the radio mast you come to the B3159 marked by the Borough of Weymouth boundary stone and continue across the road, signposted `Inland Route East'.

On reaching the A354 turn right immediately before the main road down the signposted track and after just over $\frac{1}{4}$ mile (400 m) you will find a stile in the hedge on your left. The path leads across a narrow field to cross the busy A354. Before the farm with its adjacent radio mast take care to go through the gate on the right, marked with a blue arrow. After crossing the field, leaving two tumuli to your left, you reach a metalled road. Turn right and at the next junction there is a signpost surmounted by a symbol 'Dorset - Came Wood' which, unusually, carries the six-figure map reference of the locality (687857). Here you turn right at the signpost `Bridleway to Bincombe'. At the end of the path join a metalled lane and at the junction turn left, signposted 'Inland Route East'.

Drop down the road into the village of Bincombe and where the road turns right take the track forward leaving a small church on your right. Where the path splits take the left hand fork signposted again with a blue arrow and the acorn symbol. After the overhead high-voltage power lines pass through a small signposted wooden gate and then proceed forward through one field into the next to the footpath sign. Here turn left, following the line of the old indistinct curving grassy track until it meets the road at the bottom of Combe Valley. Turn left here and follow the road until you reach the Combe Valley road sign to `Sutton Poyntz' and take this turn to the right. After 70 yards (64 m) turn left through a gate, signposted `White Horse Hill - Osmington Mills'. The path now is easy to follow with extensive views to seaward over Weymouth and Portland. On passing a ruined building on your left you reach a broad track and turn right, signposted `Osmington $1\frac{1}{2}$' and after about 200 yards (185 m) go through a gate, signposted `Inland Route Osmington'. You will shortly pass the trig point on your right and at the next field gate bear left and follow the field boundary along White Horse Hill. Just beyond the next gate fork right, signposted 'Osmington 1, Lulworth 8'.

Descend to the village of Osmington and follow the signs through the village. When you reach the main Weymouth road near the Sun Ray Inn turn left and in about 250 yards (230 m) turn right at a signpost, over a stile and footbridge, and follow the field boundary on the left through two fields and at the top look back to see the Hardy Monument in the distance and also the white horse on the hillside. Go over the stile to the footpath sign, then turn half right to cross the field at an angle to a further stile. Cross it and turn left along the hedge side to the bottom. At the end of the field there is a very short length of enclosed footpath to the road; turn right along it, descending to Osmington Mills.

ACCOMMODATION

This list of accommodation has been prepared in path order.
The following letter code is used.

Facilities

O	=	Open All Year	D =	Drying facilities for wet clothes
EM	=	Evening Meal	PL =	Packed Lunches
CP	=	Car Parking	LSP =	Long Stay Parking
DW	=	Dogs Welcome	KT =	Kit Transfer
PD	=	Pick Up/Drop Service		

Room Codes

D	=	Double	T =	Twin
S	=	Single	F =	Family
ES	=	En Suite		

Please note: The figure in brackets denotes the number of en-suite rooms e.g. 4d[2] = 4 double rooms, two of which are en-suite.

KT - Kit Transfer. A service being offered by some of our accommodation providers is to transfer your kit to your next accommodation. This could prove useful to you. Naturally a fee may be levied for this service.
PD - Pick Up/Drop. This code appears following the distance from the path and denotes a facility whereby your host is prepared to collect and return you to the coast path within reasonable distance. No fee should be charged for this service.
Distance from Path. Please remember these are only approximate and may not be accurate.

The part of the address in CAPITALS is an aid to location; it does not signify the postal town. The extreme left-hand column refers to the appropriate section in the 'Trail Description'; we feel it may help you to find addresses quickly. The amount quoted gives an **indication of the starting rate** for bed and breakfast, and may well rise. If working on a tight budget, it is best to ask first.

Tourist Information Centres can be an additional source of accommodation addresses. We have provided a list of TIC's along the coast path for your use on page 131.

The majority of our B & B addresses have been submitted by members. The fact that they are included in this book does not indicate a recommendation by The South West Coast Path Association. Their inclusion is merely for information purposes; they are there, if you want them. We cannot, for financial and practical reasons, introduce vetting, inspection or any form of `Star' rating. We do have a system whereby addresses can be removed from the list.

We wish to develop this list especially for many 'sparse' areas. Suggestions for inclusion in our next list will be welcome. Details of any new accommodation should be addressed to the Administrator. Our list is not comprehensive and walkers will find many B&B's in towns and villages along the coast path that are not recorded in this book.

It would not be out of place here to add a word of thanks from those who walk, to those who kindly board. How many times have we been thankful for a friendly welcome and good 'digs'? Maybe a note we had from one of our accommodation addresses puts it well. 'We have had quite a lot of walkers this year and we have usually managed to dry them out - and feed them up.'

Although there are a lot of addresses that state they are 'open all the year', some of these close for the Christmas period. Walkers should remember that during the holiday season many of our accommodation addresses could be fully booked up in advance by holidaymakers staying for a week or two. Conversely a walker could book for one night only in good time, thus preventing a guest house proprietor from taking a week or more booking later on. Accommodation problems can be frustrating to all parties concerned so bear these facts in mind when bed hunting **for one night only**.

Important If having booked ahead, and for any reason you are unable to get to your accommodation address, please telephone and explain your absence to your intended host. We have known instances where the host has become so worried about the non-appearance of walkers that they have informed the emergency services. The last thing we want is Police, Coastguards and Royal Navy helicopters out on a wild goose chase.

Sect.	Name and Address	Tel. No. Fax. No. Web / Email	Map Reference Opening Times	Distance from Path Starting Price Facilities Accommodation
1	Mr R Brooker 23 Chestnut Way Alcombe MINEHEAD TA24 6EB	01643 709913	972 452	1 km PD £15.00 O D EM PL CP KT 1D 1T[1]
1	Mrs D Morris Badgers 38 Summerland Road MINEHEAD TA24 6EB	01643 704583		400 mtrs £16.00 O D PL CP LSP 1D 1T 1S 1F
1	Mrs S Phillips The Old Ship Aground Quay Street MINEHEAD TA24 5UL	01643 702087 01643 709066 enquiries@oldshipaground.co.uk		500mtrs £25.00 O D EM PL CP LSP DW KT 1D 2T 1S 3F ALL ES
1	Mr & Mrs Smith 11 Glenmore Road MINEHEAD TA24 5BQ	01643 705253		1km PD O D CP KT 1D 3F
1	Mr & Mrs D Sanders 1 Glenmore Road MINEHEAD TA24 5BQ	01643 706225		700 mtr £17.00 O PL CP LSP DW KT 2D[1] 1T[1] 2S
1	Mrs J Tice Cotswold 19 Tregonwell Road MINEHEAD TA24 5DU	01643 703102 01643 703399 blizicebandb@aol.com	970 467	PD £20.00 O D EM PL CP LSP DW KT 2D[2] 2T[2] 1S
1	Mr J Murray Marston Lodge Hotel St Michael's Road MINEHEAD TA24 5JP	01643 702510 As Phone	April-Sept	400 mtrs £25.00 D CP LSP 6D 2T 2S 1F ALL ES
1	Mrs A Green 24 Ponsford Road MINEHEAD TA24 5DY	01645 703945 greenfinial@lineone.net	973 467 Mar-Oct	800 mts PD £17.00 D PL CP KT 1D 1T ALL ES
1	Mr & Mrs T V Stiles-Cox Leys The Ridge PORLOCK TA24 8HA	01643 862477 As Phone	892 469	2 kms £19.00 O D PL CP 1D 2S
1	Mr R G Steer Myrtle Cottage High Street PORLOCK TA24 8PU	01643 862978 As Phone bob.steer@talk21.com www.smoothhound@chelsoftdemon.com		100mtrsPD £22.50 O D CP LSP DW KT 5D 2T 5S 2F KT&PD Weekends Only
1	Mrs B Starr Sea View Cottage PORLOCK WEIR TA24 8PE	01643 862523	864 478	On path £19.00 O D PL CP DW KT 1D(1) 1T
2	Mrs E J Richards Silcombe Farm PORLOCK TA24 8JN	01643 862248	833 482	On path PD £18.00 O D EM PL CP LSP DW KT 2D[1] 1T[1] 1S
2	Mr & Mrs C Parker Tregonwell Riverside Guest House 1 Tors Road LYNMOUTH EX35 6ET	01598 753369 www.smoothhound.co.uk/hotels/trgonwl.html	725 493	400 mtr PD £22.00 O D PL CP LSP DW KT 7D[5] 1T[1] 1S 1F[1]
2	Mrs J Pile Oakleigh 4 Tors Road LYNMOUTH EX35 6ET	01598 752220	Mar-Nov	400 mtr £20.00 D PL CP LSP DW KT 5D 2T 2S

Sect.	Name and Address	Tel. No. Fax. No. Web / Email	Map Reference Opening Times	Distance from Path Starting Price Facilities Accommodation
2	The Bath Hotel 01598 752544 LYNMOUTH EX35 6EL	01598 752238 bathhotel@torslynmouth.co.uk www.torslynmouth.co.uk	Feb to Nov	20mtrs £27.00 D EM PL CP DW 11D 8T 1S 4F ALL ES
2	Mr & Mrs A Francis Glenville House 2 Tors Road LYNMOUTH EX35 6ET	01598 752202 tricia@glenvillelynmouth.co.uk www.glenvillelynmouth.co.uk	727 494 March to Nov	300mtrs £23.00 D PL 4D[3] 1T 1S
2	Mr&Mrs J McGowan The Denes Longmead LYNTON EX35 6DQ	01598 753573 As Phone j.e.mcgowan@btinternet.com www.thedenes.com	715 494	1km PD £16.00 O D EM PL CP KT 2D[1] 3T[2] 3F[2]
2	Mrs Mari Kirk 12 Crossmead LYNTON EX35 6DG	01598 753288		400 mtrs £18.00 O D EM PL DW 1D 1T 2S
2	Mrs P E Morgan Kingford House Longmead LYNTON EX35 6DQ	01598 752361		£21.50 O D EM PL CP DW 4D 1T 2S ALL ES
2	Mrs L Cowgill Lee House Lee Road LYNTON EX35 6BP	01598 752264 01598 752364 leehouse@freeuk.com www.smoothhound.co.uk/hotels/lee.html	717 495 Feb to Dec	400mtrs £20.00 EM PL CP LSP DW 6D 2T ALL ES
3	Mrs Dallyn Mannacott Farm Nr Hunters Inn MARTINHOE EX31 4QS	01598 763227	662 481 April to Oct	800 mtrs £16.00 D PL CP 1D 1T
3	Mr & Mrs F J Barry Glendower King Street COMBE MARTIN EX34 0AL	01271 883449 frankjbarry@netscapeonline.co.uk		100mts PD £16.00 P D PL CP LSP DW KT 2D[2] 2T[2] 1S 1F[1]
3	Mrs J Bosley Hillview Guest House The Woodlands COMBE MARTIN EX34 OAT	01271 882331 hillviewgh@appleonline.net	575 469 Easter to Oct	200 mtrs £16.00 D PL CP LSP KT 2D[2] 1T 1S
3	Mrs A Waldon Idlehour Borough Road COMBE MARTIN EX34 OAN	01271 883217	577 471 March to Oct	80mtrs £14.00 D DW 2D 1T 1F
4	Mr & Mrs W J Millington Sherborne Lodge Hotel Torrs Park ILFRACOMBE EX34 8AY	01271 862297 01271 865520 113121-222@compuserve.com www.smoothhound.co.uk/hotels/sherborn.html		200mtrs £18.00 O D EM PL DW 6D[6] 2T[1] 1S 1F[1]
4	Mr & Mrs C D Hewitt Norbury House Hotel Torrs Park ILFRACOMBE EX34 8AZ	01271 863888		200mts £20.00 O D EM PL CP LSP DW KT 4D[3] 1S 3F[3]

Sect.	Name and Address	Tel. No. Fax. No. Web / Email	Map Reference Opening Times	Distance from Path Starting Price Facilities Accommodation
5	Mrs M P Newcombe Sunnyside LEE Nr Ilfracombe EX34 8LW	01271 863189	Easter-	50mtrs PD £18.00 D PL KT 1D 1T 1S
5	Mrs F Nustedt The Grampus Inn LEE Nr Ilfracombe	01271 862906	464 483	250 mtr £21.00 O D EM PL CP LSP DW KT 1D 1T 1F ALL ES
5	Mrs G Potts The Orchard LEE Ilfracombe EX34 8LW	01271 867212 theorchard@bushinternet.com	Feb to Dec	£24.00 D PL CP LSP KT 2D[2] 1T 1S
5	Mrs S Tod Fuschia Valley House LEE BAY EX34 8LW	01271 866857 tods@supanet.com		500 mtrs PD £18.00 O D PL CP DW KT 2D[1] 1F[1]
6	Mr T Cole Lundy House Hotel Chapel Hill MORTHOE EX34 7DZ	01271 870372 01271 871001 info@lundyhousehotel.co.uk www.lundyhousehotel.co.uk	March to Oct	20 mtrs PD £24.00 D EM PL CP DW KT 5D 1T 4F ALL ES
6	Mrs A Braund Clyst House Rockfield Road WOOLACOMBE EX34 7DH	01271 870220	Mar to Oct	100 mtrs £20.00 D EM PL CP 1D 2T 1S
6	Mr & Mrs H J Riley Camberley Beach Road WOOLACOMBE EX34 7AA	01271 870231 camberley@tesco.net	465 438	600 mtrs £18.00 O D PL CP KT 4D 1T 1F ALL ES
7	Mrs G Adams Combas Farm PUTSBOROUGH Croyde EX33 1PH	01271 890398 As Phone	449 396	900 mtrs £20.00 O D EM PL CP LSP 2D[2] 1S 2F[2]
7	Mr & Mrs C Gedling West Winds Guest House Moor Lane CROYDE BAY EX33 1PA	01271 890489 As Phone chris@croydewestwinds.freeserve.co.uk www.westwindguesthouse.co.uk	On path Mar to Nov	£29.00 D EM PL CP LSP KT 3D 1T 1S ALL ES
7	Mrs J Windsor Chapel Farm Guest House Hobbs Hill CROYDE EX33 1NE	01271 890429 www.chapelfarmcroyde.co.uk	Easter to Nov	500 mtrs £20.00 D PL CP 6 ROOMS ALL ES
7	Mr & Mrs G Casban Leadengate House CROYDE EX33 1PN	01271 890373	443 388 Feb to Dec LSP Oct-May only	800 mts £22.50 D PL CP LSP DW KT 2D 1T 1S 1F ALL ES
7	Mr & Mrs A Baretta Shuna Down Road CROYDE EX33 1QE	01271 890537 as phone		100mtrs £28.00 O CP LSP KT 5D 1T ALL ES
7	Mr & Mrs P Davis Moorsands Moor Lane CROYDE EX33 1NP	01271 890781 www.croyde-bay.com/moorsands.htm	441 395	450mtrs £23.00 O D PL CP KT 2D 1T 1F ALL ES

Sect.	Name and Address	Tel. No. / Fax. No. / Web / Email	Map Reference / Opening Times	Distance from Path / Starting Price / Facilities / Accommodation
7	Mr R Tatman St Helens Priory Hobbs Hill Braunton EX33 1NE	01271 890757 st_helens_priory@lineone.net www.sthelenspriory.co.uk	Feb-Dec	800 mtrs £27.50 D EM PL CP DW 4[4] 2T
8	Mrs R C Saunders Stockwell Lodge 66 South Street BRAUNTON	01271 814338	486 362	200mtrs PD £17.00 O D PL CP LSP DW KT 4D[3] 3T[3] 1S 3F[3]
8	Mrs J Watkins North Cottage 14 North Street. BRAUNTON EX33 1AJ	01271 812703	485 367	200mtrs PD £16.00 O D PL CP DW KT 1D[1] 1T[1] 1S 1F
8	Mr & Mrs T C Stoop Hewish Moor Farmhouse Hewish Lane INSTOW Bideford EX39 4LR	01271 860450 as phone timangi@hewishfarm.fsnet.co.uk www.silverstreamukfishing.com		3km PD £20.00 O D EM PL CP LSP DW KT 2D[1] 1S PRIV BATH
8	Mr & Mrs P Borg The Wayfarer Inn Lane End Road INSTOW Bideford EX39 4LB	01271 860342 01271 860066 wayfarerinn@tinyworld.co.uk www.instow.net		20mtrs £25.00 O D EM PL CP 1D 2T
8	Mr & Mrs J Harrison Cresta Guest House Sticklepath Hill BARNSTAPLE EX31 2BU	01271 374022 as phone www.crestaguesthouse.com.uk		800 mts PD £18.00 O D PL CP DW KT 2D[2] 1T[1] 2S 2F[2]
9	Mrs H Laugharne Mount Hotel Northdown Road BIDEFORD EX39 3LP	01237 473748 01237 373813 andrew@themountbideford.fsnet.co.uk www.themount1.cjb.net		500 mts PD O D PL CP LSP KT 3D 1T 2S 1F ALL ES
9	Mr G Bower Greysands Bed & Breakfast Long Lane WATERTOWN Appledore EX39 1NQ	01237 479310	454 303	on path £20.00 O D PL CP LSP KT 1D[1] 1T 1F
9	Mrs D E George Oakwood 34 Yelland Road FREMINGTON EX31 3DS	01271 373884		1.5kms £14.50 O D EM PL CP 2D 2T 1S 1F
9	Mrs D Cope Conkers Durrant Lane NORTHAM EX39 2RL	01237 474794 www.enterprise.conkers.co.uk		350 mts PD £26.00 O D EM PL CP LSP KT 1T[1]
9	Mr & Mrs D Brewster 5 Estuary View NORTHAM Bideford EX39 1XZ	01237 478909		500mtrs £18.00 O D CP 1T[1]
9	Mrs S Clegg Mayfield Avon Lane WESTWARD HO! EX39 1LR	01237 477128 sallyclegg1@hotmail.com		400mts £14.00 O D PL CP LSP KT 2D 1T 1S
9	Mr & Mrs P Snowball Brockenhurst 11 Atlantic Way WESTWARD HO! EX39 1HX	01237 423346 As Phone snowball@brockenhurst1.freeser	432 290	200 mtrs PD £25.00 O D PL CP LSP DW KT 2D 1T ALL ES

Sect.	Name and Address	Tel. No. Fax. No. Web / Email	Map Reference Opening Times	Distance from Path Starting Price Facilities Accommodation
9	Mr & Mrs R Sharratt Eversley 1 Youngaton Road WESTWARD HO! EX39 1HU	01237 471603		200 mtrs £15.00 O D CP DW 1D 1T 1S 1F[1]
9	Mrs M Brocklesby The Puffin Inn 123 Bay View Road WESTWARD HO! EX39 1BJ	01237 473970 01237 422815 thepuffins@breathemail.net		500 mtr £25.00 O D EM PL CP LSP 2D 1T 1S 1F ALL ES
9	Mrs C Pile Culloden House Hotel Fosketh Hill WESTWARD HO! EX39 1JA	01237 479421 01237 475628 enquiries@culloden-house.co.uk www.culloden-house.co.uk		200 mtr £25.00 O D PL CP LSP DW 2D[1] 5T[4] 2F[2]
10	Mr & Mrs K.W Ryder The Old Mill BUCKS MILL EX 39 5	01237 431701 As Phone kryder 1 @ compuserve.com.	355 237	On path £21.00 O D EM PL CP LSP 2D 1T 1S
10	Mrs C Giddy Temple Bar High Street CLOVELLY EX39 5TE	01237 431438	Mar-Nov	500mts PD £20.00 D CP LSP 1D 1T 1S
10	The New Inn High Street CLOVELLY EX39 STQ	01237 431303 01237 431636 newinn@clovelly.co.uk		on path £17.50 O D EM PL CP LSP 7D 1S ALL ES
10	Ms L.J Simms Donkey Shoe Cottage 21 High Street CLOVELLY	01237 431601		200mtrs £20.00 O D PL CP LSP KT 1D 1T 1S 1F
10	Mr & Mrs T D Curtis Fuchsia Cottage Burscott Lane HIGHER CLOVELLY EX39 5RR	01237 431398 curtis@fuschiacottage.fslife.co.uk www.clovelly-holidays.co.uk	313 242	1km PD £16.00 O D PL CP LSP KT 1D[1] 1T[1] 1S
10	Mrs B May Boat House Cottage 148 Slerra Hill HIGHER CLOVELLY EX39 5ST	01237 431209	553 124	800 mtrs £16.00 O D PL CP LSP DW KT 1D 1T 1S 1F
10	Mrs P Vanstone High Banks Cottage Slerra Hill HIGHER CLOVELLY EX39 5ST	01237 431752		750 mtrs £16.00 O D PL KT 1D OR S
11	Mr & Mrs J W George Gawlish Farm GAWLISH Hartland EX39 6AT	01237 441320 As Phone		500mtrs PD £18.00 O D EM PL CP LSP DW KT 2D 1T ALL ES
11	Mrs Y Heard West Titchberry Farm WEST TITCHBERRY Hartland Point EX39 6AU	01237 441287 As Phone	242 271	250mtrs PD £18.00 O D EM PL CP LSP KT 1D 1T 1F

Sect.	Name and Address	Tel. No. Fax. No. Web / Email	Map Reference Opening Times	Distance from Path Starting Price Facilities Accommodation
11	Mr & Mrs C Johns Hartland Quay Hotel HARTLAND QUAY EX39 6DU	01237 441218 01237 441371		On Path PD £25.00 O D EM PL CP LSP DW KT 6D[5] 4T[4] 2T[1] 5F[5]
11	Mrs H Davey Stoke Barton Farm Stoke HARTLAND EX39 6DU	01237 441238	Easter to Sept	700mtrs PD £18.00 D PL CP LSP DW KT 1D(1) 1T(1)
11	Mrs B Slee Homeleigh Stoke HARTLAND EX39 6DU	01237 441465	235 247 Mar-Oct	800 mtrs £17.00 D PL CP LSP KT 1D 1T
11	Mrs M Loveridge 2 Harton Manor The Square HARTLAND EX39 6BL	01237 441670	258 245	4 kms PD £16.00 O D EM PL CP LSP DW KT 1D[1] 1T
11	Mrs T Goaman Elmscott Farm HARTLAND EX39 6ES	01237 441276 01237 441076	231 215	800mts PD £22.00 O D EM PL CP LSP KT 3D[2] 1T PTE BATH
12	Mrs Heywood Cornakey Farm CORNAKEY Morwenstow EX23 9SS	01288 331260	Jan-Nov	500mtrs £19.00 D EM PL CP LSP 1D 1T 1F[1]
12	Mrs J Hudson Little Bryaton MORWENSTOW Bude EX23 9SU	01288 331755 little.bryaton@dial.pipex.com www.little.bryaton.dial.pipex.com	221 156	1.2 kms PD £21.50 O D EM PL CP LSP DW KT 1D 1T 1F ALL ES
12	Mr & Mrs Cole Jays, WOOLLEY MORWENSTOW Bude EX23 9PP	01288 331540 cole.jays@talk21.com www.members.tripod.co.uk/jaysbarn/jaysbarn	254 168	4km PD £19.00 O D EM PL CP LSP DW KT 1D 1T 1S 1F ALL ES
12	Mrs C White Trelawney Crosstown MORWENSTOW Bude EX23 9SR	01288 331453		800 mts £20.00 O D PL CP LSP KT 1D 1T
12	Mr M E Payne Pencarrol Guest House 21 Downs View BUDE EX23 8RF	01288 352478	Jan-Nov	300 mtrs £19.00 D PL CP LSP 3D[2] 1T[1] 2S 1F[1]
12	Mr & Mrs M Curtis Atlantic Calm 30 Downs View BUDE EX23 8RG	01288 359165 atlanticcalm@btinternet www.atlanticcalm.co.uk	206 071	200 mtrs PD £17.00 O D EM PL CP LSP DW KT 5D 2T 1S ALL ES
12	Miss E Abbott St Merryn Coast View BUDE EX23 8AG	01288 352058 01288 359050 st.merryn@ukonline.co.uk www.stmerryn.org.uk		1.6km PD £15.00 O D PL CP DW 1D 1T 1S 1F

Sect.	Name and Address	Tel. No. Fax. No. Web / Email	Map Reference Opening Times	Distance from Path Starting Price Facilities Accommodation
13	Mr & Mrs M Fly Fairway Guest House 8 Downs View BUDE EX23 8RF	01288 355059 fairwayhouse@kfly.freeserve.co.uk www.fairwayguesthouse.co.uk		200 mts £15.00 O D EM PL CP DW KT 3D[2] 1T[1] 2S[1] 1F[1]
13	Mrs P Drew Surfhaven 31 Dows View Bude EX23 8RG	01288 353923 As Phone surfhaven@bude33.fsnet.co.uk www.surfhaven.info		£17.00 O D PL CP LSP DW 3D 4F ALL ES
13	Mr & Mrs J Thorne Upton Cross UPTON Bude EX23 0LY	01288 355310 As Phone		150mtrs £19.00 O D PL CP LSP 2D 1T 1F ALL ES
12	Mrs S Trewin Harefield Cottage UPTON Bude EX23 0LY	01288 352350 01288 352712 sally@coast-countryside.co.uk		220 mts £22.00 O D EM PL CP LSP DW KT 3D [2] 1T[1] 1F[1]
13	Bay View Inn Marine Drive WIDEMOUTH BAY EX23 0AW	01288 361273 enquiries@bayviewinn.co.uk www.bayviewinn.co.uk	201 022	100mts PD £18.00 O D EM PL CP LSP DW KT 3D[2] 1T 1S 3F[3]
13	Mrs A Short 5 Penkenna Close HIGHER CRACKINGTON Bude	01840 230648		1.6km PD £15.00 O D PL CP DW KT 1T 1S
13	Mr & Mrs J Cooper Coombe Barton Inn CRACKINGTON HAVEN EX23 0JG	01840 230345 01840 230788	Mar-Oct	On Path PD £25.00 D EM PL CP LSP KT 5D[3] 1T 1S
14	Mrs J Horwell High Pennycrocker Farm ST JULIOT Boscastle PL35 0BY	01840 250488 As Phone jackiefarm@aol.com	127 927	1km £18.00 O D PL CP LSP 2D[1] 1T[1]
14	Mr & Mrs G Crown Tolcarne House Hotel Tintagel Road BOSCASTLE PL35 0AS	01840 250654 As Phone crowntolhouse@eclipse.co.uk www.milford.co.uk/go/tolcarne.html	March-Oct	800 mtrs £27.00 D EM PL CP LSP DW 5D 2T 1S ALL ES
14	Mrs C Nicholls Treosewill Farm Paradise BOSCASTLE PL35 0BL	01840 250545 As Phone trerosewill@talk21.com trerosewill.co.uk	096 905 Feb-Nov	500mtrs PD £23.00 D PL CP LSP KT 3D 1T 2F ALL ES
14	Mrs D Johnson Tremorvah BOSCASTLE PL35 0AU	01840 250636 01840 250616 drawingboard@compuserve.com www.cornwall-online.co.uk/tremorvah	096 915	200mtrs PD £18.00 O D PL KT 1D 1T 1S
14	Mrs J Haddy Home Farm Minster BOSCASTLE PL35 0BN	01840 250195 jackie.haddy@btclick.com www.homefarm-boscastle.co.uk	105 906	2 kms £19.00 O D EM PL CP LSP KT 2D 1T ALL ES
15	Mrs A Jones Grange Cottage BOSSINEY Tintagel PL34 0AX	01840 770487	065 888 Mar- End Oct	200mtrs £18.00 D PL CP KT 4D[1] 1T[1] 1S 1F

Sect.	Name and Address	Tel. No. Fax. No. Web / Email	Map Reference Opening Times	Distance from Path Starting Price Facilities Accommodation
15	Mr L N Leeds Willapark Manor Hotel BOSSINEY Nr Tintagel PL34 0BA	01840 770782		100mtrs £29.50 O D EM PLCP DW 6D 2T 2S 3F ALL ES
15	Mrs P Tinney Bossinney Cottage BOSSINEY Nr Tintagel PL34 0AY	01840 770327	066 888	600 mtrs PD £17.50 O D EM PL CP LSP KT 2D 1S 1F
15	Mrs Y Clark Bosayne Guest House Atlantic Road TINTAGEL PL34 0DE	01840 770514 As Phone clark@clarky100.freeserve.co.uk www.bosayne.co.uk	890 050	30mtrs PD £17.00 O D EM PL CP LSP DW KT 3D[3] 1T[1] 3S 2F[1]
15	Mr R D Howe Pendrin House Atlantic Road TINTAGEL PL34 0DE	01840 770560 As Phone pendrin@tesco.net	056 888 Mar-Nov	400 mtrs £16.00 D EM PL CP 4D[3] 2T 1S 2F[1]
16	Mrs A. May Challock Guest House TREKNOW Tintagel PL34 0EN	01840 770273	057 867 Easter-Oct	400mtrs £19.00 D EM PL CP DW 2D 1T
16	Mrs L S Von Lintzgy Fairholme 30 Trewetha Lane PORT ISAAC PL29 3RW	01208 880397 01208 880189	001 805	200 mtrs PD £17.00 O D EM PL CP LSP DW 2D[1] 1T 2F[2]
16	Mrs M Andrews Hathaway Bed and Breakfast Roscarrock Hill PORT ISAAC PL29 3RG	01208 880416 marionandrews@talk21.com www.cornwall-online.co.uk/hathaway	Easter-Oct	30 mts £19.00 D CP DW 1D 3T[2] 1S
16	Mrs M Durston Anchorage 12 The Terrace PORT ISAAC PL29 3SG	01208 880629 As Phone the_anchorage@hotmail.com	001 809	On path PD £19.50 O D EM PL CP LSP KT 3D[1] 1T[1] 2S 1F
16	Mr & Mrs D Jennings Courtyard CafE Pendragon House New Road PORT ISAAC PL29 3SB	01208 880715 courtyardpi@btopenworld.com	998 809 Feb-Nov	100 mts £22.00 D EM PL CP KT 1D 1T ALL ES
16	Mr D Goodbourn Compass Rose 56 New Rd PORT ISAAC PL29 3SD	01208 880767 compassrose@supanet.com	808 995	300mtrs PD £17.00 O D PL CP KT 1D 1T
17	Mrs P White Seaways POLZEATH PL27 6SU	01208 862382 pauline@seaways99.freeserve.co		500mtrs PD £25.00 O D EM CP LSP KT 2D[1] 2T[1] 1S 1F
18	Mr M Martin Silvermead ROCK Nr Wadebridge PL27 6LB	01208 862425 01208 862919	936 758	300mtrs £20.00 O D EM PL CP LSP DW 3D[3] 2T[1] 2S 2F[2]
18	Roskarnon House Hote ROCK Nr Wadebridge PL27 6LD	01208 862785	Mar-Oct	100mtrs £25.00 D EM CP LSP 4D 4T 1S 1F ALL ES

Sect.	Name and Address	Tel. No. Fax. No. Web / Email	Map Reference Opening Times	Distance from Path Starting Price Facilities Accommodation
18	Mr E. Champion Estuary Views 8 Treverbyn Road PADSTOW PL28 8DW	01841 532551		1km £22.50 O D PL CP DW KT 2D 1T ALL ES
18	Mrs M R Romer 23 Barry's Lane PADSTOW PL28 8AU	01841 532178 maryrose@rhodesia.freeserve.co.uk	917 754 Apr-Oct	500mtrs £20.00 D DW 1D 1T[1]
18	Mr P A Tamblin Hemingford House 21 Grenville Road PADSTOW PL28 8EX	01841 532806 peter@ptamblin.freeserve.co.uk www.padstow-bb.co.uk	913 751	1km £24.00 O D PL CP 2D[1] 1T 1S DW By Arrang.
19	Mr & Mrs J Stock Woodlands Close TREATOR Padstow PL28 8RU	01841 533109 john@stock65.freeserve.co.uk www.cornwall-online.co.uk/woodlands-close		1km £18.00 O D PL CP LSP KT 1D[1] 1T[1] 1S
19	Mrs S Hamilton Trevone Bay Hotel TREVONE Nr Padstow PL28 8QS	01841 520243 01841 521195 hamilton@trevonebay.demon.co.uk	892 755 Easter to MidOct	400mtrs £26.00 D EM PL CP DW 6D 3T 3S 2F ALL ES
19	Mrs J Loosemore Caradon Windmill Nr Padstow PL28 8QS	01841 520120	896 752	2.4kms PD £16.00 O D CP LSP 1D 1T 1S 1F
19	Mrs S A Mills Well Parc Hotel TREVONE Nr Padstow	01841 520318 sally@wellparc-demon.co.uk		400mtrs PD £20.00 O EM PL CP LSP KT 4D[2] 1T 1S 4F[4]
20	Treyarnon Bay Hotel TREYARNON BAY PL28 8JN	01841 520235 01841 520239 www.treyarnon-bay-hotel.co.uk	Mar-Oct	100mtrs £25.00 EM PL CP LSP DW KT 4D[3] 2T[2] 4F[4]
20	Mr & Mrs A.S. Etherington The Waterbeach Hotel TREYARNON BAY Nr Padstow PL28 8JW	01841 520292 01841 521102 waterbeach@aol.com	Easter-Oct	150 mtrs £32.00 D EM CPDW 6D 2T 2S 9F ALL ES
20	Mrs S Shadbolt Trelooan Treporth PORTHCOTHAN BAY PL28 8LS	01841 521158	858 716	300mtrs £18.00 O D PL CP KT 1D 1T
20	Mrs J Cook Quoit Treburrick ST EVAL Porthcothan Bay PL27 7UR	01841 540935	858 716	1.5 km PD £16.00 O D CP LSP 2D
21	Mr M Ward Malmar Hotel TRENANCE Mawgan Porth TR8 4DA	01637 860324 as phone malmarhotel@supanet.com www.malmarhotel.com	851 679	400 mtrs £23.00 O D EM PL CP DW 4D[3] 3T[2] 2S[1] 1F[1]
21	Mr & Mrs D Cross Sea Vista Hotel MAWGAN PORTH TR8 4AL	01637 860276 crossd@supanet.com www.seavistahotel.co.uk	Mar-Oct	500mtrs £20.00 PL CP DW 5D[4] 3S[1] 1F[1]

Sect.	Name and Address	Tel. No. Fax. No. Web / Email	Map Reference Opening Times	Distance from Path Starting Price Facilities Accommodation
21	Mr P Carthew Shore-Leas MAWGAN PORTH Nr Newquay TR8 4BA	01637 860851 pcarthew@ntlworld.com	851 670	100 mtrs £15.00 O D CP 1T[1]
21	Mr & Mrs R Brake Bre - Pen Farm BRE-PEN Mawgan Porth TR8 4AL	01637 860420 jill.brake@virgin.net	849 667	300 mtrs £18.00 O D EM PL CP DW 3D[2] 1T
21	Mr C Goss Porth Beach Hotel Beach Road	01637 872447 01637 872469 enquire@porthbeach-hotel.co.uk	830 627 March-Dec	20mtrs PD £20.00 D EM PL CP LSP DW KT 8D 6T 7F ALL ES
21	Mr N Pedlar The Homestead Porthbean Road NEWQUAY TR7 3LU	01637 876918 neilpedlar@hotmail.com	830 627	20 mtrs PD £15.00 O D CP KT 1D 1T 1S
21	Mr & Mrs D Youlden Bothwicks House 3 Bothwicks Road NEWQUAY TR7 1DY	01637 851580	812 619	On Path £20.00 O PL CP 1D 1T 1F[1]
21	Mrs S R Harper Chichester Guest House 14 Bay View NEWQUAY TR7 2LR	01637 874216 As Phone sheila.harper@virgin.net http://freespace.virgin.net/sheila.harper	813 614	750mtrs £16.50 O D EM PL CP 2D 2T 2S 1F PRIV SHOWER
21	Mrs P Williams Roma Guest House 1 Atlantic Road NEWQUAY TR7 1QJ	01637 875085	803 616	500 mtr £14.00 O D EM PL CP LSP KT 4D[1] 1T 1S 1F[1]
21	Mr D Grant The Corisande Manor Hotel Riverside Avenue Pentire Newquay TR7 1PL	01637 872042 david@corisande.com www.corisande.com	On Path	£69.00 O D EM PL CP DW 8D 2T 1S ALL ES
22	Mr & Mrs D Eyles Crantock Bay Hotel WEST PENTIRE Crantock TR8 5SE	01637 830229 01637 831111 stay@crantockbayhotel.co.uk crantockbayhotel.co.uk	777 607 Feb-Nov	50mtrs £35.00 D EM PL CP LSP DW KT 8D 13T 9S 3F ALL ES
22	Mrs J Robinson St Marys West Pentire Road CRANTOCK TR8 5RZ	01637 830257 As Phone joyrobinson@compuserve.com#http://joyrobin		400 mts PD £18.00 O D EM PL CP LSP KT 2D[1] 1F[1]
22	Mr & Mrs R Boston Highfield Lodge Hotel Halwyn Road CRANTOCK Newquay TR8 5TR	01637 830744 01637 830568 info@highfieldlodge.co.uk www.highfieldlodge.co.uk		800mtrs PD £18.00 O EM CP LSP KT 7D[5] 1T 1S
23	Mr & Mrs W Woodcock Chy An Kerensa Cliff Road PERRANPORTH TR6 0DR	01872 572470 As Phone	755 543	20 mtr £17.00 O D PL CP LSP DW KT 2D[1] 2T[1] 2S[1] 3F[3]
23	Mrs M Crofts Tremore Liskey Hill Crescent PERRANPORTH TR6 0HP	01872 573537 As Phone tremore@totalise.co.uk www.tremore.co.uk	Apr-Sept	400mtrs £20.00 D PL CP LSP 3D[2] 1T[1] 1S

Sect.	Name and Address	Tel. No. Fax. No. Web / Email	Map Reference Opening Times	Distance from Path Starting Price Facilities Accommodation
23	Mr & Mrs R Honey Perranova Guest House Cliff Road PERRANPORTH TR6 0DR	01872 573440	Jan-Oct	100 mtr £18.00 D PL CP KT 1D 1T 1S 1F
23	Mrs A Snow Gull Rock 25 Tywarnhayle Road PERRANPORTH TR6 0DX	01872 573289 0870 1312570 holiday@gullrock.co.uk www.gullrock.co.uk	755 544	100 mtr £17.00 O CP DW 1D 1T ALL ES
24	Dorothy Gill-Carey Penkerris Penwinnick Road ST AGNES	01872 552262 As Phone info@penkerris.co.uk www.penkerris.co.uk		1 kmPD £17.50 O D EM PL CP LSP DW 3D[3] 3T[3] 2S 3F[3]
24	Mrs F Appleton Glen Cottage Quay Road ST AGNES TR5 0RP	01872 553546 glencott_2000@yahoo.co.uk		500 mtrs PD £15.00 O D PL CP LSP DW KT 2D 1T 1F
24	Mr & Mrs G Treleaven Driftwood Spars Hotel Trevaunance Cove ST AGNES TR5 0RT	01872 552428 01872 553701 driftwoodspars@hotmail www.driftwoodspars.com		on path PD £32.00 O D EM PL CP LSP DW KT 8D 1T 1S 5F ALL ES
25	Mrs V Parkinson Buzby View Forthvean Road PORTHTOWAN TR4 8AY	01209 891178 As Phone buzbyview@cornwall-county.com	691 473 Easter-Oct	500 mtr PD £19.00 D PL CP KT 2D 1T 1S
25	Mrs S Hardwick The Beach Hotel PORTHTOWAN TR4 8AE	01209 890228 As Phone colin@hardwick63.freeserve.co.uk www.thebeachhotel.net		On Path PD £22.50 O D EM PL CP LSP DW KT 3D 2T 1S 4F ALL ES
26	Mr & Mrs A Keast Fountain Springs Glenfeadon House PORTREATH TR16 4JU	01209 842650 As Phone	Feb to Dec	50mtrs £20.00 D EM PL CP LSP DW 2D[2] 1T 1S[1] 3F[3]
26	Mr & Mrs C J Healan Cliff House The Square PORTREATH TR16 4LB	01209 842008	656 455	On path £20.00 O D PL 1D 1T 2S ALL ES
26	Mr & Mrs P Smythe Benson's 1 The Hillside PORTREATH TR16 4LL	01209 842534 01209 843578	Easter-Oct	On path £20.00 D PL CP LSP 2D 2S ALL ES
26	Mr C Symonds Suhaili 14 Forth-an-Nance PORTREATH TR16 4NQ	01209 842110		on path PD £18.00 O D CP LSP DW KT 2D(1) 1T(1) 1F
27	Mr T Greenaway Godrevy House GWITHIAN St Ives Bay TR27 5BW	01736 755493		500 mts PD £0.00 O D PL CP LSP DW KT 5D 2T ALL ES
27	Mrs L Davies Nanterrow Farm GWITHIAN Hayle TR27 5BP	01209 712282 nanterrow@hotmail.com www.nanterrowfarm.co.uk	599 412	1.5km PD £17.00 O D PL CP LSP KT 1D 1T 1S 1F

Sect.	Name and Address	Tel. No. Fax. No. Web / Email	Map Reference Opening Times	Distance from Path Starting Price Facilities Accommodation
27	Mrs J Cooper 54 Penpol Terrace HAYLE TR27 4BQ	01736 752855	Jan-Nov	500mtrs PD £18.00 D PL CP LSP KT 1D 1T 1S
28	Mr & Mrs D O'Sullivan Hindon Hall LELANT St Ives TR26 3EN	01736 753046 As Phone hindonhall@talk21.com www.hindonhall.co.uk	543 369	on path £23.00 O D PL CP LSP 4D ALL ES
28	Mr T Park Wild Thyme Parc Owles Carbis Bay St Ives TR26 2RE	01736 795717 As Phone	Mar-Oct	150mtrs £20.00 CP 2D[2]
28	Mrs L Bowden Carlill 9 Porthminster Terrace ST IVES TR26 2DQ	01736 796738 lynne@lgpa.freeserve.co.uk www.travelcheck/hotel/1518.htm		250 mtrs £18.00 O D EM PL CP LSP DW KT 4D[3] 1T 1S 2F[1]
28	Ms L Dean-Burrows Ten Steps 11 Fish Street ST IVES TR26 1LT	01736 798222 As Phone		1.5km £20.00 O D PL CP LSP KT 1D 1T 1S 1F ALL ES
28	Mrs S Martin 6 Barnoon Terrace ST IVES TR26 1JE	01736 793172	517 407	100mtrs £16.00 O D PL 1T[1] 1S[1]
28	Mr D S Tremelling Chy-An-Creet Hotel Higher Stennack ST IVES TR26 2HA	01736 796559 As Phone walk@saint-ives.com www.saint-ives.com	507 399 Easter-Oct	1km PD £21.00 D EM PL CP LSP DW KT 4D 2T 2F ALL ES
28	Mr R Smith St Ives Backpackers ST IVES	01736 799444 As Phone st.ives@backpackers.co.uk www.backpackers.co.uk		100mtrs £8.00 O 2D 2T 11 DORMS
28	Ms K Daines Chy Lelan Bunkers Hill ST IVES TR26 1LJ	01736 797560 As Phone chylelan@dainesk.fsnet.co.uk		800 mtrs £18.00 O 4D 1T 2S 1F
28	Mrs Clifford Seagulls Guest House Godrevy Terrace ST IVES TR26 1JA	01736 797273 01736 799297 seagullsstives@aol.com www.seagullsstives.com		20 mts £20.00 O D PL CP LSP 6D[4] 1T[1] 2S[2] 1F[1]
29	Mrs N Mann Trewey Farm TREWEY Zennor TR26 3DA	01736 796936	454 384	1.5kms £20.00 O D PL CP DW 2D 1T 1S 2F
29	Mr P Whitelock The Old Chapel Backpackers Hostel ZENNOR TR26 3BY	01736 798307 zennorbackpackers@btinternet.com www.backpackers.co.uk	455 385 As Phone	500mtrs £10.00 O D EM PL CP LSP 1F 5 DORMS
29	Dr Gynn Boswednack Manor BOSWEDNACK Zennor TR26 3DD	01736 794183	443 378 Mar-Oct	1 km £18.00 D PL CP LSP KT 3D[2] 1T 1S

Sect.	Name and Address	Tel. No. Fax. No. Web / Email	Map Reference Opening Times	Distance from Path Starting Price Facilities Accommodation
29	Mr & Mrs I Hamlett Rosmorva BOSWEDNACK Zennor St Ives TR26 3DD	01736 796722	443 378	900 mtr £17.00 O D PL CP LSP 1D 1F[1]
29	Mrs Berryman Treen Farm GURNARDS HEAD Zennor TR26 3DE	01736 796932	436 377 Easter-Oct	400 mtr £18.50 D PL CP LSP DW KT 1D 1T
29	Mrs J Kell The Gurnards Head Hotel TREEN Zennor TR26 3DE	01736 796928 01736 795313 enquiries@gurnardshead.free-on www.gurnardshead.fsnet.co.uk		800 mtr £25.00 O D EM PL CP LSP DW KT 4D 1T 1F ALL ES
29	Mrs J Davey Pendeen Manor PENDEEN TR19 7ED	01736 788753 As Phone		250mtrs PD £18.00 O D PL CP LSP DW KT 5D[2] 1T 1S 1F[1]
29	Mrs P W Cass The Radjel Inn PENDEEN TR19 7DS	01736 788446 theradjelinn@aol.com	385 344	850mtrs PD £17.00 O D EM PL CP LSP KT 1D 1T 1S 1F
29	Mrs S M Russell Bojewan House PENDEEN TR19 7TR	01736 787312 01736 787242 sheila.russell@btinternet.com	393 347	1 km PD £17.00 O D EM PL CP KT 1D[1]
29	Mr & Mrs T Dymond The Old Count House BOSCASWELL DOWNS Pendeen TR19 YED	01736 788058	383 344 Easter to Oct	1.2kms £16.00 D PL CP LSP 1D 1F
30	Miss V A Bailey Field House TREWELLARD Pendeen TR19 7ST	01736 788097 As Phone fieldhousetrewellard@talk21.com www.cornwall-online.co.uk	338 377	1.5kms £18.00 O D EM PL 2D[2] 1T EM April-Sept
30	Mr R Harvey Rannick Studio HIGHER TREWELLARD Pendeen TR19 7TE	01736 787335	385 337 April-Oct	2.5 km PD £16.00 D EM PL CP LSP DW KT S/C CARAVAN SLEEPS 4
30	Boswedden House Hote CAPE CORNWALL St Just TR19 7NJ	01736 788733 As Phone relax@boswedden.org.uk www.boswedden.org.uk	359 53185	200 mts £20.00 O D PL CP LSP DW 1D 4T 2S 1F ALL ES
31	Mrs J Cargeeg Manor Farm BOTALLACK TR19 7QG	01736 788525		300 mtrs £23.00 O CP LSP 2D 1T ALL ES
31	Mrs E Lawry Llawnroc 1 Truthwall Villa St Just TR19 7QL	01736 788814		400mts PD £16.00 O D PL CP KT 3D 2T 1F
31	Mrs V Prentice The Retreat 13 Boswedden Terrace ST JUST TR19 7NF	01736 788221	364 315	800 mts £20.00 O D EM PL CP LSP KT 1T 1S
31	Mr & Mrs P Michelmore 2 Fore Street St JUST TR19 7LL	01736 787784 As Phone Dogs by Arrang.	372 313	1.5 kms £17.50 O PL 1D 1T

Sect.	Name and Address	Tel. No. Fax. No. Web / Email	Map Reference Opening Times	Distance from Path Starting Price Facilities Accommodation
31	Mrs C Collinson Bosavern House BOSAVERN St Just in Penwith Penzance TR19 7RD	01736 788301 As Phone marcol@bosavern.u-net.com www.bosavern.u-net.com	371 305	1 km PD £21.00 O D PL CP LSP DW KT 3D[3] 2T[1] 1S[1] 2F[2]
31	Mr & Mrs M Adams Homefields MAYON Sennen TR19 7AD	01736 871418 01736 871666 homefield1BandB@AOL.com www.homefieldsguesthouse.co.uk		500 mts £15.00 O D PL CP DW 3D[3] 2T[1] 1F[1]
32	Mr T Ellison Whitesands Lodge SENNEN TR19 7AR	01736 871776 As Phone info@whitesandslodge.co.uk www.whitesandslodge.co.uk	366 264	400 mts £11.00 . O D EM PL CP LSP DW KT 2D[1] 1T 1S 2F[1] 25 Dorm Beds
32	Mrs P Jones Sunnycroft SENNEN TR19 7AP	01736 871744 as phone	365 260	800mts PD £18.00 O D EM PL CP LSP DW KT 1D[1] 1T PRIV BATH
32	Mr & Mrs R Davis Sea View House The Valley PORTHCURNO TR19 6JX	01736 810638 seaview.porthcurno@tinyworld.co.uk www.seaviewhouseporthcurno.com	383 227	350mtrs PD £22.50 O D EM PL CP LSP KT 4D 1T 1S ALL ES
32	Mr & Mrs T Goss The Porthcurno Hotel The Valley PORTHCURNO TR19 6JX	01736 810119 01736 810711 porthcurnohotel@netscapeonline.co.uk www.porthcurnohotel.co.uk		250 mtrs £22.00 O D EM PL CP LSP DW KT 5D[3] 6T[4] 1F[1]
32	Mrs R Thomas Grey Gables PORTHCURNO TR19 6JT	01736 810421 As Phone		100mtrs PD £19.50 O D EM PL CP LSP KT 3D[3] 2T[1]
32	Mrs J Green Mariners Lodge Hotel PORTHCURNO St Levan Penzance TR19 6JU	01736 810236 01736 810840 themarinerslodge@aol.com www.marinerslodgehotel.co.uk		50mtrs PD £22.00 O D EM PL CP LSP DW KT 3D[2] 1T[1] 2S 1F[1]
33	Mrs E Jilbert Penver Houses Farm TREEN Nr Porthcurno TR19 6LG	01736 810778 As Phone	394 231 April to Oct	750mtrs £16.50 D PL CP LSP DW KT 1D 1T
33	Mrs P Hall Treen Farmhouse TREEN Nr Porthcurno TR19 6LF	01736 810253 paulachrishall@treenfarm.fsnet.co.uk	394 231	750mtrs £15.00 O D PL CP LSP DW KT 1D[1] 1T 1S
33	Mrs S White Cove Cottage ST LOY St Buryan Penzance TR19 6DH	01736 810010	424 232	on path £30.00 O D EM CP 1D[1]
33	Mrs D Hardy Pridden ST BURYAN Penzance TR19 6EA	01736 810801 01736 810054 doana.hardy@priddenfarm.co.uk www.priddenfarm.co.uk	415 265	8 kms PD £17.00 O D EM PL CP LSP KT 1D[1] 1T 1F

Sect.	Name and Address	Tel. No. Fax. No. Web / Email	Map Reference Opening Times	Distance from Path Starting Price Facilities Accommodation
33	Mr & Mrs Rowley Lamorna Guest House LAMORNA Nr Penzance TR19 6XL	01736 731367 As Phone lamornalodge@eurobell.co.uk www.lamornalodge.eurobell.co.uk		500mtrs £24.00 O D EM PL CP KT 4D[2] 2F[2]
33	Mrs P Richardson Pipers Cottage LAMORNA Penzance TR19 6BQ	01736 810881 As Phone patrickatpipers@aol.com		1km PD £20.00 O D PL CP LSP 1D[1] 1T[1]
34	Mr M Male Lowenna Raginnis Hill MOUSEHOLE TR19 6SL	01736 731077 mm4lowenna@aol.com	468 262	On path £19.50 O D PL 1F(1)
34	Mrs M Maiden 1 Paul Lane MOUSEHOLE Penzance TR19 6TR	01736 731406 As Phone	Mar-Mid Dec	250 mts £17.50 D PL 1D 2T
34	Mrs A J Waters Sunrise Commercial Road MOUSEHOLE TR19 6QG	01736 731457		200mtrs £15.00 O D PL DW 2D 1S
34	Mrs Buswell Penalva Alexandra Road PENZANCE TR18 4LZ	01736 369060 As Phone	298 468	500mts PD £16.00 O D KT 2D[2] 1T[1] 1S 1F[1]
34	Mr & Mrs J Maddern The Tarbert Hotel & Restaurant Clarence Street PENZANCE TR18 2NU	01736 363758 01736 331336 reception@tarbert-hotel.co.uk www.tarbert-hotel.co.uk	819 325 Feb-Nov	1 km £32.00 D EM PL CP 7D 2T 2S 1F ALL ES
34	Mr & Mrs J Leggatt Cornerways 5 Leskinnick Street PENZANCE TR18 2HA	01736 364645 As Phone enquires@cornerways-penzance.co.uk www.penzance.co.uk/cornerways	Mar-Jan	800mtrs £19.00 D EM PL CP DW 1D 1T 1S 1F ALL ES
34	Mr & Mrs R Stacey Lynwood Guest House 41 Morrab Road PENZANCE TR18 4EX	01736 365871 As Phone lynwoodpz@aol.com www.penzance.co.uk/lynwood-guesthouse		200 mtrs £13.50 O D PL DW KT 2D[1] 2T[1] 2S[2] 2F[2]
34	Mr P R Taylor Penzance Backpackers Blue Dolphin PENZANCE TR18 4LZ	01736 363836 01736 363844 pzbackpack@ndirect.co.uk www.penzancebackpackers.ndirect.co.uk	467 299	400 mtr £10.00 O D 2D 4DORMS[3]
34	Mr & Mrs M Russell Chy-an-Mor 15 Regeant Terrace PENZANCE TR18	01736 363441 As Phone mikeandjan@chyanmor.co.uk www.chyanmor.co.uk	475 298 Feb-Nov	100 mts £25.00 D CP LSP 4D 3T 1S 2F ALL ES
34	Mr & Mrs P Bashford Kimberley House 10 Morab Road PENZANCE TR18 4EY	01736 362727 As Phone kimberley.house@faxvia.net	Feb-Dec	£15.00 PL CP 2D[2] 3T[1] 1S 2F

Sect.	Name and Address	Tel. No. Fax. No. Web / Email	Map Reference Opening Times	Distance from Path Starting Price Facilities Accommodation
34	Mr J Smalley Chy Bowjy CHY SAUSTER Penzance TR20 8XA	01736 368815 01736 363440 jj@jj-associates.co.uk www.chy-bowjy.co.uk	350 470	4.5 kms PD £18.00 O D EM PL CP LSP DW KT 1D
36	Mr & Mrs P Leeper Quilkyns 1 St Pirans way Perranuthnoe Penzance TR20 9NJ	01736 719141 paul@quilkyns.co.uk www.quilkyns.co.uk	Feb-Nov	150mtrs £17.00 D PL KT 2T
36	Mrs M Foy Mzima Penlee Close PRAA SANDS TR20 9SR	01736 763856	588 281	800mtrs PD £17.00 O D PL CP KT 1T 1F
36	Mrs G Garraghan Bodeeve PRAA SANDS Penzance TR20 9TQ	01736 763246 gillieg75541410@aol.com		On path £13.00 O D PL CP LSP 2T 2S
36	Mr & Mrs K Allen Gwynoon Guest House Chy-An-Dour Road PRAA SANDS TR20 9SY	01736 763508 keithrallen@hotmail.com www.theaa/hotels/106540.html		50 mtrs £25.00 O D PL CP LSP KT 2D 2T 2S 2F ALL ES
37	Mr F P Hallam Seefar Peverell Terrace PORTHLEVEN TR13 9DZ	01326 573778 seefar@talk21.com www.cornwall-online.co.uk	March to Nov	200mtrs £16.00 D PL CP LSP DW KT 2D[1] 1T[1] 1S
37	Miss S Kelynack & Mr R Perdins An Mordros Hotel Peverell Terrace PORTHLEVEN TR13 9DZ	01326 562236 As Phone info@anmordroshotel.com www.anmordrashotel.com		On Path £18.50 O D EM PL KT 4D[2] 1T[1] 1S 2F[1]
37	Mr & Mrs P Ingham Anchor Cottage Cliff Road PORTHLEVEN TR13 9EZ	01326 574391	629 254	On Path £17.50 O D KT 1D[1] 1T
37	Ms S Flanagan The Copper Kettle Tea Rooms 33 Fore Street PORTHLEVEN TR13 9HQ	01326 565660 01326 564772		100mtrs £21.00 O D EM PL CP 2D[1] 1T 1S 1F
37	Mrs C Budd Sandpipers Loe Bar Road PORTHLEVEN TR13 9EL	01326 564542	April to Sept	On path £18.00 D PL CP KT 1D 1T 1S
38	Mr & Mrs T Tucker Lyndale Guest House 4 Greenbank Meneage Road HELSTON TR13 8JA	01326 561082 01326 565813 enquiries@lyndale1.freeserve.co.uk www.lyndale1.freeserve.co.uk		4.5 kms PD £17.00 O D EM PL CP LSP DW KT 3D[2] 2T[1] 2S[1] 1F
38	Mrs J Tyler-Street Trenance Farmhouse D PL CP LSP DW MULLION TR12 7HB	01326 240639 As Phone trenancefarm@cwcom.net www.trenancefarmholidays.co.uk	673 185 Apr-Sept	500mtrs £21.00 3D 1T ALL ES
38	Mr & Mrs P Dann Ridgeback Lodge Hotel & Restaurant Nansmellion Road MULLION TR12 7DH	01326 241300 As Phone Ridgebacklodge@compuserve.com www.business.thisiscornwall.co.uk/ridgeback	677 185	100mtrs £19.50 O D EM LSP DW KT 3D[1] 1T[1] 1S 2F[2]

Sect.	Name and Address	Tel. No. Fax. No. Web / Email	Map Reference Opening Times	Distance from Path Starting Price Facilities Accommodation
38	Mr M Bolton Criggan Mill MULLION COVE TR12 7EU	01326 240496 0870 1640549 info@crigganmill.co.uk www.crigganmill.co.uk	667 180	200 mtrs £17.00 O D EM PL CP KT 10D 10T 10S 10F ALL ES
39	Mrs I Sowden The Most Southerly House LIZARD POINT TR12 7NU	01326 290300 As Phone	702 115	on path £18.00 O D PL CP LSP KT 2D[1]
39	Mr & Mrs P Brookes Parc Brawse House Penmenner Road. THE LIZARD TR12 7NR	01326 290466 01326 290894 lindabrookes@cwcom.net www.cornwall-online.co.uk/parcbraw	701 121	300mtrs PD £17.00 O D EM PL CP LSP DW KT 4D[3] 2T[1] 1F[1]
39	Mr D Macbride Kynance Bay House Penmenner Road THE LIZARD TR12 7NR	01326 290498 01326 291079 david.macbride@btinternet.com	700 120	400mtrs PD £28.00 O D PL CP LSP KT 2D[2] 2T[1] 1S
39	Mrs P James Carmelin Pentreath Lane THE LIZARD TR12 7NY	01326 290677 pjcarmelin@aol.com	699 126	500 mtrs PD £20.00 O D PL CP LSP DW KT 1D(1)
39	Mrs K Thirlaway Green Cottage THE LIZARD TR12 7NZ	01326 290099		750mtrs £16.00 O D CP LSP DW 2D
39	Mrs G Rowe Trethvas Farmhouse THE LIZARD Helston TR12 7AR	01326 290720 As phone	709 136 Mar-Oct	300mtrs £20.00 D PL CP LSP 1D 1T 1F ALL ES
40	Mrs R Whitaker Wych Elm PONSONGATH Coverack TR12 6SQ	01326 280576	756 179	1 km PD £18.00 O D EM PL CP LSP DW KT 1T ES
40	Mrs T Carey Tamarisk Cottage COVERACK TR12 6TG	01326 280638	Easter-Oct	On path £18.00 D PL CP LSP DW 1D 1T 1S
40	Mr P Cheze-Brown The Croft Lowland Lane COVERACK TR12 6TF	01326 280387 As Phone www.cornwall-online.co.uk/the.croft	783 187	On Path £18.00 O D EM PL CP LSP DW 3T[2]
40	Mrs M E Daw Bakery Cottage Polcoverack Lane COVERACK TR12 6TD	01326 280474		On path £18.00 O D EM PL CP LSP DW 1D 1F
40	Mrs W Watters Boak House COVERACK TR12 6SA	01326 280608	Mar-Nov	50mts PD £18.50 D CP DW KT 1D 1T 1S 2F
40	Ms T Hone Trevenwitt Farm Coverack Helston TR12 6SL	01326 290873 tracyhone@onetel.net.uk	740 171 Apr-Oct	400mtrs £18.50 D EM PL CP LSP DW KT 1D 1S 1 STUDIO
41	Mrs R Kelly Trevinock PORTHOUSTOCK St Keverne TR12 6QP	01326 280498 www.trevinock_guesthouse_thelizard.co.uk	802 216 Mar-Oct	1.5kms PD £19.00 D EM PL CP LSP KT 2D[1] 2S

Sect.	Name and Address	Tel. No. Fax. No. Web / Email	Map Reference Opening Times	Distance from Path Starting Price Facilities Accommodation
41	Ms A Strickland Gallen-Treath Guest House PORTHALLOW TR12 6PL	01326 280400 gallentreath@btclick.com www.gallen-treath.com	797 232	150mtrs PD £22.00 O D EM PL CP LSP DW KT 2D 1T 1S 1F ALL ES evening meal winter only
41	Mrs P Hawthorne Valley View House Porthallow Cove St Keverne TR12 6PN	01326 280370 As Phone hawthorne@valleyviewhouse.freeserve.co.uk www.smoothhound.co.uk/hotels/valleyvi.html	796 232	20 mtrs pd £19.00 O D EM PL CP LSP KT 2D[1] 1T
41	Mrs L Jenkin Landrivick Farm MANACCAN 1D[1] 1T 1S Helston TR12 6HX	01326 231686		1.6 kms PD £21.00 O D EM PL CP LSP
41	Mrs P Julian Landrivick Farm LANDRIVICK Manaccan TR12 6HX	01326 231249		1.6kms PD £21.00 O D EM PL CP LSP 1D 1T 1S 1F ALL ES
41	Mrs J Jane Higher Roscadden Vicarage Lane MANACCAN Helston TR12 6JH	01326 231423	767 252	On Path £19.50 O D CP DW 2D 1T PRIV FACIL
41	Mrs B H Taylor Holmes Lean Farmhouse St Martin Helston TR12 6BZ	01326 231022 holmes@leanfarmhouse.fsnet.co.uk www.cornwall-online.co.uk/leanfarm	759 255 Feb_Nov	2kms PD £35.00 D EM PL CP LSP KT 2D[1]
41	Mrs J Davies Pengwedhen HELFORD TR12 6JZ	01326 231481 nandjdavies@hotmail.com	755 265 Easter-Oct	500 mtrs £22.00 D CP LSP KT 1D 1T 1S
41	Mrs P Royall POINT Helford Nr Helston TR12 6JY	01326 231666 info@helfordcottages.co.uk www.helfordcottages.co.uk	758 262	on path £25.00 O D CP 1T[1]
42	Mr & Mrs T Cooke Hideaway Rosevear MAWGAN TR12 6AZ	01326 221392	697 245	2kms PD £20.00 D CP LSP 2D 1T ALL ES
42	Mrs C Spike Carwinion Vean Grove Hill MAWNAN SMITH TR11 5ER	01326 250513		1.6 km £20.00 O D PL CP LSP DW 3D[1] 2T[1] 1F
42	Mrs S P Annan Chynoweth Carwinion Lane MAWNAN SMITH TR11 5JB	01326 250534 01326 251010 sannan@lineone.net	781 283	800 mtrs PD £20.00 O D PL CP KT 2T[1] 1F
42	Mrs Dugdale Trevean MAWNAN SMITH Nr Falmouth TR11 5JD	01326 250100 01326 250543 nicola.dugdale@btclick.com www.cornwalltouristboard.co.uk	781 283	800 mtrs PD £20.00 O D PL CP DW KT 1D 1T ALL ES
42	Mrs C Lake Gold Martin Car Lidnak Road MAWNAN SMITH Falmouth TR11 5HA	01326 250666 gold_martin@hotmail.com		1.6kms PD £20.00 O D EM PL CP LSP DW KT 1D 1T OWN FACIL

Sect.	Name and Address	Tel. No. Fax. No. Web / Email	Map Reference Opening Times	Distance from Path Starting Price Facilities Accommodation
42	Mr & Mrs G Cummins Grove Hotel Grove Place FALMOUTH TR11 4AU	01326 319577 As Phone guests@grovehotel.freeserve.co.uk grovehotel.freeserve.co.uk		On path £24.00 O D EM PL CP DW 4D 4T 4S 3F ALL ES
42	Mr & Mrs I Carruthers The Clearwater 59 Melvill Road FALMOUTH TR11 4DF	01326 311344 clearwater@lineone.net www.clearwaterhotel.co.uk	Feb-Dec	500mtrs £19.00 D PL CP LSP 5D[4] 2T 1S 2F[1]
42	Mr & Mrs J Appleyard Rosemary Hotel 22 Gyllyngvase Terrace FALMOUTH TR11 4DL	01326 314669 As Phone rosemaryhotel@lineone.net www.cornwall-online.co.uk/rosemary	810 318 Feb-Nov	50mtrs £24.00 EM PL CP 6D 1T 1S 2F ALL ES
42	Mr & Mrs R Picken The Lerryn Hotel De Pass Road FALMOUTH TR11 4BJ	01326 312489 thelerrynhotel@tesco.net www.thelerrynhotel.co.uk		20mtrs £28.00 O EM PL CP LSP DW KT 8D 8T 3S 1F ALL ES
42	Mr & Mrs D Burd Esmond House Emslie Road Falmouth	01326 313214		100mts £19.00 O 3D[2] 2T[2] 1S
42	Mr & Mrs D Bowerman Arwenack Hotel 27 Arwenack Street Falmouth TR11 3JE	01326 311185 arwenack@hotmail.com www.falmouth-hotels.co.uk		£22.00 O D PL CP LSP DW
43	Mrs K Moseley Braganza Grove Hill ST MAWES TR2 5BJ	01326 270281 as phone braganzakf@aolcom	Closed Nov 3D[3] 1S	300 mtrs £27.00 D PL CP LSP DW KT
44	Mrs J Milnes Bohurrow Farmhouse Bohortha ST ANTHONY IN ROSELAND Porthscatho TR2 5EY	01872 580966		800 mts £18.00 O D CP LSP DW 1D[1] 1T 1S
44	Mr & Mrs R Hart Hillside House 8 The Square PORTSCATHO TR2 5HW	01872 580526	353 877	30 mtrs PD £20.00 O D PL DW KT 2D 1T
44	Mrs W A Penhaligon Trewithian Farm PORTSCATHO Truro TR2 5EJ	01872 580293 penhaligon@trewithian.freeserve.co.uk		800mts £15.00 O D PL CP LSP DW KT 2D 1S 1F SHARED BATH
44	Mr & Mrs A Sievwright The Royal Standard Inn 5 The Square GERRANS Nr Truro TR2 5EB	01872 580271 As Phone		800 mts £17.00 O EM CP LSP 1D 1S
44	Mrs A Palmer Trenestrall RUAN HIGH LANES Portscatho TR2 5LX	01872 501259	Feb-Nov	2.5km PD £18.00 D EM PL CP DW 1D 1T 1F ALL ES
45	Mr & Mrs K Righton Broom Parc CAMELS Truro TR2 5PJ	01872 501803 01872 501109 www.broomparc.freeserve.co.uk	930 390	On Path PD £25.00 O D EM PL CP LSP DW KT 1D 2T[2]

Sect.	Name and Address	Tel. No. Fax. No. Web / Email	Map Reference Opening Times	Distance from Path Starting Price Facilities Accommodation
45	Mr & Mrs M Rawling Treverbyn House Pendower Road VERYAN Truro TR2 5QL	01872 501201 mike-ali@treverbyn.fsbusiness.co.uk www.cornwall-online.co.uk/treverbyn		2 kms PD £22.50 O D PL CP 1D 1T 1S ALL ES
45	Mrs P Ollerearnshaw Fuglers The Gow PORTLOE TR2 5RE	01872 501482	940 395	On Path £20.00 O PL DW KT 1T 1F[1]
47	Mr & Mrs A Freeman Llawnroc Inn GORRAN HAVEN St Austell PL26 6NU	01726 843461 01726 844056 llawnroc@mevagissey.com www.llawnroc.mevagissey.com		100 mts £20.00 O D EM PL CP LSP DW 3D 3T 2F ALL ES
47	Ms G Mott Piggy Pantry The Willows GORRAN HAVEN	01726 843545 piggyspantry@hotmail.com www.piggyspantry.co.uk		200 mtrs £20.00 O D PL CP LSP DW 1D 1T
47	Mr & Mrs R J Smith 'Homestead' 34 Chute Lane GORRAN HAVEN PL26 6NU	01726 842567		On Path £25.00 O CP 1D 1T ALL ES
47	Miss S Chubb The Granary Boswinger GORRAN St Austell PL26 6LL	01726 844381 holidays@thegranaryboswinger.freeserve.co.uk www.cornwallbandb.co.uk	991 410	500mts PD £22.00 O D EM PL CP 2D 1T 1S
47	Mrs J O Lucas Mount Pleasant Farm GORRAN HIGH LANES Gorran Haven PL26 6LR	01726 843918 mpfarm@vispa.com 2D[1] 1T 1S www.vegetarian-cornwall.co.uk	987 432 April-Oct	2kms PD £17.00 D EM PL CP LSP KT
48	Ms J Connolly Mandalay Hotel School Hill MEVAGISSEY PL26 6TQ	01726 842435 as phone joe@mandalayhotel.freeserve.co.uk		300mtrs PD £18.00 O D PL CP LSP DW KT 6D 1T 2F ALL ES
48	Mr & Mrs A Parsloe Tregorran Guest House Cliff Street MEVAGISSEY PL26 6QW	01726 842319 patricia@parsloep.freeserve.co.uk www.tregorran.homestead.com/home.html	Jan-Nov	100mtrs PD £20.00 O D PL LSP DW KT 4D 1T 1F ALL ES KT by arrangement
48	Mrs C J Avent Wild Air Polkirt Hill MEVAGISSEY PL26 6UX	01726 843302		On path PD £22.50 O D PL CP KT 3D[2]
48	Mrs W Bennett Mount Pleasant House Cross Park Terrace Mevagissey PL26 6TA	01726 843777 wenbennett@hotmail.com		700mtrs PD £16.00 O D PL CP LSP KT 1D 1T 1S
49	Mr & Mrs P Jenkin Treburthick Higher Porthpean St Austell PL26 7AY	01726 73689 pamattreburthick@hotmail.com	029 505	300mtrs PD £20.00 O D CP LSP DW KT 2D[2] 1T 1S
49	Mr & Mrs R Callis Ardenconnel 179 Charlestown Road CHARLESTOWN PL25 3NN	01726 75469 ardenconnel@hotmail.com		400mtrs £21.00 O D PL CP KT 2D[1] 2T[1] 3S[1] 2F[1]

Sect.	Name and Address	Tel. No. Fax. No. Web / Email	Map Reference Opening Times	Distance from Path Starting Price Facilities Accommodation
49	Miss S Mathieson Coastguard House 11 Coastguard Terrace ST AUSTELL PL25 3NJ	01726 72828 01726 73954	039 515	50 mtrs £15.00 O D PL CP LSP DW KT 1D 1T
49	Mrs D A Best Broad Meadow House Quay Road ST AUSTELL PL25 3NX	01726 76636 As Phone Best.Tribe@btopenworld.com	039 517	150mtrs PD £22.50 O D PL CP LSP KT 1D[1]
50	The Cliff Head Hotel Sea Road O EM PL CP LSP CARLYON BAY PL25 3RB	01726 812345 01726 815511 cliffheadhotel@btconnect.com www.cornishriviera.uk/cliffhead	53520	on path £45.00 30D 15T 15S 4F ALL ES
50	Mrs M.H Ball Polbrean House Woodland Ave, Tywardreath PAR PL24 2PL	01726 812530 www.smoothhound.co.uk		2 kms £20.00 O D PL CP LSP KT 2D 1S
50	Mrs B D Burgess 55 Polmear Road PAR PL24 2AW	01726 812967	086 535	500mtrs £15.00 O D CP LSP 1T 2S
51	Mr & Mrs R M Bullock Trevanion Guest House 70 Lostwithiel Street FOWEY PL23 1BQ	01726 832602 As Phone trefoy@globalnet.co.uk www.users.globalnet.co.uk/~trefoy/fowey.htm	124 518 March to Nov	800 mtr £22.50 D CP 2D[1] 1T[1] 1F[1]
51	The Ship Inn Trafalgar Square FOWEY PL23 1AZ	01726 832230 As Phone	125 515	On path £20.00 O EM 2D 2T 2F[1]
51	Mr & Mrs D Turner Topsides Esplanade FOWEY PL23 1HZ	01726 833715	123 515	50mtrs £16.00 O D PL DW 2D 1S
51	Mrs C Eardley St Keverne 4 Daglands Road FOWEY PL23 1JL	01726 833164 carol@stkeverne1.fsnet.co.uk www.fowey.com/stkeverne.htm	124 518 Feb-Nov	500mtrs £22.00 D PL KT 2D ALL ES
52	Mr & Mrs Rogers Quayside House POLRUAN PL13	01726 870377		on path PD £30.00 O D PL LSP KT 3D[3] 1T
52	Mrs P Moore Chyavallon Landaviddy Lane POLPERRO PL13 2RT	01503 272788 as phone www.polperro.org		350mtrs £19.00 O D PL CP DW 2D 1T ALL ES
52	Mrs P Wilcox The Watchers The Warren POLPERRO PL13 2RD	01503 272296 as phone www.polperro.org		On Path PD £19.00 O D EM DW KT 2D 1T ALL ES DW by Arrang.
52	Mr & Mrs P C Warren Schooner Guest House 1 Trelawney Terrace West Looe PL13 2AG	01503 262670 As Phone enquiries@schoonerpoint.co.uk www.schoonerpoint.co.uk	252 537	150mtrs PD £14.00 O D PL CP DW KT 4D[2] 1T[1] 2S 1F[1]

Sect.	Name and Address	Tel. No. Fax. No. Web / Email	Map Reference Opening Times	Distance from Path Starting Price Facilities Accommodation
53	Mr & Mrs C Eveleigh Grasmere St Martins Road EAST LOOE PL13 1LP	01503 262556	254 544	400mtrs £16.00 O D EM PL CP 3D[1] 1T[1] 1F
53	Mr E Mawby Marwinthy Guest House East Cliff EAST LOOE PL13 1DE	01503 264382 eddiemawby@lineone.net www.marwinthy.co.uk	256 533 March-Oct	On Path £17.00 D DW 3D[2] 1T 1F
53	Mr & Mrs J Jenkin Sea Breeze Lower Chapel Street EAST LOOE PL13 1AT	01503 263131 As Phone johnjenkin@sbgh.freeserve.co.uk www.cornwallexplore.co.uk/seabreeze	256 351	100mtrs £16.00 O D PL DW 4D[3] 1T 1S
54	Mrs P Rowlandson Blue Haven Hotel Looe Hill SEATON PL11 3JQ	01503 250310 bluehaven@btinternet.com www.smoothhound.co.uk/hotels/bluehave.html		300mtrs £20.00 O D.EM PL CP DW KT 3D[3] 1T[1] 1S 1F[1] EM PL DW by arrange.
54	Mr D Maynard The Inn On The Shore Seafront DOWNDERRY PL11 3JY	01503 250210 01503 250660	314 539	800 mts O EM PL CP LSP 2D 2T 1S ALL ES
54	Mrs A J Harvey The Bungalow Cliff Road PORTWRINKLE PL11 3BY	01503 230334	355 541 March to Oct	On Path £15.00 D PL CP 1D 1T
54	Mrs D Hughes B & B by the C 39 Whitsand Bay View PORTWRINKLE PL11 3DB	01503 230947 01503 230946 darrylhughes@hotmail.com www.bandbbythec.com		100 yds £20.00 O D CP LSP 2D[2] 1T 1S
54	Mrs K Ridpath Fir Cottage LOWER TREGANTLE Crafthole PL11 3AL	01752 822626 As Phone		200 mtrs PD £17.50 O D EM PL CP LSP DW KT 1T 3F
55	Mr C Collins Avon House Garrett Street CAWSAND PL10 1PB	01752 822229 collins@cawsand.f9.co.uk	435 502	300 mtr £15.00 O D PL CP LSP DW KT 2D[1] 2S
55	Mrs D Goodwright Clarendon Garrett Street CAWSAND PL10 1PD	01752 823460	435 502	On Path £17.00 O D PL 1D 1T 1S
55	Mr D Riggs The Halfway House Inn Fore Street KINGSAND PL10 1NA	01752 822279 01752 823146 www.connexions.co.uk/halfway/		500mtrs £28.50 O D EM PL CP LSP DW 3D 1S 1T 1F ALL ES
56	Mrs J Moulds Berkeley's of St James 4 St James Place East PLYMOUTH PL1 3AS	01752 221654 As Phone www.smoothhound.co.uk/hotels/berkely2.html		on path £20.00 O D CP 3D 1T 1S 1F ALL ES
56	Mrs M Emery Acorns & Lawns Guest House 171 Citadel Road PLYMOUTH PL1 2HY	01752 229474 As Phone		100mtrs £18.00 O D PL 5D[5] 3T[2] 1S 1F[1]

Sect.	Name and Address	Tel. No. Fax. No. Web / Email	Map Reference Opening Times	Distance from Path Starting Price Facilities Accommodation
58	Miss F Kempt West Hanover Lodge HOLBETON PL8 1JN	01752 830582	617 502 April1-Sept30	4.5kms £17.00 D CP 1D(1)
58	Miss L Price Mildmay Colours Inn HOLBETON Plymouth PL8 1NA	01752 830248 01752 830432 www.mildmay-colours.co.uk		2 kms £30.00 O D EM PL CP DW 3D 3T 2F ALL ES
58	Mrs L Wallis Windlestraw Penquit ERMINGTON PL21 OLU	01752 896237 As Phone wallispenquit@beeb.net Will PD Yealm Erme Avon	646 544	2kms PD £21.00 O D PL CP LSP KT 1T 1S
58	Mrs P J Brunskill Cliff Path RINGMORE Nr Kingsbridge TQ7 4HR	01548 810654	651 456	800 mtrs £16.00 O D PL CP 1T
58	Mrs I Dodds Ayrmer House RINGMORE Nr Kingsbridge	01548 810391		1.2kms £25.00 O D CP LSP 2D[2] 1T
58	Mr M Walker Blackadon Barns Nr Ivybridge PL22 0HB	01752 897034 mwalkone@aol.com www.blackadonbarns.co.uk	665 577	12kms PD £20.00 O D EM PL CP LSP DW KT 5D[4] 6T Will Pick Up/Drop
58	Mrs C Walsh Folly Foot CHALLABOROUGH Bigbury-On-Sea TQ7 4JB	01548 810036 carolwalsh@freenet.co.uk www.bigburyonsea.co.uk	652 447 Mar-Oct	50 mtrs PD £20.00 D PL CP LSP KT 2D[2] 1S 1F
58	Mr & Mrs M A Farrell Warren Cottage Marine Drive BIGBURY-ON-SEA TQ7 4AS	01548 810210 As Phone	650 444	On path PD £18.00 O D EM PL CP LSP KT 1T 1S
58	Mrs J Hughes Warren Point Marine Drive BIGBURY-ON-SEA TQ7 4AS	01548 810616	649 445 Mar-Oct	On Path £24.00 PL CP LSP KT 2D 2T 1S 1F 3 rooms in total
58	Mrs R van der Heiden Avonlea 3 Folly Hill BIGBURY ON SEA TQ7 4AR	01548 810926 01548 810153 hansvheiden@eurobell.co.uk		20mts PD £25.00 O D CP 2D[1] 1T 1S
59	Mr & Mrs J Litchfield Beacon Point Hotel THURLESTONE SANDS TQ7 3JY	01548 561207	676 411 Jan-Oct	10mtrs £23.00 D EM PL CP DW 2D[2] 1T[1] 3F[1]
59	Mr & Mrs C Barclay The Sand Pebbles Hotel Grand View Road HOPE COVE Kingsbridge TQ7 3HF	01548 561673	Apr-Oct	250 mtrs £30.00 D EM PL CP DW 8D 3T 1F ALL ES
60	Mr & Mrs R Petty-Brown Rocarno Grenville Road SALCOMBE TQ8 8BJ	01548 842732 rocarno@c.s.com	736 389	500mtrs £19.50 O D PL DW 1D 1T ALL ES

Sect.	Name and Address	Tel. No. Fax. No. Web / Email	Map Reference Opening Times	Distance from Path Starting Price Facilities Accommodation
60	Mr & Mrs A J Bouttle Torre View Hotel Devon Road SALCOMBE TQ8 8AJ	01548 842633 as phone bouttle@torreview.eurobell.co.uk www.SmoothHound.co.uk/hotes/torreview.html	735 385 Mar-Oct	500 mtrs £28.50 D EM PL 5D[4] 2T[2] 1S 1F[1]
60	Mrs J Dean Furzehill Moult Road SALCOMBE TQ8 8LG	01548 843319 as phone	Apr-Oct	500mtrs £21.00 D PL CP LSP 1D 1T
60	Mrs P Snelson Lyndhurst Hotel Bonaventure Road SALCOMBE TQ8 8BG	01548 842481 as phone lyndhursthotel@salcombe_online.co.uk www.salcombeinformatione.co.uk/lyndhurst.html	Mar-Oct	400 mtrs £25.00 D PL CP 3D 3T 1S 1F ALL ES
60	Mr & Mrs R Vaughan Trennels Hotel Herbert Road SALCOMBE TQ8 8HR	01548 842500 trennels_hotel@btinternet.com www.btinternet.com/~r.vaughan/trennels-hotel	Mar-Oct	400mtrs £23.00 CP KT 5D ALL ES
60	Mrs E M Weymouth Motherhill Farm Main Road SALCOMBE TQ8 8NB	01548 842552 As Phone djw@dweymouth.fsnet.co.uk	730 393 Easter-Oct	1.5 kms £18.00 D CP LSP 1D 1T 1S
60	Ms A Woodhatch Rainbow's End 11 Platt Close SALCOMBE TQ8 8NZ	01548 843654 thewoodhatches@hotmail.com		800mtrs PD £18.00 O D CP DW 1D[1] 1T[1]
61	Mr & Mrs N Alen Ashleigh House Ashleigh Road KINGSBRIDGE TQ7 1HB	01548 852893 as phone reception@ashleigh-house.co.uk www.ashleigh-house.co.uk	731 439	6 kms PD £21.00 O D EM PL CP LSP DW 5D 1T 2F ALL ES
61	Mr & Mrs M Mitchelmore Sunnyside EAST PRAWLE TQ7 2BY	01548 511387 As Phone	Jan-Nov	1.6kms £17.00 D CP LSP 1D 1T 2S
61	Mrs J Foss Down Farm START POINT Kingsbridge	01548 511234 As Phone	806 377 1Jan-30Nov	600mtrs £18.00 D PL CP LSP 1D[1] 1T
61	Mrs P Wolstenholme Widget North Hallsands Kingsbridge TQ7 2EX	01548 511110	819388	on path £20.00 O D PL CP LSP KT 2D[1] 1T
61	Mr & Mrs B Smith Waterside TORCROSS Kingsbridge TQ7 2TQ	01548 580280 As Phone waterside.house@virgin.net www.watersidehouse.com	824 421	On path £19.00 O PL CP 3D[3] 1T[1] 2S 1F[1]
61	Mr & Mrs R Rose-Price Startlea House TORCROSS Kingsbridge TQ7 2TQ	01548 580724 Rose-Price@startlea.co.uk www.startlea.co.uk	823 422	5 mts £25.00 O D CP 1D 1T ALL ES
61	Ms C Ley Linger Lodge TORCROSS TQ7 2TJ	01548 580599	421 822	300mts £22.50 O D CP 2D ALL ES

Sect.	Name and Address	Tel. No. Fax. No. Web / Email	Map Reference Opening Times	Distance from Path Starting Price Facilities Accommodation
62	Mrs V A Mercer Old Walls SLAPTON Nr Kingsbridge TQ7 2QN	01548 580516	822 449	1 km PD £18.00 O D PL DW KT 2D[1] 1T
62	Mrs J Makepeace Skerries STRETE Nr Dartmouth TQ6 0RH	01803 770775 01803 770950 jamskerries@rya-online.net		500mtrs £22.50 O D PL CP KT 2D 1T ALL ES
62	Mr & Mrs C Tonkin Fairholmes Bay View Estate STOKE FLEMING Dartmouth TQ6 0QX	01803 770356 As Phone fairholme@tonkin.fslife.co.uk	861 481	500mtrs PD £20.00 O D CP LSP KT 3D[3]
62	Miss S Leach Sunny Banks Guest House 1 Vicarage Hill sue@sunnybanks.com DARTMOUTH TQ6 9EW	01803 832766 As Phone www.sunnybanks.com	Feb-Dec	1 km £21.00 EM PL CP DW 5D[4] 2T[2] 1S 2F[2]
62	Mrs G Platts The Anchorage 73 Victoria Road DARTMOUTH TQ6 9RX	01803 835046		1.5km £18.00 O D 2D 1T
62	Mrs A Cardwell The Maitland 28 Victoria Road DARTMOUTH TQ6 9SA	01803 835854	875 513	2.4 kms £16.00 O D CP 2D[2] 1T 1S
63	Mr & Mrs L Congdon Carlton House Higher Street KINGSWEAR TQ6 0AG	01803 752244		100 mtrs £15.00 O D PL CP LSP DW 2D 1T 1S 2F
63	Mr & Mrs P Hancock Melville Hotel 45 New Road BRIXHAM TQ5 8NL	01803 852033 melvillehotel@brixham45.fsnet.co.uk	March to Dec	500 mtrs £16.00 D EM PL CP 4D[3] 3S 2F[2]
63	Mr & Mrs T Boulton Sampford House 57/59 King Street BRIXHAM TQ5 9TH	01803 857761 As Phone carole@boulton.fsbusiness.co.uk		50mtrs £20.00 O D EM PL CP DW 5D 1T ALL ES
64	Mr & Mrs P Gibbs Benbows Hotel 1 Alta Vista Road ROUNDHAM Paignton TQ4 6DB	01803 558128 petergibbs@lineone.net		200mts £14.50 O EM PL CP LSP DW 5D[2] 1T[1] 3F[1]
64	Mrs P Kingdon Bruce Lodge Guest House 2 Elmsleigh Road PAIGNTON TQ4 5AU	01803 550972 As Phone roger_kingdon@lineone.net www.paigntondevon.co.uk/brucelodge	891 610 Easter-Sept	500mtrs £16.00 D EM PL CP LSP 2D 2T 1S 1F
64	Mrs R Leysinger Cedar Court 3 St Matthews Road Torquay TQ2 6JA	01803 607851	903 634	700 mts £22.00 O D EM PL CP 5D 3S 2F ALL ES
64	Ansteys Cove Hotel 327 Babbacombe Road TORQUAY TQ1 3TB	01803 200900 01803 211150 info@torquaydevon.com www.torquaydevon.com		On Path £30.00 O EM CP LSP 6D 1T 2S ALL ES

Sect.	Name and Address	Tel. No. Fax. No. Web / Email	Map Reference Opening Times	Distance from Path Starting Price Facilities Accommodation
64	Mrs A French The Meadfoot Bay Hotel Meadfoot Sea Road Torquay TQ1 2LQ	01803 294722 01803 214473 stay@meadfoot.com www.meadfoot.com	Feb-Oct	150mtrs £26.50 EM PL CP 10D 7T 4S 1F ALL ES
65	Ms J Hobday Beech Close Guest House 53 Babbacombe Road BABBACOMBE TQ1 3SN	01803 328071		100 mtrs £16.00 O D PL CP LSP 4D[1] 1S
65	Mr T P Pinder Birch Tor 315 Babbacombe Road TORQUAY TQ1 3TB	01803 292707 As Phone terry@birchtor.co.uk www.birchtor.co.uk	932 648	50 mts £15.00 O EM PL CP DW 3D[1] 1T[1] 1S 1F
65	Mr & Mrs K A James Suite Dreams Hotel Steep Hill MAIDENCOMBE TQ1 4TS	01803 313900 01803 313841 suitedreams@suitedreams.co.uk www.suitedreams.co.uk		200 mtrs £22.00 O D CP 9D 3T ALL ES
65	Mrs D Sibthorp The Beehive Steep Hill MAIDENCOMBE Torquay	01803 314647	927 687	250 mtrs £20.00 O D CP LSP 1D 1T ALL ES TQ1 4TS
65	Mr P Hockings Brunswick House 5 Brunswick Street Teignmouth TQ14 8AE	01626 774102 margrethehockings@hotmail.com Dogs by arrangement	941 727	100 mtrs £18.50 O D PL DW 4D 3T 1S 3F ALL ES
66	Mrs A Ferris The Blenheim 1 Marine Parade DAWLISH EX7 9DJ	01626 862372		10 mtrs £21.50 O D PL CP DW 3D ALL ES
66	Mr & Mrs M Hayes The Old Vicarage STARCROSS EX6 8PX	01626 890206 As Phone maggie@theoldvicarage.clara.co.uk www.theoldvicarage.clara.net	March-Oct	On path £21.00 D CP LSP 2D 1T ALL ES
66	Mr I Stewart The Croft Guest House Cockwood Harbour STARCROSS EX6 8QY	01626 890282 01626 891768	975 808	On Path O D EM PL CP LSP DW 6T[6] 2S[1]
66	Mrs M Lambert Wixels Ferry Road TOPSHAM EX3 0JH	01392 876785		On path £16.00 O D DW 1D
66	Mr J Dobinson The Barn Hotel EXMOUTH EX8 2DF	01395 224411 01395 225445	014 801	100 mtrs £30.00 O EM PL CP 4D 1T 2S 4F ALL ES
66	Mrs P M Garwood St Aubyns 11 Hartley Road EXMOUTH EX8 2SG	01395 264069		1km £18.00 O D PL CP LSP DW 3D 1T 1S
66	Ms A Jones Sholton Guest House 29 Morton Road EXMOUTH EX8 1BA	01395 277318	999 807	100 mtrs £17.00 O D PL CP DW 3D[3] 2T[1] 1S 2F[2]

Sect.	Name and Address	Tel. No. Fax. No. Web / Email	Map Reference Opening Times	Distance from Path Starting Price Facilities Accommodation
67	Mrs S Freeman 10 Knowle Village BUDLEIGH SALTERTON EX9 6AL	01395 445807	050 825	1.5KM PD £18.00 O D PL CP LSP DW KT 1D 1T 1S
67	Mrs H J Simmons Chapter House 6 Westbourne Terrace BUDLEIGH SALTER EX9 6BR	01395 444100	May-Dec	100mtrs £20.00 O D PL CP LSP DW 1D 1T 1F ALL ES
68	Mr M C Penaiuna Canterbury Guest House Salcombe Road SIDMOUTH EX10 8PR	01395 513373 cgh@eclipse.co.uk	127 878	600 mtr £18.00 O D EM PL CP DW 3D 2T 1S 2F ALL ES
68	Mrs L Lever Larkstone House 22 Connaught Road SIDMOUTH EX10 8TT	01395 514345		500 mtrs £17.50 O D CP DW 1D 1T[1] 1S
68	Mrs J Young Avalon Guest House Vicarage Road SIDMOUTH EX10 8UQ	01395 513443 owneravalon@aol.com www.avalonsidmouth.co.uk		500mtrs £22.00 O D CP 4D 1T ALL ES EM not peak season
68	Mr & Mrs P Scorey Cranmere House 2 Fortfield Place SIDMOUTH EX10 8NX	01395 513933		200 mtrs £19.50 O D PL CP 4D 1T 2S 1F ALL ES
68	Mr & Mrs D Haslam Bramley Lodge Guest House Vicarage Road SIDMOUTH EX10 8UQ	01395 515710 haslam@bramleylodge.fsnet.co.uk		750mtrs PD £19.00 O D EM PL CP DW KT 2D[2] 1T[1] 3S[1] 1F
68	The Manager The Royal York & Faulkner Hotel Esplanade SIDMOUTH EX10 8AZ	Free 0800 220714 01395 577472 yorkhotel@eclipse.co.uk www.royalyorkhotel.net	Feb-Dec	500 mts £30.00 D EM PL CP DW 9D 30T 22S 7F ALL ES
69	Mr & Mrs P R Manning Pendennis South Down Road BEER EX12 3AE	01297 23395 Easter-End Sept	228 889	30mts £20.00 D EM PL CP LSP 4D[3] 2T[1] 1S 1F
68	Mr & Mrs B Rosewarne Sea Glimpses Burrow Road SEATON EX12 2NF	01297 22664 As Phone	250 899	30mtrs £18.00 O D PL CP LSP 1D 1T 1F
69	Mr & Mrs P R Webber The Tors Guest House 55 Harbour Road SEATON EX12 2LX	01297 20531		£18.00 O CP 3D[1] 1T[1] 1S 1F
69	Mrs E D Jordan Lyndhurst Manor Road SEATON EX12 2AQ	01297 23490		800 mtr £17.00 O CP LSP DW 1D 1T 1S
69	Mr & Mrs R Webber Axe Farm AXMOUTH Seaton EX12 4BG	01297 24707 axe.farm@ic24.net www.axefarm.co.uk	256 911	1km £18.00 O D PL CP LSP DW 2D OR 2T ALL ES

Sect.	Name and Address	Tel. No. Fax. No. Web / Email	Map Reference Opening Times	Distance from Path Starting Price Facilities Accommodation
69	Mrs J Calvert 13 Southcombe Terrace AXMOUTH Seaton EX12 4AT	01297 22749 Jkmacalvert@yahoo.co.uk		500mts £15.00 O D CP 1D 1T
70	Ms M Bolton Cliff Cottage Tea Garden Cobb Road LYME REGIS DT7 3JP	01297 443334 merry.bolton@btinternet.com	Easter-Nov	25 mtrs £20.00 D EM PL CP DW 2D[2] 1T
70	Mr & Mrs W Bradbury Charnwood Guest House 21 Woodmead Road Lyme Regis DT7 3AD	01297 445281 charnwood@lymeregis62.freeserve.co.uk www.lymeregisaccommodation.com	339 924	500mtrs £21.00 O D CP 4D[3] 2T[2] 1S[1] 1F[1]
72	Mr A Hardy Britmead House West Bay Road BRIDPORT DT6 4EG	01308 422941 465 913 01308 422516 britmead@talk21.com www.britmeadhouse.co.uk		800mts £22.00 D CP DW KT 3D 2T 2F ALL ES
72	Mrs G R Bramah 143 Victoria Grove BRIDPORT DT6 3AG	01308 456617 467 934		3km PD £18.00 O D CP LSP KT 1T
73	Mr M B Hoare Burton Cliff Hotel BURTON BRADSTOC DT6 4RB	01308 897205 01308 898111 www.burtoncliffhotel.com.uk		on path PD £21.00 O D EM PL CP LSP DW KT 7D(5) 8T(6) 3S(1)
73	Mrs N Millard Blegberry Swyre Road WEST BEXINGTON DT2 9DD	01308 897774 532 872 01308 898300 normamillard@aol.com		500 mts PD £20.00 O D PL CP LSP 1D 1F PRIV FACIL.
73	Mr & Mrs R Harris The Berries Beach Road WEST BEXINGTON DT2 9DG	01308 897329 532 867		250mtrs PD £22.50 O D CP LSP DW KT 2D 1F ALL ES
73	Mrs M Harman Linton Cottage ABBOTSBURY DT3 4JL	01305 871339 queenbee@abbotsbury.co.uk www.lintoncottage.co.uk		1km £25.00 O D PL CP LSP 3D(3)
73	The Swan ABBOTSBURY	01305 871249		1km O EM PL CP LSP DW 3D[1] 2T[1]
73	Mr & Mrs F Harber The Keep Back Street ABBOTSBURY DT3 4JP	01305 871294 578 854 mayling.thirlaway@which.net		50mtrs £18.00 O D CP LSP KT 1D(1) 2S
73	Mrs P Crockett 21 Rodden Row ABBOTSBURY DT3 4JL	01305 871465 855 579		750mtrs £19.00 O D PL CP LSP 1D 1T
74	Mrs A Martin The Old Fountain 36 Front Street PORTESHAM DT3 4ET	01305 871278 603 860 as phone		2 kms PD £20.00 O D PL KT 1D 1T
74	Mrs P Westcott Stonebank 14 West Street CHICKERELL DT3 4DY	01305 760120 643 807 01305 760871 sww@stonebank-chickerell.co.uk www.stonebank-chickerell.co.uk	Apr-Sept	2 kms £22.50 D PL CP 2D ALL ES

Sect.	Name and Address	Tel. No. Fax. No. Web / Email	Map Reference Opening Times	Distance from Path Starting Price Facilities Accommodation
75	Mr D Fox The Pulpit Inn PORTLAND DT5 2JT	01305 821237		on path £25.00 O D EM CP LSP 2D 1S 1F
76	Mrs Harvey Florian 59 Abbotsbury Road WEYMOUTH DT4 0AQ	01305 773836 01305 750160 clare@florian-guesthouse.co.uk www.florian-guesthouse.co.uk		500 mtrs £19.00 O D EM PL CP 3D 2T 1S 1F ALL ES
75	Mr & Mrs G Tatlow The Cunard Guest House 45/46 Lennox Street Weymouth DT4 7HB	01305 771546 As Phone		50mtrs PD £17.00 O D EM PL CP KT 6D[2] 4T[1] 2S 2F[1]
76	Mrs K Legg Rosedale Church Lane OSMINGTON DT3 6EW	01305 832056	Mar-Oct	on path £18.00 D CP 2D[1] 1T 1F
76	Mrs J Ravensdale Elads-Nevar West Road Wareham BH20 5RZ	01929 400467	824 806	800 mtrs £16.00 O D PL CP LSP DW 1D[1] 1T
76	Mr & Mrs R J Foote Lulworth Cove Hotel WEST LULWORTH BH20 5RQ	01929 400333 01929 400534 hotel@lulworth-cove.com www.lulworth-cove.com		on path £27.50 O D EM PL CP LSP DW 14D[10] 1S[1] 2F[2]
76	The Shirley Hotel 01929 400167 WEST LULWORTH Nr Wareham BH20 5RL	01929 400358 durdle@aol.com www.shirleyhotel.co.uk	824 806 Feb-Nov	400mtrs £37.00 D EM PL CP DW 9D 4T 1S 1F ALL ES
76	Mrs C Miller Cromwell House Hotel WEST LULWORTH BH20 5RJ	01929 400253 01929 400566 catriona@lulworthcove.co.uk www.lulworthcove.co.uk		on path £30.00 OD EM PL CP LSP DW 7D 5T 2S 3F ALL ES
76	Mr & Mrs P Brachi West Coombe Farmhouse COOMBE KEYNES Wareham BH20 5PS	01929 462889 01929 405863 west.coombe.farmhouse@barclays.net www.westcoombefarmhouse.co.uk	842 842	4km PD £22.00 O D PL CP KT 1D[1] 1T 1S
76	Mr & Mrs R T Cooper April Thatch COOMBE KEYNES Lulworth Cove BH20 5PP	01929 463412 admin@aprilthatch.co.uk www.aprilthatch.co.uk	842 843	4.8kms PD £20.00 O D PL CP 1D 1T 1S ALL ES
77	Mr M Francis East Burton House WOOL Wareham BH20 6HE	01929 463857 01929 463026 mikefr@ntlworld.com www.eastburton.free-yellow.com	870 834	3km PD £25.00 O D PL DW 2D 1T
77	Mrs E Braisby Blackmanston Farm STEEPLE Kimmeridge BH20 5NZ	01929 480743 as phone	916 808	1.5km PD £22.00 O D EM PL CP LSP DW KT 2D[1] 2T 2S 1F
78	Mrs G Hole Bradle Farm CHURCH KNOWLE Kimmeridge BH20 5NU	01929 480712 01929 481144 bradlefarmhouse@farmersweekly.net www.smoothhound.co.uk/hotels/brundle.html	930 805	3.5kms PD £23.00 O D PL CP LSP 2D 1T ALL ES

Sect.	Name and Address	Tel. No. Fax. No. Web / Email	Map Reference Opening Times	Distance from Path Starting Price Facilities Accommodation
78	Mrs S Amos Dorset's West Country B&B 12 Rempstone Road SWANAGE BH19	01929 423271		1 km O D PL CP 5D 2T 2F ALL ES
78	Mr & Mrs A Preston Sunny Bay 17 Cluny Crescent SWANAGE BH19 2BP	01929 422650 gillgc@aol.com.		200mtrs £16.00 O CP 2D[1] 1T[1]
78	Mrs E Hine Perfick Piece Springfield Road SWANAGE BH19 1HD	01929 423178 01929 423558 perfick-piece@supanet.com www.perfick-piece.supanet.com	028 788	400mtrs £15.00 O D EM PL CP DW 1D 1T 1S 1F[1]
78	Amberlea 36 Victoria Avenue SWANAGE BH19 1AP	01929 426213 amberlea-guesthouse@excite.co.uk	026 792	PD £18.00 O PL CP KT 4D 1T ALL ES
78	Mr & Mrs M S Cooper Sunny South 118 Kings Road West SWANAGE BH19 1HS	01929 422665 SunnySouth@btinternet.com www.sunnysouth.btinternet.co.uk	023 790 May-Sept	812 mtr £16.00 D PL 2D[2]
79	Mrs J Small 11 Durlston Point 78 Park Road SWANAGE BH19 2AE	01929 421717 je.small@virgin.net	033 782	100 mts PD £20.00 O D EM PL CP LSP KT 1D[1] 1T
79	Mrs North The Laurels 60 Britannia Road POOLE BH14 8BB	01202 265861 martin@thelaurelspoole.freeserve.co.uk thelaurelsbandb.freeservers.com	033 913 Jan-Nov	1km £20.00 D CP 1D 1T 1S 1F ALL ES

CAMPSITES

A list of campsites has been prepared in path order.

The following letter code is used;

T	=	Toilets	S	= Showers
G	=	Grocery Shop	CP	= Car Parking
LSP	=	Long Stay Parking	LY	= Laundry
O	=	Open All Year	DW	= Dogs Welcome
KT	=	Kit Transfer	PD	= Pick Up/Drop

KT - Kit Transfer. A service being offered by some of our accommodation providers is to transfer your kit to your next accommodation. This could prove useful to you. Naturally a fee may be levied for this service.
PD - Pick Up/Drop. This code appears following the distance from the path and denotes a facility whereby your host is prepared to collect and return you to the coast path within reasonable distance. No fee should be charged for this service.
Distance from Path. Please remember these are only approximate and may not be accurate.

The part of the address in CAPITALS is an aid to location; it does not signify the postal town. The extreme left-hand column refers to the appropriate section in the 'Trail Description'; we feel it may help you to find addresses quickly. The amount quoted gives an **indication of the starting rate per** night, and may well rise. If working on a tight budget, it is best to ask first.

Individuals - but we stress **not parties** - usually find no problem in obtaining leave to camp away from official camp sites if they request permission to do so. In fact, our correspondence has many examples of extra kindnesses extended by farmers and others to campers. We would, however, very much emphasize the requesting of permission first. It would be so easy for the thoughtlessness of a few to undo the good relationships of many others built up over some years.

This list is thin in many areas. Suggestions for inclusions in future lists will always be welcome. Information of any new sites should be addressed to the Administrator.

Sect.	Name and Address	Tel. No. Fax. No. Email Web	Map Ref. Distance from Path	Facilities Starting Price Opening Times
1	The Holiday Site Manager Camping Club Site North Hill MINEHEAD TA24 5LB	01643 704138 www.campingandcaravaningclub.co.uk	958 471	T S LY DW £6.90 Mar - Sep
3	Mr & Mrs T Greenaway Newberry Farm Touring Caravans & Camping Woodlands COMBE MARTIN EX34 0AT	01271 882334 01271 882880 www.newberrycampsite.co.uk	574 470 200 mts	T S LY CP £6.50 Easter - End Oct
4	Mr & Mrs D S Dovey Hele Valley Holiday Park HELE BAY Caravans also avail. Ilfracombe EX34 9RD	01271 862460 01271 867926 holidays@helevalley.co.uk www.helevalley.co.uk	600 mts	O T S LY G CP DW £6.00 Apr-Oct S/C Cottage and Static
4	Mr D L Wassell Big Meadow Camp Site WATERMOUTH ILFRACOMBE EX34 9SJ	01271 862282 www.big-medow.co.uk	558 483 On path	T S LY G CP LSP DW £3.00 Easter-Oct
8	Mrs Stansmore Chivenor Cross Caravan Park BARNSTAPLE EX31 4BN	01271 812217 01271 812644	505 350 100 mts	T S LY G CP DW KT £6.00 15 Mar-15 Nov
8	Lobb Fields Caravan & Camping Park Saunton Road BRAUNTON EX33 1EB	01271 812090 As Phone lobbfields@compuserve.com www.lobbfields.com	380 443 1.6kms	T S LY CP DW £6.00 Mar to Oct
9	Mr Clements Knapp House Activity Centre Churchill Way NORTHAM EX39 1NT	01237 474804	50mts	T S LY CP LSP DW £4.00 Apr - Oct
10	Mr R Croslegh Steart Farm Touring Park Horns Cross Bideford EX39 5DW	01237 431836 steartcamping@tinyworld.co.uk	356 229 1 km	T S LY CP LSP DW £3.00 Easter-30 Sept
11	Mrs H Davey Stoke Barton Farm STOKE Tearoom on site Hartland EX39 6DU	01237 441238	234 246 700 mtsPD	T S CP LSP DW KT £3.50 Easter - End Sept
12	Mr & Mrs J M Cloke Upper Lynstone Camping & Caravan Park BUDE EX23 0LP	01288 352017 01288 359034 reception@upperlynstone.co.uk www.upperlynstone.co.uk	205 053 100 mts	T S LY G CP LSP DW £7.00 Easter - Oct
13	Mrs J Onions Coxford Meadow St Gennys CRACKINGTON HAVEN EX23 0NS	01840 230707 01840 230451	161 967 1 km PD	T S CP LSP DW KT £3.00 Easter - Oct
13	Mrs S Weller Hentervene Camping & Caravan Park CRACKINGTON HAVEN EX23 0LF	01840 230365	155 944 3.2 kms	T S LY CP LSP DW £4.50 Open All Year
15	Mr & Mrs R L Wickett Bossiney Farm Caravan & Camping Park BOSSINEY Tintagel PL34 0AY	01840 770481 01840 770025 www.bossineyfarm.co.uk	067 888 200mtrs	T S LY G CP LSP DW April to Oct

Sect.	Name and Address	Tel. No. Fax. No. Email Web	Map Ref. Distance from Path	Facilities Starting Price Opening Times
17	Mrs R Harris South Winds Camping & Caravan Park POLZEATH PL27 6QU	01208 863267 01208 862080 www.rockinfo.co.uk	948 790 On path	T S LY CP LSP DW £10.00 Mar to Sept
17	Mr R Harris Tristram Caravan & Camping Park POLZEATH PL27 6UG	01208 862215 01208 862080 www.rockinfo.co.uk	948 790 On path	T S LY G CP LSP DW KT £10.00 Mar to Nov
18	Mr & Mrs B Harris Dennis Cove Campsite Dennis Cove PADSTOW PL28 8DR	01841 532349	920 745 500 mts Apr - Sept	T S LY DW
20	Carnevas Farm Holiday Park PORTHCOTHAN BAY PL28 8PN	01841 520230 as phone	862 728 800mtrs	T S LY G CP DW £6.00 1 Apr to 31 Oct
21	The Holiday Site Manager The Camping & Caravan Club Site TREGURRIAN Newquay TR8 4AE	01637 860448 www.campingandcaravanningclub.co.uk	853 654 800 mts	T S LY CP DW Mar-Sept
24	Ms J. Sawle Beacon Cottage Farm Touring Park Beacon Drive ST AGNES TR5 0NU	01872 552347/553381 Mobile 07879 413862	705 505 400mtrs	T S LY CP LSP DW £5.00 Apr to oct
25	Mr J Barrow Rosehill Touring Park PORTHTOWAN Truro TR4 8AR	01209 890802 reception@rosehillcamping.co.uk www.rosehillcamping.co.uk	693 473 800 mts	T S LY G CP £8.50 Apr-End Oct
26	Mr H Williams & Son Magor Farm Caravan Site TEHIDY Camborne	01209 713367	632 427 15mtrs	T S LY G CP LSP DW £5.00 Apr - Oct
28	Mr R Osborne Trevalgan Family Camping Park ST IVES TR26 3BJ	01736 796433 01736 799798 trevalgan@aol.com www.trevalganholidayfarm.co.uk	490 402 400mtrs	T S LY G CP LSP DW £7.00 1 May to 30 Sept
30	Mr J Boyns Levant House Camp Site TREWELLARD Pendeen TR19 7SX	01736 788795	375 337 500mtrs	T S CP DW £2.50 1 Apr to 31 Oct
30	Kelynack Caravan & Camping Park KELYNACK Penzance	01736 787633 As Phone steve@kelynackholidays.co.uk www.ukparks.co.uk/kelynack	372 301 1.5kms PD	O T S LY G CP LSP DW £3.00 Bunk Barn also avail from £7 pppn
30	Mr & Mrs P Whitelock The Old Chapel Backpackers Hostel ZENNOR TR26 3BY	01736 798307 As Phone zennorbackpackers@btinternet.com www.backpackers.co.uk	455 385 500mtrs	O T S LY CP LSP £3.50 Open All Year. Winter by
30	Mr P Eachus Trevaylor Camp Site BOTALLACK Penzance TR19 7PU	01736 787016 bookings@trevaylor.com www.trevaylor.com	370 328 500 mts	T S LY G DW £6.50 Apr to Oct
31	Mr T Ellison Whitesands Lodge Lands End Backpackers SENNEN TR19 7AR	01736 871776 As Phone info@whitesandslodge.co.uk www.whitesandlodge.co.uk	366 264 400 mts	O T S LY CP LSP DW KT £6.00 Open All Year

Sect.	Name and Address	Tel. No. Fax. No. Email Web	Map Ref. Distance from Path	Facilities Starting Price Opening Times
33	Mr J Hall Treen Campsite TREEN Nr Penzance TR19 6LF	01736 810526	392 228 80mtrs	T S G CP LSP DW £5.00 end Mar - end Oct
38	Mr A B Thomas Tenerife Farm Caravan & Camping Park Predannack MULLION TR12 7EZ	01326 240293 as phone	672 166 800 mts	T S LY CP LSP DW £6.00 Easter to Oct
39	Mr & Mrs R H Lyne Henry's Campsite Caerthillian Farm THE LIZARD TR12 7NX	01326 290596 01326 290080	125 701 500mtrs PD	O T S CP LSP DW KT £5.00 Open all year
40	Mr & Mrs K G Bonser Silver Sands Holiday Park Gwendreath Kennack Sands Ruan Minor, Helston TR12 7LZ	01326 290631 As Phone enquiries@silversandsholidaypark.co.uk www.silversandsholidaypark.co.uk	729 169 1km	T S LY CP DW £5.00 May to Sept
40	T Gibson Caravan Park Gwendreath Farm KENNACK SANDS Helston TR12 7LZ	01326 290666 tom.gibson@virgin.net www.tomandlinda.co.uk	729 168 1km	T S LY G CP DW £4.20 Easter to Oct
40	Mrs M Mita Little Trevothan Caravan and Camping Park COVERACK	01326 280260 As Phone trevothan@connexions.co.uk www.connexions.co.uk/trevothan/index.htm	770 180 1 km	T S LY CP LSP DW £5.50 Apr-Oct
44	Mr & Mrs V Barry Treloan Coastal Farm PORTSCATHO Truro TR2 5EF	01872 580989/580899 as phone holidays@treloan.freeserve.co.uk www.coastalfarmholidays.co.uk	874 348 300 mtrs PD	O T S LY CP LSP DW KT £5.00 Open All Year Camping Barn available
47	Dr J Whitter Trelispen Camping Park GORRAN HAVEN	01726 843501 As Phone trelispen@care4free.net	005 421 750 mts	T S LY CP LSP DW £7.00 Apr to Oct
47	Mrs M Parkhouse Treveor Farm GORRAN St Austell PL26 6LW	01726 842387 As Phone	987 418 1.6 kms	T S LY CP DW £6.00 Apr - Oct
53	Tencreek Caravan Park LOOE PL13 2JR	01503 262447 01503 262760 tencreek@aol.com www.tencreek.co.uk	234 525 1.6 km 1.6km in land via public footpath	O T S LY G CP DW £8.00 Open All Year
53	Miss R Davey Camping Caradon Touring Park Tralawn Looe PL13 2NA	01503 272388 As Phone	542 218 2.4kms PD	T S LY G CP LSP DW KT £6.50
53	Mr & Mrs R Haywood Talland Caravan Park TALLAND BAY Nr Looe PL13 2JA	01503 272715 01503 272224	515 234 100 mts Apr-Oct	T S LY G CP LSP DW £3.00
58	Mr J Tucker Mount Folly Farm BIGBURY ON SEA TQ7 4AR	01548 810267 as phone	661 447 on path	O T CP LSP DW £4.00 Open All Year

Sect.	Name and Address	Tel. No. Fax. No. Email Web	Map Ref. Distance from Path	Facilities Starting Price Opening Times
59	Mr P Higgin Karrageen Camping Site BOLBERRY Nr Kingsbridge TQ7 3EN	01548 561230 01548 560192 phil@karrageen.co.uk www.karrageen.co.uk	689 394 1.2 kms	T S LY G CP DW £7.00 15 Mar to 15 Nov
60	Mrs S Rogers Ilton Farm Camp Site As Phone MALBOROUGH TQ7 3BZ	01548 842858	722 403 2.25kms	T S CP DW £5.50 Easter to Oct
60	Mrs S M Squire Higher Rew Camping Park MALBOROUGH Kingsbridge TQ7 3DW	01548 842681 01548 843681 enquiries@higherrew.co.uk www.higherrew.co.uk	714 382 1.5 kms	T S LY G CP LSP DW £6.50 Easter-End Oct
60	Mrs F Stidston Bolberry House Farm Caravan & Camping Park Bolberry Nr Kingsbridge TQ7 3DY	01548 561251 as phone bolberry.house@virgin.net www.bolberryparks.co.uk	800mtrs	T S LY G CP LSP DW
60	Mr & Mrs B Sweetman Sun Park Caravan & Camping SOAR MILL COVE Nr Salcombe TQ7 3DS	01548 561378 As Phone	1200 mts	T S LY CP DW KT £6.00 Easter - Sept
64	Marine Park Holiday Centre Grange Road PAIGNTON TQ4 7JR	01803 843887 01803 845427 info@beverley-holidays.co.uk www.beverley-holidays.co.uk	888 587 1km	T S LY CP £9.00 EASTER-OCT
64	Beverley Park Holiday Park Goodrington Road PAIGNTON TQ4 7JE	01803 843887 01803 845427 info@beverley-holidays.co.uk www.beverley-holidays.co.uk	888 588 1.2kms	T S G CP CF LY £7.30 Mar - Oct
66	Mrs V Jeffery Cofton Country Holiday Park STARCROSS Nr Dawlish EX6 8RP	01626 890111 info@coftonholidays.co.uk www.coftonholidays.co.uk		T S LY G CP DW Easter-End October
68	Mr A Franks Oakdown Caravan Park Weston SIDMOUTH EX10 0PH	01297 680387 01297 680541 oakdown@btinternet.com www.bestcaravanpark.co.uk	167 902 2 kms	T S LY CP DW £8.00 Apr to Oct
69	Mr D. Boyce Salcombe Regis Caravan & Camping Park SALCOMBE REGIS Sidmouth EX10 0JH	01395 514303 as phone info@salcombe-regis.co.uk www.salcombe-regis.co.uk	151 892 1.5kms	T S LY G CP DW £7.00 15 Apr - 28 Oct
69	Mr J M Salter Manor Farm Camping & Caravan Site Seaton Down Hill SEATON EX12 2JA	01297 21524	1km	T S LY CP LSP DW £7.00 15 Mar to 31 Oct
69	Mr R K Webber Axmouth Camping Site Axe Farm SEATON EX12 4BG	01297 24707 axe.farm@ic24.net www.axefarm.co.uk	256 911 1 km	T S G CP LSP DW £5.00 Mid Mar-Mid Oct

Sect.	Name and Address	Tel. No. Fax. No. Email Web	Map Ref. Distance from Path	Facilities Starting Price Opening Times
70	Mr & Mrs A Morgan Hook Farm Caravan & Camping Park Hook Farm Gore Lane Lyme Regis DT7 3UU	01297 442801 www.hookfarm-uplyme.co.uk	323 929 1.5 kms	T S LY G CP DW £8.00 Open all Year
71	Mr R Loosmore Manor Farm Holiday Centre CHARMOUTH DT6 6QL	01297 560226 enq@manorfarmholidaycentre.co.uk www.manorfarmholidaycentre.co.uk	368 937 500mtrs	O T S LY G CP LSP DW £8.00 Open All Year
71	Mrs J Ireland Newlands Camping Park CHARMOUTH DT6 6RB	01297 560259 01297 560787	373 935 500mtrs	O T S LY G DW £8.00 Open All Year
71	Ms J. Pointing Wood Farm Caravan & Camping Park Axminster Road CHARMOUTH DT6 6BT	01297 560697 01297 561243 holidays@woodfarm.co.uk www.woodfarm.co.uk	355 940 1km	T S LY G CP LSP DW £8.00 Mar to Oct
72	Mr & Mrs M Cox Golden Cap Holiday Park SEATOWN Bridport DT6 6JX	01308 422139 01308 425672 holidays@wdlh.co.uk www.wdlh.co.uk	424 919 100mtrs	T S LY G CP DW £8.50 17 Mar to 5 Nov
73	Mr R Condliffe Freshwater Beach Holiday Park BURTON BRADSTOCK Nr Bridport DT6 4PT	01308 897317 01308 897336 enquiries@freshwaterbeach.co.uk www.freshwaterbeach.co.uk	898 479 200mtrs	T S LY G DW £9.00 17 Mar - 12 Nov
74	Mr & Mrs M J Coombe Sea Barn Farm Camping FLEET Weymouth DT3 4ED	01305 782218 01305 775396	624 814 200mtrs	T S LY G CP LSP DW £6.00 Easter to 31 Oct
76	Pebble Bank Caravan Park 90 Camp Road Weymouth DT4 9HF	01305 774844 As Phone info@pebblebank.co.uk www.pebblebank.co.uk	657 775 400mtrs	T S LY CP LSP DW £7.00 April - October
78	Mr & Mrs J Wootton Toms Field Campsite Toms Field Road SWANAGE BH19 3HN	01929 427110 As Phone tomsfield@hotmail.com www.tomsfieldcamping.co.uk	995 785 1.5kms	T S LY G CP LSP DW £7.50 Mid Mar to Oct Bunk Barn also avail £7pppn
78	Mrs J M Scadden Ulwell Cottage Caravan Park ULWELL Swanage BH19 3DG	01929 422823 01929 421500 www.ulwellcottagepark.co.uk	3 kms	T S LY G CP DW 1 Mar - 7 Jan

YOUTH HOSTEL ASSOCIATION

There is an amazing variety of youth Hostels along the South West Coast Path, 21 in total and all offering comfortable, friendly accommodation. Prices start from £5.15 per night, including bed linen, the use of self-catering kitchens, drying rooms and cycle sheds. The YHA is a membership organisation, however non-members are welcome to join on arrival at the hostel. Membership enables you to take advantage of the 5000 Youth Hostels world wide, regular member's magazine 'Triangle', annual YHA Accommodation Guides and discounts at YHA Adventure Shops and local tourist attractions. YHA annual membership costs are currently: Under 18 - £6.50, adult - £13.00 and family (2 adults & 2 children) - £26.00. The meals are excellent value, at around £3.40 for breakfast, Packed Lunches £3.00 to £3.90 and Evening Meals £5.00.

Book directly with the Youth Hostel of your choice of for further assistance, please contact English Regions Office, P O Box 11, Matlock, Derbyshire, DE4 2XA. Telephone 01629 825850, fax 0162 824571 or email Englishregions@YHA.org.uk, or why not visit their website at www.YHA.org.uk

Prices range from £4 to £9.75 for bed and bed linen, but please remember to check with each individual hostel before booking.

YOUTH HOSTELS

Minehead Youth Hostel Alcombe Combe	MINEHEAD	TA24 6EW	Phone:01643 702595	Grid Ref: 973 442	
Lynton Youth Hostel Lynbridge	LYNTON	EX35 6AZ	Phone:01598 753237	Grid Ref: 720 487	
Elmscott Youth Hostel Hartland	HARTLAND	EX39 6ES	Phone:01237 441367	Grid Ref: 231 217	Self Catering Only
Boscastle Youth Hostel Palace Stables	BOSCASTLE	PL35 0HD	Phone:01840 250287	Grid Ref: 096 915	
Tintagel Youth Hostel Dunderhole Point	TINTAGEL	PL34 0DW	Phone:01840 770334	Grid Ref: 047 881	Self Catering Only
Treyarnon Bay Youth Tregonnan Treyarnon	PADSTOW	PL28 8JR	Phone:01841 520322	Grid Ref: 859 741	
Perranporth Youth Hostel Droskyn Point	PERRANPORTH	TR6 0GS	Phone:01872 573812	Grid Ref: 752 544	Self Catering On
Land's End Youth Hostel Letcha Vean	ST JUST	TR19 7NT	Phone:01736 788437	Grid Ref: 364 305	
Penzance Youth Hostel Castle Horneck, Alverton	PENZANCE	TR20 8TF	Phone:01736 362666	Grid Ref: 457 302	
Coverack Youth Hostel Park Behan, School Hill	HELSTON	TR12 6SA	Phone:01326 280687	Grid Ref: 782 184	
Boswinger Youth Hostel Boswinger	GORRAN	PL26 6LL	Phone:01726 843234	Grid Ref: 991 411	
Golant Youth Hostel Penquite House, Golant	FOWEY	PL23 1LA	Phone:01726 833507	Grid Ref: 118 557	
Plymouth Youth Hostel Belmont House, Belmont Place	PLYMOUTH	PL3 4DW	Phone:01752 562189	Grid Ref: 461 555	May close in 200
Salcombe Youth Hostel Sharpitor	SALCOMBE	TQ8 8LW	Phone:01548 842856	Grid Ref: 728 374	
Maypool Youth Hostel Maypool House, Galmpton	BRIXHAM	TQ5 0ET	Phone:01803 842444	Grid Ref: 877 546	
Exeter Youth Hostel 47 Countess Wear Road	EXETER	EX2 6LR	Phone:01392 873329	Grid Ref: 942 897	
Beer Youth Hostel Bovey Combe, Townsend	SEATON	EX12 3LL	Phone:01297 20296	Grid Ref: 223 896	
Litton Cheney Youth Litton Cheney	DORCHESTER	DT2 9AT	Phone:01308 482340	Grid Ref: 548 900	Self Catering Only No Smokin
Lulworth Cove Youth School Lane	WEST LULWORTH	BH20 5SA	Phone:01929 400564	Grid Ref: 832 806	
Portland Youth Hostel Hardy House, Castletown	PORTLAND	DT5 1BJ	Phone:01305 861368	Grid Ref:	
Swanage Youth Hostel Cluny Crescent	SWANAGE	BH19 2BS	Phone:01929 422113	Grid Ref: 031 785	

TOURIST INFORMATION CENTRES

Town	Address		Postcode	Phone	Fax
MINEHEAD	17 Friday Street		TA24 5UB	Phone: 01643 702624	Fax: 01643 707166
MINEHEAD	17 Friday Street		TA24 5UB	Phone: 01643 702624	Fax: 01643 707166
LYNTON	Town Hall	Lee Road	EX35 6BT	Phone: 01598 752225	Fax: 01598 752755
COMBE MARTIN	Sea Cottage	Cross Street	EX34 0DH	Phone: 01271 883319	Fax: 01271 883319
ILFRACOMBE	The Promenade		EX34 9BX	Phone: 01271 863001	Fax: 01271 862586
WOOLACOMBE	Red Barb Cafe Car Park	Barton Road		Phone: 01271 870553	Fax:
BRAUNTON	The Bakehouse Centre	Caen Street	EX33 1AA	Phone: 01271 816400	Fax: 01271 816947
BARNSTAPLE	36 Boutport Street		EX31 1RX	Phone: 01271 375000	Fax: 01271 374037
BIDEFORD	Victoria Park	The Quay	EX39 2QQ	Phone: 01237 477676	Fax: 01237 421853
BUDE	Visitor Centre	The Crescent	EX23 8LE	Phone: 01288 354240	Fax: 01288 355769
PADSTOW	Red Brick Building	North Quay	PL28 8AF	Phone: 01841 533449	Fax: 01841 532356
NEWQUAY	Municipal Offices	Marcus Hill	TR7 1BD	Phone: 01637 871345	Fax: 01637 852025
PERRANPORTH	Beiners Arms Hotel		TR6 0DP	Phone: 01872 573368	Fax:
PENZANCE	Station Road		TR18 2NF	Phone: 01736 362207	Fax:
FALMOUTH	28 Killigrew Street		TR11 3PN	Phone: 01326 312300	Fax: 01326 313457
FOWEY	4 Custom Hill House		PL23 1AB	Phone: 01726 833616	Fax: 01726 833616
ST IVES	The Guildhall	Street an Pol	TR26 2DT	Phone: 01736 796297	Fax: 01736 798309
LOOE	The Guildhall	Fore Street	PL13 1AA	Phone: 01503 262072	Fax: 01503 265426
PLYMOUTH	Island House	9 The Barbican	PL1 2LS	Phone: 01752 264849	Fax: 01752 257955
IVYBRIDGE	Leonards Road		PL21 0SL	Phone: 01752 897035	Fax:
SALCOMBE	Council Hall	Market Street	TQ8 8DE	Phone: 01548 843927	Fax: 01548 842736
DARTMOUTH	The Engine House	Mayors Avenue	TQ6 9YY	Phone: 01803 834224	Fax: 01803 835631
KINGSBRIDGE	The Quay			Phone: 01548 853195	Fax: 01548 854185
BRIXHAM	The Old Market House	The Quay	TQ5 8TB	Phone: 01803 852861	Fax:
TORQUAY	Vaughan Parade		TQ2 5JG	Phone: 01803 297428	Fax:
PAIGNTON	The Esplanade		TQ4 6ED	Phone: 01803 558383	Fax: 01803 551959
TEIGNMOUTH	The Den	Sea Front	TQ14 8BE	Phone: 01626 779769	Fax: 01626 779770
DAWLISH	The Lawn		EX7 9EL	Phone: 01626 863589	Fax:
EXMOUTH	Alexandra Terrace		EX8 1NZ	Phone: 01395 222299	Fax:
BUDLEIGH SALTER	Fore Street		EX9 6NG	Phone: 01935 445275	Fax:
SIDMOUTH	Ham Lane		EX10 8XR	Phone: 01395 516441	Fax: 01395 516441
SEATON	The Underfleet		EX12 2TB	Phone: 01297 21660	Fax: 01297 21689
LYME REGIS	Guildhall Cottage	Church Street	DT7 3BS	Phone: 01297 442138	Fax: 01297 443773
BRIDPORT	32 South Street		DT6 3NQ	Phone: 01308 424901	Fax: 01308 421060
WEYMOUTH	King's Statue	The Esplanade	DT4 7AN	Phone: 01305 785747	Fax: 01305 788092
SWANAGE	The White House	Shore Road	BH19 1LB	Phone: 01929 422885	Fax: 01929 423423
WAREHAM	Trinity Church	South Street	BH20 4LU	Phone: 01929 552740	Fax: 01929 554491
POOLE	Tourism Centre	The Quay	BH15 1HE	Phone: 01202 253253	Fax: 01202 684531

SOUTH WEST COAST PATH ASSOCIATION - HISTORY

We are sometimes asked what we have done and we set out below some of the things in which we have been involved in one way or another. We do as well send a steady flow of reports on path deficiencies, both as regards maintenance and the route of the path to the local authorities and the Countryside Agency.

1973   Official Formation in May.
Attendance Cornish Opening at Newquay.
Comments to Sports Council on proposed Countryside Park at Northam Burrows.
First Information Sheets produced.

1974   Evidence submitted to Mr Yepp for his report to the Countryside Commission on Long Distance Footpaths.
We welcomed Devon N.F.U. representation on our Committee.
Attendance at South Devon and Dorset Opening in September at Beer.
Registration as a Charity.
First Description issued.

1975   Mark Richard's book 'Walking the North Cornwall Coastal Path' published - a work in which we may fairly say we played a part.
Clematon Hill, Bigbury, small new section of Coast Path agreed at SWWA's instigation.
Article on SWW in 'Rucksack'.
Attendance at Opening of so-called Exmoor Coastal Path.
Bideford Public Enquiry - successful opposition to Golf Course on the Coastal Path at Abbotsham.
Hartland Point Success at last in getting path south from Hartland Point over Blagdon and Upright Cliffs. Walk over new Lulworth Range Walk.

1976   First Footpath Guide issued.
Thurlestone Diversion opposed.
Evidence submitted to House of Commons Expenditure Committee Environment sub-committee.
North Cliffs Improvements between Portreath and Hayle secured, thanks to National Trust.
Public Enquiry with R.A. at Kingswear on the section Kellys Cove to Man Sands.
Consulted by Devon County Council on path at Watermouth and Dorset County Council about Abbotsbury.
Goodbye to our first Chairman, Mr Walter - we lose a tower of strength.

1977   SWWA mentioned in the YH. Handbook.
Publications of Letts Guides in three volumes. The first satisfactory books to whole path in which we can say our information helped a little.
Attendance at Coverack Youth Hostel official opening.
Evidence presented to Lord Porchester's Exmoor Study.
Badges produced.
Evidence given to Devon County Council for Taw/Torridge Estuary Survey.

1978   First Printed Footpath guide.
Attendance at Westward Ho! Somerset/North Devon Opening.
Dean Quarry, St Keverne, Cornwall Opposition to diversion.
Pentewan Lack of Path submitted to Local Ombudsman.
Hartland New path seaward of Radar Station obtained, thanks to South West Way Association.

1979   Evidence given at Public Enquiries at Abbotsbury and Lulworth Cove.
Submission to Mr Himsworth for his report on Areas of Outstanding Natural Beauty.
First printed News Letters and Descriptions, and the first illustrated description.
Pine Haven to Port Quin gap submitted to Local Ombudsman.
Assistance to Letts for their Guide reprint.

1980   Result of 1976 Public Enquiry at Kingswear published.
Discussion Dean Quarry, St Keverne, Cornwall.
Dialogues with Countryside Commission about path deficiencies.
Alternative coastal path open Glenthorne Estate, Somerset and we submit proposals for rerouting in Exmoor National Park.
St Loy, Cornwall Special report submitted.
Attendance at Widmouth Head, North Devon, Public Enquiry.
Opinions expressed to Department of Environment on draft 'Wildlife and Countryside Bill'.

1981 Annual Guide 'State of the Path' section improved.
Attendance at second Kingswear Public Enquiry.
Countryside Commission decide that path wardenship will be greatly extended.
Duckpool, North Cornwall Bridge provided.
Path improvements at Watermouth; Braunton to Barnstaple; Dean Quarry; Clematon Hill; Bigbury; Mothecombe and Maidencombe.

1982 Wardenship of coastal path in Cornwall completed.
Further openings at: Cleave Farm in North Cornwall, Pentewan with its unfortunate execution and Mount Edgecombe in South Cornwall, Higher Brownstone Farm, Kingswear and a short section west of Berry Head in South Devon.
Agreement was also reached for a high tide route at Mothecombe in South Devon.
The 1982 Guide incorporates a new 'Itinerary Suggested' section.

1983 Opening of the Widmouth Head section in North Devon and a second long section in South Devon between Kingswear and Man Sands.
Crackington Haven, North Cornwall Major improvements to the Path on the western side.
Cornwall's 10th Anniversary Walk.

1984 **New Section** A new section of the Path opened on the east bank of the mouth of the River Dart close to Kingswear and giving access to Mill Bay Cove and a splendid stretch of coastal walking.
Trebarwith Strand to Backways Cove in North Cornwall A coastal route opened.

1985 **Culbone - Foreland Point** The alternative coastal path at the Glenthorne Estate was waymarked as the official route, which is a great improvement.
Pinehaven - Port Quin (North Cornwall) The new path was opened and is a vast improvement, although the substantial fence and barbed wire detracts from the scene.

1986 **Minehead to Porlock Weir** New alternative path between North Hill and Hurlstone Point signposted and waymarked.
Black Head, Cornwall Now purchased by the National Trust.

1987 **Barnstaple/Bideford/Northam** The new route completed along the railway lines and open.
Bude Attendance at Public Enquiry to prevent development adjacent to footpath.
Chynhalls Point Coast path moved to seaward of hotel.
Branscombe Attendance at Public Enquiry to urge true coast path instead of inland route. Preferred route adopted.
Bidna/Northam Owing to breach in sea wall an acceptable diversion is negotiated.

1988 **Woody Bay to Trentishoe** Devon County Council adopts our recommended, nearer the coast route as the official coast path.

1989 **Culbone** On site exploration with Countryside Commission and Exmoor National Park Authority to discover an acceptable alternative to the long unnecessary Culbone diversion.
Chynhalls Cliff On site exploration for a more coastal trail.
Fire Beacon Point/Pentargon Cornwall County Council installs grand new path.
Wembury Attend public meeting at Down Thomas to successfully oppose erection of locked gates across Coast Path by Royal Navy.
Strete Gate/Warren Cove Attend public meeting and give evidence to support proposals by Countryside Commission and Devon County Council for an improved and more true coast path.

1990 **Membership** Now over 1000.

1991 **Buckator** At our request Cornwall County Council re-route official path around the headland.
Worthy/Culbone On site explorations for a preferable diversion to that proposed by Exmoor National Park Authority.
Strete Gate/Warren Cove Continuing our strong argument with Devon County Council for a coast path.
Lyme Regis Continued pleas to Dorset County Council to reinstate the coast path along the golf course.
We estimate the Coast Path to be about 613 miles (982 km) long.

1992 **Watcombe and Maidencombe** Our recommended route put in by Devon County Council.
Worthygate Wood Our suggested path installed by National Trust.
Commenced discussions with Countryside Commission to examine sections of coast suitable for 'Set Aside'.

1993   **Foreland Point** Successful opposition to an application to close path on west side.
Buck's Mills Success with our request for a coast path avoiding the holiday complex.
Port Quin Our suggested path is installed by National Trust.
Write and produce the 'trail description' in this book the 'Other Way Round'.

1994   Invited by the Countryside Commission to become a member of the South West Coast Path
Steering Group to review the management of our Coast Path.
Association acquires a computer.

1995   Membership reaches 2,000
Culbone section re-opened by Exmoor National Park.
Strete Gate/Warren Point - continuous pressure causes Devon County Council to explore
again for a route that will provide an acceptable coast path.
Continuing involvement in the 'Coast Path Project'.
Association details on the Internet. See Web address on page 2.

1996   Path descriptions for the whole SWW written and printed.
Continuing involvement in the coast path project and production of the strategy document
Lyme Regis - Golf Course Route reinstated by Dorset County Council.
Strete Gate/Warren Point - Devon County Council decides to install our preferred route but
rejected by Countryside Commission.

1997   **Red River at Gwithian** A new footbridge put in by Cornwall County Council.
The SWCP Project published its strategy for the future management of the Coast Path.
The Association becomes a member of the SWCP Management Group.

1998   Our Silver Jubilee Year (25 years old). Application made, jointly with R.A. to Minister for the
Environment requesting he use his powers to create a coast path between Strete Gate and
Warren Point. Application refused.
Mountbatten Point, Plymouth opened as a coast path.
Jennycliff Plymouth City Council installs an off-road coast path.
South West Way Association launches its Silver Jubilee Appeal to raise funds toward
markers at each end of the coast path.
South West Way Association produces a Development Plan for the next three years.

1999   Name changed to South West Coast Path Association.
Membership Secretary becomes known as Administrator.
Publications Officer appointed.   Membership passes 3,000.
Continued involvement with celebratory markers at each end of the coast path.
A history of the coast path written and published.

2000   Global Positioning reveals the length of the Coast Path (1014 km - 630 miles) - it is Britain's
only National Trail to exceed 1000 km.
Strete Gate / Warren Point - South West Coast Path Team undertakes a complete review of
this section.
St German's Beacon - progress made in realising an acceptable Coast Path.
Crock Pits - Exmoor National Park installs a coastal route sought by us for many years.
Revised Path Descriptions now produced in-house.

2001   Eight Winter Cliff Falls Disrupt Line of Dorset Coast Path.
Whole Coast Path Closed for 3 months due to Foot and Mouth Crisis.
Introduction of Credit Card facilities for members.
11 August - Whole Coast Path walked on one day by Association members to
celebrate the re-opening of the Coast Path.
Countryside Agency Board accept the review by the South West Coast Path Team that
recommends vital Coast Path realignments between Strete Gate and Stoke Fleming

A CALLIGRAPHIC MAP OF THE SOUTH WEST COAST PATH

This quality produced calligraphic map of the South West Coast Path, Britain's longest footpath was designed, illustrated and written by James Skinner of Gloucester. He is a keen rambler and member of a number of walking organisations including the South West Coast Path Association, the Backpackers' Club and the Ramblers' Association.

James, and his wife Linda have spent many holidays walking the Coast Path - experiencing at first hand the incredible diversity of scenery. The South West Coast Path passes through five areas of outstanding natural beauty, numerous heritage coasts, through wild isolated countryside, across high cliffs and wide estuaries - yet touching small villages, towns and popular resorts.

The printed calligraphic map has been written entirely by hand complemented by fine pen and ink drawings illustrating many of the sights to be found whilst walking the path.

The **COLOUR** indicating the relief of the peninsular was achieved through using professional quality colour pencils. James has been interested in calligraphy since the mid 1980s when he attended a local summer school. More recently he has completed a full-time professional course in Calligraphy and Book-binding at Digby Stuart College, London. At present, James teaches the craft to adults at a variety of centres in his home county and the South West of England. This calligraphic map would make a superb gift, or an ideal memento for anyone having walked part or all of the path.

Overall size (approximately): 560mm deep x 760mm wide.

Image size : 464mm deep x 675mm wide.

ALL PRICES ARE INCLUSIVE OF POSTAGE AND PACKING
Calligraphic Map:- LAMINATED : UNLAMINATED - suitable for framing UK £8.95 USA $21; other overseas countries £12.50 (payable by sterling draft drawn on a London bank). Allow 28 days for delivery. Please make cheques payable to James Skinner and send to: James Calligraphy Services 49 Appleton Way Hucclecote. GLOUCESTER GL3 3RP England.

OFFA'S DYKE PATH - A MONUMENTAL TRAIL

Walkers on the Offa's Dyke Path glimpse the sea only twice as they progress from Sedbury Cliffs on the Severn estuary to Prestatyn on Liverpool Bay, or vice versa. In between their first and last day, however, they pass through a very varied landscape as they follow the approximate historic border of England and Wales. Unspoilt moorland, rolling hills and farmland are crossed by the path between the tourist areas of the Wye Valley and the North Wales coast. Across the plains of Gwent, over the Black Mountains, the river valleys of Radnor, the Severn and Dee valleys, the limestone hills round Llangollen and the Clwyddian ridges; the list of varied attractions is long. For nearly half the route, the Offa's Dyke ancient monument is a silent companion, sometimes almost eroded away, but at others an impressive 6 1/2 yards (6 metres) from ditch to the bank top as the earthwork rolls across the hills of the Clun area. Many ancient hill-forts, castles and abbeys lie on or near the route whose 177 miles (285 km) can be covered in a week, although most visitors will prefer a longer period in which to absorb its varied attractions.

Offa's Dyke Association was formed in 1969 as a pressure group to press for the establishment of the trail. When the route was officially opened in 1971, the Association continued its voluntary work by providing information services to walkers in the form of 'strip maps', route notes, guide books and its 'Where to Stay' accommodation and camping booklet. Pressure group activities continued to ensure the maintenance of the route, as its system of volunteers watched over lengths of the path.

Since 1982 the trail has been maintained by a professional service for which the Association lobbied. This has developed into the 'Offa's Dyke Management Service' financed by the Countryside Council for Wales and the Countryside Agency through Powys and Shropshire County Councils. ODA helps this body, with whom it shares premises at the recently opened Offa's Dyke Centre at Knighton, whilst also continuing to support walkers, run the Knighton TIC, and provide educational services based on the Offa's Dyke Interpretive Exhibition.

For details of membership and services offered, contact Offa's Dyke Association (SW), Knighton, Powys, LD1 1EN. Tel: 01547 528753. E-mail oda@offasdyke.demon.co.uk

INTRODUCTION TO THE SOUTH WEST COAST PATH ASSOCIATION

Whilst walking the path, or on any other occasion, should you meet someone interested in this book, the Association, or the coast path, do not worry if no one has a pencil and paper - just tear off one of these:

The South West Coast Path Association was formed 29 years ago to promote the interest of users of our coast path. We continue to press the authorities to maintain it properly and to complete the path. We produce guide books which are issued to members and can be purchased through the Administrator.

Administrator, Sarah Vincent, 25 Clobells, South Brent, Devon. TQ10 9JW
Tel / Fax: (01364) 73859, e-mail: coastpath.swcpa@virgin.net

Secretary, Eric Wallis, Windlestraw, Penquit, Ermington, Devon, PL21 OLU (01752 896237), e-mail: wallispenquit@beeb.net

The South West Coast Path Association was formed 29 years ago to promote the interest of users of our coast path. We continue to press the authorities to maintain it properly and to complete the path. We produce guide books which are issued to members and can be purchased through the Administrator.

Administrator, Sarah Vincent, 25 Clobells, South Brent, Devon. TQ10 9JW
Tel / Fax: (01364) 73859, e-mail: coastpath.swcpa@virgin.net

Secretary, Eric Wallis, Windlestraw, Penquit, Ermington, Devon, PL21 OLU (01752 896237), e-mail: wallispenquit@beeb.net

The South West Coast Path Association was formed 29 years ago to promote the interest of users of our coast path. We continue to press the authorities to maintain it properly and to complete the path. We produce guide books which are issued to members and can be purchased through the Administrator.

Administrator, Sarah Vincent, 25 Clobells, South Brent, Devon. TQ10 9JW
Tel / Fax: (01364) 73859, e-mail: coastpath.swcpa@virgin.net

Secretary, Eric Wallis, Windlestraw, Penquit, Ermington, Devon, PL21 OLU (01752 896237), e-mail: wallispenquit@beeb.net

The South West Coast Path Association was formed 29 years ago to promote the interest of users of our coast path. We continue to press the authorities to maintain it properly and to complete the path. We produce guide books which are issued to members and can be purchased through the Administrator.

Administrator, Sarah Vincent, 25 Clobells, South Brent, Devon. TQ10 9JW
Tel / Fax: (01364) 73859, e-mail: coastpath.swcpa@virgin.net

Secretary, Eric Wallis, Windlestraw, Penquit, Ermington, Devon, PL21 OLU (01752 896237), e-mail: wallispenquit@beeb.net

NOTES

NOTES

NOTES

NOTES

NOTES

NOTES

NOTES